Advice on the Art of Governance

67
64
63
61

73.
Since people are in great danger

81, don't trust humanity

84, Question your faults
- Who to befriend, rules
enemy's / friends

85 - $

86, No social mobility
be content

89, travel if you cannot succeded locally

SUNY Series in Near Eastern Studies
Said Amir Arjomand, Editor

Advice on the Art of Governance

MAU'IẒAH-I JAHĀNGĪRĪ
Of Muḥammad Bāqir Najm-i S̱ānī

AN INDO-ISLAMIC MIRROR FOR PRINCES

Persian Text with Introduction, Translation, and Notes by

SAJIDA SULTANA ALVI

State University of New York Press

The preparation of this volume was made possible by a grant from the Translation Program of the National Endowment for the Humanities, an independent federal agency.

Published by
State University of New York Press, Albany

Printed in the United States of America

For information, address State University of New York Press, State University Plaza, Albany, N.Y., 12246

Library of Congress Cataloging-in-Publication Data

Muḥammad Bāqir Najm Ṣānī, d. 1637.
[Maw' iẓah-i Jahāngīrī. English & Persian]
Advice on the art of governance: an Indo-Islamic mirror for princes: Mau' iẓah-i Jahāngīrī of Muḥammad Bāqir Najm-i Ṣānī/ Persian text with introduction, translation, and notes [by] Sajida S. Alvi.
p. cm.—(SUNY series in Near Eastern studies)
Includes bibliographical references and index.
ISBN 0-88706-918-5 ISBN 0-88706-919-3 (pbk.)
1. Education of princes. 2. Mogul Empire—Kings and rulers. I. Alvi, Sajida S. (Sajida Sultana), 1941- . II. Title. III. Title: Mau' iẓah-i Jahāngīrī. IV. Series.
JC393.C3M8413 1989
321.6—dc19 88-16342
CIP

10 9 8 7 6 5 4 3 2 1

DEDICATED TO ANNEMARIE SCHIMMEL

CONTENTS

PREFACE AND ACKNOWLEDGMENTS

Mughal India is one of the most extensively discussed periods in the history of Islam in India. Nevertheless, many questions remain unanswered. A number of fundamentally important texts dealing with the sociopolitical history, religion, and literature are still in manuscript form, lying scattered all over the subcontinent. Scholars interested in the social, cultural, and literary dimensions of the Indo-Islamic heritage are often deterred by the difficulties in acquiring, reading, and interpreting unpublished texts. In such an important area of inquiry as the evolution of Islamic political thought in the pluralistic society of medieval India, there is little published material. Publication of some texts discussed in the Introduction has generated an interest in the subject. Editing and annotation of *Mau'iẓah-i Jahāngīrī*, an unpublished Persian text, along with its English translation in this volume, is one more step in this direction.

Many colleagues and friends have given me support and encouragement over the years in completing this project. My special thanks are due to Annemarie Schimmel, John F. Richards, Bruce Lawrence, Donald P. Little, Charles J. Adams, and M. A. R. Barker.

Amongst the institutions that have helped me, I am indebted to the National Endowment for the Humanities, Translation Program for its generous research grant, and to the Faculty of Graduate

Studies and Research, McGill University, and the College of Liberal Arts, University of Minnesota, for their travel grants.

I would also like to thank Linda Perry and Hugh Oliver for carefully reading the manuscript and suggesting many editorial improvements.

Lastly, I express my gratitude to my husband, Sabir, and our sons, Farzad and Suroosh, for their understanding and patience at my spending endless hours away from home in completing this work.

Sajida Sultana Alvi

INTRODUCTION

Mau'iẓah-i Jahāngīrī (Admonition of Jahāngīr or Advice on [the art of] Governance), written by Muḥammad Bāqir Najm-i S̱ānī in 1612-1613, provides valuable insights into political and ethical thought in India during the reign of the Mughal emperor Jahāngīr (1605-1627). Works on the ethics of statecraft, written in Islamic languages by men of affairs and letters who were eager to advise rulers on various aspects of government, are often known by the European term *Mirrors for Princes*. Since such description is widely used and understood as a reference to this body of literature, I have used it in my discussion below. This introductory essay is probably the first comprehensive and comparative study of available Indo-Islamic Mirror literature from the thirteenth to the early part of the seventeenth century; at the same time, it provides a detailed analysis of the content of the *Mau'iẓah*.[1]

MIRRORS AS A GENRE

Writers dealing with Islamic political thought—from Ibn Khaldūn[2] in the fourteenth century to Rosenthal[3] and Lambton[4] in the twentieth—have not given enough importance to the Mirrors literature, primarily because of its literary character. It is true that this genre neither offers a systematic interpretation of political thought in a given period nor ventures upon a systematic treatment of the problems of government, state, and society. However, it can complement other historical and philosophical works. Reflecting the prevailing political trends among the ruling elite and the social norms of the period, it can be used as a rich resource of social, intellectual, and religious trends. The writer of a Mirror, by the very nature of the subject matter, usually belongs to the ruling class, is familiar with the mechanics of government, and quite often holds an important administrative position. Inevitably, then, the literature is elitist.

In the absence of a clearly defined format for the genre of Mirrors, the writer enjoys certain flexibility in expressing his views. He can choose an anecdotal style or write a didactic narrative—unlike a historian, who cannot ignore the chronological sequence of events or overlook the protagonists of his narrative. Robert Dankoff, in his recent study, considers the Mirrors "useful during times of crisis in the state . . . a change of dynasty, an outside threat or inner disintegration."[5] However, Mirrors literature should not be equated with the poetic genre lamenting social and political chaos (*shahr āshobs*)[6] or books of warning (*'ibrat nāmahs*).[7]

The evolution of the genre of Mirrors in Arabic and Persian is discussed by, among others, Lambton and Dawood.[8] Our focus here will be on its development in Islamic India.

INDO-ISLAMIC MIRRORS BEFORE THE SEVENTEENTH CENTURY

With the establishment of Muslim rule in India, the Persian literary tradition of Mirrors was transplanted in the subcontinent. Like political theorists, the writers of Mirrors were concerned with the Islamic character of the state. However, in their search for political expediency, they suggested remedial steps that were sometimes antithetical to the spirit of divinely revealed Islamic law (*Sharī'ah*). The personal, familial, and biographical influences that turned the writers to the Mirrors genre in the first place also determined the focus of their works.

Three important Iranian works that influenced the writings of Mirrors in India were: *Qābūs Nāmah*, written in 1082 by Kaykā'ūs b. Iskandar b. Qābūs, a Ziyarid prince; *Siyāsat Nāmah*, written in 1091-1092 by the shrewd Saljūq wazir Niẓām al-Mulk; and al-Ghazālī's *Naṣīḥat al-Mulūk*, written between 1105 and 1111.[9] However, the problems confronting the Muslim community in India were of a different nature and magnitude from those in Iran. Consequently, the ideas on statecraft discussed in the three major Indian works of the early medieval period differ from those written in Iran.

Among the earliest extant Indian works is the *Ādāb al-Ḥarb wa al-Shujā'at* of Muḥammad b. Manṣūr Mubārak-shāh Fakhr-i Mudabbir,[10] written during a time of confusion and political instability. The threat of Mongol invasion loomed large, and the Turkish slaves were trying to outwit and outmaneuver each other in their efforts to seize political power. Sultan Iltutmish (1211-1236), after subduing his rivals, asked Fakhr-i Mudabbir to write a manual for him. And who could have been more qualified? The writer claimed to be a descendant of Abū Bakr (d. 634) on his paternal side and of Abū Muslim (killed in 755) and Maḥmūd of Ghazna (d. 1030) on his maternal side—in other words, half Semitic and half Aryan—and he was also well versed in Islamic learning and a logical heir to the Turco-Iranian heritage.[11]

Over a century later, Żiyā al-Dīn Baranī (died after 1357) wrote his well-known *Fatāwā-i Jahāndārī* when the threat of the Mongol invasion had subsided and Muslim rule had gained a foothold in the subcontinent. Baranī, a *nadīm* of Sultan Muḥammad bin Tughluq (1325-1351) for seventeen years, wrote the *Fatāwā* following the death of his patron as "an atonement for his sins" and as a shield for his salvation.[12] According to Baranī, he (Baranī) had acquired a good education by learning Arabic, traditional logic, *tafsīr, ḥadīth, fiqh,* and *taṣawwuf* but had learned no philosophy or science.[13] He remained an elitist, unsympathetic to the non-Muslims and untouched by the prevailing mystical thought around him.[14]

The last significant work written during the Sultanate period was Sayyid 'Alī Hamadānī's *Ẕakhīrat al-Mulūk*. A Ṣūfī saint, Hamadānī (d. 1385), though not directly involved in politics, had among his followers the rulers and ruling polity. It was at their request that he wrote this work to serve as a manual for their guidance.[15] The *Ẕakhīrah* bears witness to its author's profound mystical view of a good state and worthy statesmanship or rule.

Major themes in these works include the sovereign and his responsibilities; the community and the minorities; right religion versus justice; ruling polity and behavioral code; and rebellion and holy war (*jihād*) to promote the cause of Islam. Ideological, cultural, and sociopolitical developments play an important role in determining thematic emphases in the Mirrors.

In contrast to the juristical and philosophical works on statec[illegible] these Mirrors do not address the concept and theory of the s[illegible] It is understood that the state is Islamic and the sovereign a Mu[illegible] Nevertheless, most of the authors, prompted by their first-[illegible] knowledge of the workings of administrative apparatus, compromise with the utopian view of the ruler and the state and express their opinion on how a ruler might be successful. Thus, understandably, discussions revolve primarily around the personality and conduct of the ruler.

By Baranī's time, the concept of the *khalīfah/imām* and his functions (as put forth by al-Māwardī—d. 1058) had been revised as a result of political change.[16] Indeed, the concept of the relationship between the caliph and the sultan had already been modified by al-Ghazālī.[17] With the fall of the Caliphate, men of affairs became concerned more with stability and order than with any particular brand of government. To achieve that goal, the pre-Islamic Sasanid political ethic remained attractive to such writers as Baranī. Without apparent fear of arousing controversy, Baranī categorically stated that, because of the transformation of the city-state of Medina to a large empire in the classical period of Islamic history, effective rule could not be achieved simply by adhering to the Prophet Muḥammad's *sunnah* and his tradition of poverty (*faqr*) and piety.[18] Baranī's near contemporary Ṣūfī Hamadānī was diametrically opposed to Baranī's views. He admonished his contemporary rulers to follow the example of the *Khulafā'-i Rāshidīn* in practicing self-denial in their private and public lives.[19] All writers are in full agreement with the jurists in suggesting that it is the ruler who must ensure implementation of the *Sharī'ah* and enhancement of the cause of Islam; however, there are subtle differences in their perceptions of the personality and role of an ideal ruler.

Mudabbir, like his predecessors (especially those in Iran), considered the ruler to be the shadow of God on Earth.[20] Baranī also regarded the ruler as one of the wonders of God's creation. Once designated by God to rule other human beings, he is blessed with divine grace and becomes superhuman.[21] Hamadānī, however, believed that it was not the office but the *Sharī'ah*-oriented policies of the ruler which earned for him the lofty position of God's viceregent on Earth.[22] Al-Ghazālī, Mudabbir, and Hamadānī ranked rulers next to the prophets. It was the might of their arms which ensured implementation of the *Sharī'ah.* Hamadānī could not hide his disdain for some contemporary rulers who compromised their religious beliefs and ethical values for the sake of maintaining their worldly power.[23]

True faith or right religion was a matter of concern to all writers, but the importance of personal piety varied for each. According to Baranī, a ruler with strong faith ranked among the pivots/poles (*quṭubs*) and saints (*abdāls*). He was painfully aware that the Sasanid traditions in court etiquette adopted by contemporary sultans were against the spirit of Islam, although such traditions were understandably necessary for effective control of the empire and the people. In Baranī's view, power, not personal piety, represented the most effective way to implement laws of the *Sharī'ah.*[24] Baranī's concern for the ruler's conduct and his emphasis on the preservation of the *Sharī'ah* reflect the thinking of India's Muslim intellectual elite endeavoring to maintain cultural and religious identity in an alien land. The advice of Baranī's contemporary Hamadānī, as well as that of his predecessor al-Ghazālī, on personal conduct and behavior is quite different and couched more specifically in an Islamic idiom. The theological element in the *Naṣīḥat* and the *Ẕakhīrah* is more profound than in any of the other Mirrors under discussion, and frequent mention of the Day of Judgment simply intensifies their religious character. But regardless of the idiom and orientation of these works, sovereignty remained the most important institution to all writers, because it protected religion and ensured stability.

Like their predecessors, the Mirror writers in India considered justice very important for the ideal ruler. Baranī's concept of justice was, however, tied to the notion of true faith. The communalistic approach in his work is discernible even in his discussion of the dispensation of justice. Baranī wished the state to become theocratic, and to prescribe for the Hindus—the majority—either acceptance of Islam or death.[25] He recognized, however, that it was not possible to completely eradicate polytheists.[26] In his scheme of government, the citizens did not have equal rights. He proposed that the Hindus and other non-Muslim groups should be humiliated and denied positions of responsibility in the administration.[27] Mudabbir, by contrast (writing at the time of unstable Muslim rule), considered it incumbent upon the ruler to dispense justice to all subjects regardless of their religion or race. Justice for him was the [illegible]

[illegible] private, public, and religious lives, reiterating the position taken by al-Māwardī in *al-Aḥkām al-Sulṭāniyyah.*[29] In the dispensation of justice, however, Hamadānī did not suggest discriminatory action against non-Muslim subjects.[30]

That religion and politics are counterparts was repeatedly expressed in the manuals of the medieval period. The individuals who supposedly guided the ruler in religious matters were the *'ulamā'*—the religious elite.[31] Perceptions about this group among the writers were influenced by the general mood and attitude during their respective periods. Writing at the time of the ascendancy of the Chishtiyyah order, Mudabbir showed special reverence for the virtuous people (*ahl-i ṣalāh*) and the *'ulamā.'* He advised the ruler to fulfill the needs of these groups and to respect them so as to receive their blessings. Mudabbir believed that the *'ulamā'* should be incorporated into the sultan's retinue so that their prayers could bring victory and success to the ruler.[32] While Baranī did not write detailed instructions about the *'ulamā'* for his addressee (Sultan Feroze Shāh—1351-88), he referred to the religious elite in several contexts, and advised the ruler, for his personal salvation, to be generous to this class.[33] Hamadānī discussed two groups of the *'ulamā'*, the worldly *'ulamā'* (*'ulamā'-i dunyā*) and the other-worldly *'ulamā'* (*'ulamā'-i ākhirat*), and criticized those who degraded themselves by selling their knowledge for material gain and who engaged in mutual rivalries.[34] He pointedly warned the rulers in stern language against the damaging effects of associating with the this-worldly *'ulamā.'*[35]

The importance of the political elite in successfully running the government was recognized by all writers, but the qualities and attributes of the nobles and their relations with the ruler received differing emphases from period to period. Baranī, in his scheme of government, was concerned with the lineage of the ruling polity. He proposed that the high-born—mainly the Turks—should be in charge of the administration while the low-born, including the Hindus and Indian Muslims, should not be considered worthy of royal patronage or given positions of responsibility.[36] Such thinking was probably fostered by the rival cliques that surrounded Baranī. Mudabbir, too, recognized that the offspring of nobility should be patronized and given opportunities to serve the state.[37] He added, however, that the doors to state employment should be open to capable and loyal individuals of any background, although they should not be given parity with experienced and senior administrators.[38] Hamadānī, in his pursuit of an ideal Islamic order, hoped to see righteous, God-fearing, and conscientious nobility in all departments of the government administration.[39]

Army elite and political elite were one and the same during the medieval period. High-ranking nobles were commanders of troops as well, and the prestige of a noble depended on the might of his arms. Since political stability, social order, and territorial expansion were contingent upon the quality and quantity of the armed forces of a ruler, his dependence upon the army elite was quite natural. Consequently, the army elite is an important topic of discussion among all writers. The very title of Mudabbir's work, *Ādāb al-Ḥarb wa al-Shujā'at*, reflects the attitudes of the period, especially the importance attached to the art of warfare in the early part of the thirteenth century. The author devotes twenty-five of thirty-four chapters to war-related themes, ranging from the role of the horse to the building of defenses. He states unequivocally that for any stable government, full knowledge of the art of warfare is a prerequisite.[40] Compared to Mudabbir, Baranī devoted less attention to the army. However, he recognized the importance of fighting forces for a successful government and referred to troops as the wealth of a ruler. Baranī was particularly interested in the personal qualities of an army elite, believing that a powerful commander could pose a serious threat to the reigning sovereign.[41]

Jihād, another topic discussed by the writers, is important in the context of India. According to Mudabbir, *jihād* was obligatory for the collective body of Muslims (*farḍ kifāyah*) but need not be applied to non-Muslims if they countenanced Islam or agreed to pay poll tax (*jizyah*). He insisted upon the collection of *jizyah* from the idol worshippers and, by implication, granted the Hindus a status of belonging to the "people of the book" (*dhimmīs*).[42] Such an attitude reflects a sense of insecurity among the Muslim elite at this critical time. In the face of the Mongol threat, Mudabbir could not prescribe for the Hindus a choice between "Islam or the sword."[43] However, over a century later, Baranī expressed the view that the responsibility for completely annihilating the Hindus rested with the ruler. Acceptance of *jizyah* by the sultan was not prudent because it could impede the spread of Islam.[44] Baranī also found it difficult to accept the Hindus as "people of the book" (*ahl al-kitāb*).[45]

In the suppression of violence or rebellion (*fitnah*), the writers do not draw any distinction between Muslim or non-Muslim rebels. *Fitnah* is a threat to political stability and social order and must be suppressed with the might of arms. Hamadānī proposed the death penalty for a traitor or rebel.[46]

At the same time, Mudabbir and Baranī did not ignore the close relationship between state policies and the health of the economy. Mudabbir stressed that revenue collectors should be honest and righteous to ensure the well-being of the peasantry. Strict control of the army—the largest consumer of commodities—was necessary for lawful dealings with the business community and peasantry. Hoarding of money by the artisans had to be stopped. It was the responsibility of the state to standardize currency and weights and to make the trade routes safe for the transportation of commodities.[47] Along with the factors highlighted by Mudabbir, Baranī discussed the advantages of price and wage controls. One of Baranī's recommendations was that the state should crush monopolists who dictated market prices through their control of transportation and credit. He believed that prices and wages should be fixed for the sake of social security, basing his belief on the success of price and wage controls introduced by one of the ablest sultans of Delhi, 'Alā' al-Dīn Khaljī (1296-1316).[48]

From this brief overview, it should be clear that the Mirrors can be used as a valuable supplement to historical chronicles for understanding the political, social, and intellectual history of the Sultanate period in Indo-Islamic history. Historical necessity, political expediency, and practical utility are the main characteristics of this genre. The works reflect the idealistic views of the writers and provide glimpses of the machinations of the political apparatus.

THE MUGHAL ERA

The surviving works on political thought written during the

Mughal era (1526-1707), give us only a fragmentary and hazy account of the period. However, scholars are unanimous in their belief that the 'interconfessional Islamicate culture' (to use Hodgson's terminology[49]) achieved a high level during this time because of its well-run ruling institutions, well-knit and centralized bureaucracy, and economic prosperity. Mughal culture transcended ethnic, linguistic, and religious identities. Richards has rightly stated that the Mughals were able to achieve what the previous ruling Muslim dynasties in India had been unable to do—to create an elaborate ideology of royal authority and legitimacy and to introduce for the ruling elite, the rank-holders (*manṣabdārs*), a new meaning of honor and pride and a new code for their behavior.[50] In any discussion on political thinking, the *manṣabdārs* are of central importance. Because of their role in political and cultural spheres, they were the empire. This empire, according to Pearson, consisted of eight thousand individuals (which could be further reduced to a core of one thousand) who were directly tied through patronage to the person of the emperor. They provided a "level of integration or solidarity and a distinctive membership status."[51] Thus, what we see in Mughal India is a successful application of Ibn Khaldūn's concept of group solidarity (*'aṣabiyyah*).[52]

Most of the authors of Mirrors of the Mughal period belonged to the polity and were successfully integrated into the sociopolitical structure. Because of their close ties to political power, they could hardly be seen as impartial critics of the regime: their aspirations and hopes were too closely tied with the emperors or *manṣabdārs* who were their patrons. As writers and often *manṣabdārs* as well, they were instrumental in enforcing the political philosophy of the Mughals and in enhancing their composite culture. They enjoyed power, influence, and the intellectual freedom to express their views.

Extant Mirrors of the Mughal Era (1556-1627)

There is only one work—*Akhlāq-i Ḥakīmī*[53] by Ḥasan 'Alī al-Munshī al-Khāqānī, or as he is called at the end of the work, Ḥasan 'Alī bin Ashraf Tajāwuz-Allāh—known to have been completed during Akbar's reign. It was written for Akbar's half-brother Muḥammad Ḥakīm. Very little is known about the writer (referred as Munshī). It is only through his work that we learn of his service with Muḥammad Ḥakīm. He wrote this work in 987-88/1579-80, when his patron was engaged in the successful campaign against the ruler of Badakhshan. The writer could not accompany Ḥakīm, but as a token of his appreciation for the favors of his patron, he compiled the work.[54] In its content and form, *Akhlāq-i Ḥakīmī* reflects the writer's religious and mystical background. Divided into fourteen chapters, the *Akhlāq* covers such topics as justice (*'adālat*), patience (*ṣabr*), generosity (*sakhāwat*), discipline (*siyāsat*), forgiveness (*'afv*), and consultation (*mashwarat*). Munshī acknowledged that other writers before him had explored similar major themes, but he claimed that his contribution was in his narrow focus on the ethical conduct of the rulers, and in his condensation, verification, and correction of the didactic stories recorded by his predecessors.[55] A noteworthy point is that he cites his sources of information.[56] The stories and maxims in the work are drawn from *ḥadīth* and mystical literature, pre-Islamic and post-Islamic Iranian history, pre-Islamic Arabian and classical Islamic history, and to a lesser extent from Indo-Islamic history. At the beginning or at the end of chapters, the author praises his patron, Muḥammad Ḥakīm, the governor of Kabul, for being a good ruler.

Abū'l Fażl (d. 1602), the master historian of emperor Akbar, presented his views on his philosopher king (Akbar) in a philosophical tradition and on the perfect man in a mystical tradition. While his monumental work, *Akbar Nāmah*, represents the major historical account of Akbar's period, it has some elements of a Mirror. It cannot, however, be strictly included in this genre, and thus it is not analyzed here.[57]

In addition to the *Mau'iẓah* come two other noteworthy works from Jahāngīr's period: Qāḍī Nūr-Allāh Khāqānī's *Akhlāq-i Jahāngīrī*[58] and Shaykh 'Abd al-Ḥaqq Muḥaddith's *Risālah-i Nūriyyah-i Sulṭāniyyah*.[59] Khāqānī, an *'ālim*, jurist, and son of Shaykh Mu'īn al-Dīn,[60] was probably a second-generation immigrant from Herat. While serving as the *qāḍī* of Lahore, between 1620 and 1622, he wrote his voluminous work *Akhlāq-i Jahāngīrī*,[61] (comprising 526 fols.) to admonish rulers in general and Jahāngīr in particular about the art of government.[62] The writer's religious and juristical background strongly influenced the form and content of the *Akhlāq*. In style, it is more like the *Akhlāq-i Jalālī* of Muḥammad Jalāl-al Dīn Dawwānī (d. 1501), which was an important part of the curriculum during this period.[63] The didactic text is interspersed with philosophical and mystical discussions; it is also illustrated with maxims and stories from classical Islamic history and pre-Islamic Iran and frequent quotations from the Qur'ān and *ḥadīth*. The writer consciously adopted this form so that Jahāngīr, by learning from the experiences of former rulers,[64] could himself rule effectively. In the twenty-two chapters, some of the topics discussed are: divine love; virtue of knowledge; blessings of repentance (*taubah*); trust in God (*tawakkul*); generosity and condemnation of stinginess and jealousy; justice; bravery; virtues of consultation; and discipline. The work was dedicated to Jahāngīr as a token of the writer's gratitude for the favors of his patron.[65] We have no evidence that it was ever presented to the emperor, but the writer consistently praised Jahāngīr's various qualities as a ruler, and therefore probably wrote it with the intention of doing so.

Shaykh 'Abd al-Ḥaqq (1551-1642), the author of *Risālah-i Nūriyyah-i Sulṭāniyyah*, was a leading scholar of *ḥadīth* and a prolific writer, but he was not affiliated with Jahāngīr's court.[66] However, after his return from Mecca in 1000 A.H./1591 A.D. and after Jahāngīr's accession, 'Abd al-Ḥaqq (a member of the class of *'ulamā'*) considered it his duty to write a treatise on the art of government to guide Jahāngīr. Based on the Qur'ān, *ḥadīth*, and the ethical writings of former prominent scholars, the *Risālah* was considered by 'Abd-al Ḥaqq to be the best offering he could make to the emperor as a token of his support.[67] A short (30 printed pages) and concisely written manual, it differs in format from the other Mirrors. It is divided into five sections: the pillars (*arkān*) of empire; means of solidifying those pillars; the code of conduct (*ādāb*) of rulers; points crucial to running the state; and stories of former rulers on topics such as justice, forgiveness, forbearance, benevolence, strength, and valor. Despite the juristical background of the writer, the tenor of his work, as compared to *Akhlāq-i Jahāngīrī*, is not overly religious containing few quotations from the Qur'ān and *ḥadīth* literature. The didactic stories in the fifth section are drawn primarily from classical Islamic history. As is the case with the *Akhlāq*, we do not know if this work was ever presented to Jahāngīr.

MAU'IẒAH-I JAHĀNGĪRĪ AND ITS AUTHOR

An emigre from Iran, the author of *Mau'iẓah-i Jahāngīrī*, Muḥammad Bāqir Najm-i Ṣānī (d. 1637), was a descendant of Amīr Yār Muḥammad Khān Najm-i Ṣānī (the powerful *wakīl* of the founder of the Ṣafavid dynasty, Shāh Ismā'īl Ṣafavī—d. 1524). Bāqir, son of Muṣṭafā Bēg,[68] came to India in dire financial straits either towards the end of Akbar's reign (1556-1605) or at the beginning of Jahāngīr's.[69]

Bāqir entered the imperial service at the rank of one hundred or three hundred *sawār* and rose rapidly in the administrations of Jahāngīr and Shāhjahān. After serving as the governor of Patna, Bihar, Bengal, Orissa, Gujarat, Delhi, Jaunpur, and Allahabad,[70] his political career ended with his death in 1637.[71] He was linked to the Mughal family through his marriage to the niece of queen Nūrjahān; Jahāngīr affectionately called him son (*farzand*).[72] A man of both the pen and the sword, Bāqir symbolized the Indo-Persian social and cultural norms of the ruling elite. Among his extant works are the *Mau'iẓah, Kulliyāt* (collected poetry and prose works),[73] and *Sirāj-al-Manāhij* (a work on Shī'ī theology [*kalām*] written in Persian).[74]

Bāqir's contemporaries remember him as extremely capable in political affairs[75] and highly versatile in his literary and cultural pursuits. Balkhī, in particular, highlights Bāqir's literary skills, his mastery of epistolary writing (*inshā'*), history, and calligraphy, and his love of music.[76] The extant works of Bāqir demonstrate his very sophisticated style of writing as well as his interest in philosophy, mathematics, religion, and ethics.[77] Maintaining the tradition of the Mughal nobility, Bāqir extended his patronage to poets and litterateurs, and he actively contributed to the enrichment of Mughal culture.[78]

Written in concise and lucid prose, the *Mau'iẓah* represents a pragmatic approach to political problems. Bāqir covers a wide range of topics in the two chapters (*bāb*). The first is divided into six sections (*faṣl*) and two sub-sections (*qism*) and includes the personal qualities of the ruler, such as generosity, valor, and sound judgment of people; the use of diplomacy in statecraft and in dealing with enemies and rivals; the significance of such state policies as dispensation of justice, virtues of consultation, high standards in recruitment, and training of advisers and officials; and the merits of a patriarchal relationship between the ruler and high-ranking officials that generates intense loyalty of subjects toward their patron. In the second chapter, Bāqir addresses the subjects (*zīr dastān*) and peers (*akhwān-i zamān*). In the four sections of this chapter, he discusses many general topics (including the qualities and virtues of friendship), and he emphasizes both the power of wealth and the need for contentment and spiritual ascendancy. Drawing upon his personal experience, he also describes the agonies of a first-generation immigrant. He ends the *Mau'iẓah* with praise for the ideal rule of his patron, Jahāngīr, and a conventional prayer for his long life and growth in might and grandeur.[79] The *Mau'iẓah* was written in 1612 to satisfy Bāqir's intellectual interests and was named after his patron.[80] There is, however, no indication that this work was ever presented to Jahāngīr.

The ideas on politics and society in the *Mau'iẓah* refer particularly to such topics as the ruler, the state, the nobility, justice, the religious elite, the strata of society (*ṭabaqāt*), and various skills required for running the state. More precisely, the following themes are discussed.

Sovereignty

The work opens with praise of God—of His omnipotence and powers of creativity, as demonstrated in the creation of the universe and man. Following the Islamic tradition, Bāqir expresses great reverence for the Prophet Muḥammad. In the introduction, instead of highlighting the crucial role of *Imāms* after the prophet, Bāqir (himself a Shī'ī) unequivocally states: "And after the Prophet—the last of the prophets and seal of apostles—there ought to be no alternative but to have a prudent and powerful ruler with exalted authority, maintaining order and strengthening the pillars of the true religion, regulating the activities and conveniences for mankind, and achieving the blessings of peace and security."[81] In viewing the rulers as successors to the Prophet Muḥammad and as the shadow of God on earth, Bāqir is in agreement with his predecessors (Niẓām al-Mulk, al-Ghazālī, Miskawaih, Naṣīr al-Dīn Tūsī) and his contemporaries (Khāqānī and 'Abd al-Ḥaqq).[82]

In the following statement about Jahāngīr's rule, Bāqir demonstrates his familiarity with the classical theory of an Islamic state based on the three elements of community, the state as a protector of the community and its faith, Islam, and implementation of the *Sharī'ah*.[83] Bāqir says:

> In his attempt to enforce the precepts of sovereignty, to dispense the obligations of empire, to spread the rulings of illustrious *Sharī'at*,

> and to consolidate the foundations of the Muslim community, [the emperor] has opened to the masses the doors of kindness and beneficence with hands of immeasurable benevolence.[84]

Bāqir concurred with other writers and theorists that a temporal sovereign was central to the survival of the community and promulgation of Islam. He urges the ruler to uphold the good name of Islam through laudable deeds that would ensure salvation.[85] In his words:

> It is incumbent upon the Almighty's chosen creation, whom they call an emperor, to inculcate in himself the morals of the custodian of the *Sharī'ah* (Prophet Muḥammad). Waging his campaigns and conducting the business of his dominion and sovereignty according to the injunctions of Islamic law, the ruler should develop in himself qualities that beautify the attire of power.[86]

In his discussion of the centrality of a ruler in the affairs of a Muslim community and an Islamic state, Bāqir uses the religious idiom in accordance with the tradition of historical and religious writing in medieval India. However, compared with earlier writers, Bāqir does not place undue stress on Islamic orientation in government; nor does he advise the ruler on the preservation of the *Sharī'ah*.[87] Unlike the writers of the Sultanate period, he is not overly concerned about the personal lifestyle of the ruler—only in the passage cited above does he remind the ruler to be a good Muslim.

In general, Bāqir considered the Perso-Islamic court ethics to be appropriate for the ruler and polity. Writing on sovereignty, however, he reiterates the Sunnī theory of rulership instead of the Shī'ī juristical concept of *Imāmat*.[88] He believed that one could not reach the lofty position of rulership through one's own efforts—it was a divine gift and entailed heavy burden of responsibility. The ruler occupied the throne not to lead an indolent life[89] but to dispense justice, maintain harmony, and ensure the well-being of his subjects.[90]

Discussing Jahāngīr's ascendancy to the throne, the author alludes to the theory of legitimacy and authority developed by Abū'l Fażl, the court historian, for Akbar. Jahāngīr was the recipient of divine effulgence and of a special enlightenment that passed to him through his father and a chain of ancestors from Adam to Tīmūr.[91] He was, according to Bāqir, "the auspicious reigning emperor of the Īlkhānid Court, the illuminator of [Amīr Tīmūr] Gūrgān's lamp, [and] the supporter of the pillars of Caliphate and of prosperity."[92] It was because of these special qualities combined with his keen sense of justice that "famous sovereigns had willingly submitted themselves to his authority and emperors with exalted powers had heartily accepted servitude to him."[93]

As a footnote, it should be added that in the *Mau'iẓah*, Bāqir addresses the rulers or nobility in a direct manner without reference to the examples of previous rulers to substantiate his viewpoint.

The Sovereign and His Personality

The behavior of a ruler—his actions and reactions, his dealings with nobility, and his handling of his enemies—influenced societal norms, economic prosperity, and social harmony and equilibrium among various classes and communities within the state. Writers sensitive to the behavior of their patrons always gave a pointed advice on how the ruler should deal with the population; in addition, there were certain basic universal virtues which all writers extolled. Bāqir concurred with al-Ghazālī, Niẓām al-Mulk, and others in considering generosity, valor (*shujā'at*), and magnanimity (*ḥilm*) among those virtues. Valor took precedence over generosity because from valor emanated altruism. High-mindedness (*himmat-i buland*) made the rulers loftier in power. Vigilance, firm resolve, sound judgment, forbearance, forgiveness, and self-control were other characteristics that ensured stability of power. Bāqir stated unequivocally that

> [The imperial] ordinances govern the lives, possessions, properties, and honor of the people; [similarly], royal edicts and prohibitions are evenly enforced on the low-born and high-born, on plebeians and grandees. [Therefore] if the rulers do not grace their days with altruism and perseverance, do not capitalize on these qualities, and do not distinguish their conduct with magnanimity and affability, in a fit of rage they might disturb and inflict suffering on their subjects and cause property and lives of many to perish.[94]

He also added that the ruler could extend his benevolence to the peasantry and army and earn the loyalty and affection of all his subjects through his benign and congenial attitude.

Administrative Policies

As a Mirror, *Mau'iẓah-i Jahāngīrī* is not directed to the specifics of state administrative policies. From his perspective as a member of the ruling elite, Bāqir recorded his perceptions of the government and offered suggestions for promoting social harmony and economic prosperity. However, the sections on justice, administrative control, consultation and planning, and nobility are relevant to the proper operation of administration.

Justice: Bāqir stressed that the governmental control should be based on justice (*siyāsah 'adālah*). He did not follow the juridical definition of justice as *dār al-Islām* and the realm of justice as *dār al-'adl*, according to which an Islamic state is just by following the precepts of Islam. Bāqir propounded the Perso-Islamic concept of justice popularized, among others, by Niẓām al-Mulk and al-Ghazālī.[95] Bāqir devoted the first chapter of his treatise to the importance of justice in a successful and stable government. He reiterated the following *ḥadīth*, quoted by his predecessors al-Ghazālī and Ḥusayn Wā'iẓ Kāshifī: "On a pair of scales, one hour of justice outweighs sixty years of worship."[96] The enforcement of justice was crucial to the proper functioning of religious and ruling institutions.[97] The following statement presents Bāqir's views:

> In systematizing rules and in maintaining their procedures, the ruler must exercise utmost care to achieve justice and impartiality. If the judge (ruler) does not regulate the affairs of the people, a clandestine rebel, abetted by tyranny, will destroy the lives of nobility and plebian alike. If the light from the candle of justice does not illuminate the somber cell of the afflicted, the darkness of cruelty will blacken the entire country just as it does the hearts of tyrants.[98]

It should be added that Mughal emperors in general and Jahāngīr in particular are remembered for their skill in dispensing justice. Among the twelve ordinances Jahāngīr issued after his accession, the first was to provide his subjects with direct access to their ruler for redress of their grievances.[99]

Discipline: The discussion of justice is intertwined with the ruler's ability to implement his policies—or *siyāsah* as Bāqir uses the term. "The roots of the tree of justice are invigorated and watered by showers from the clouds of discipline, because [governmental] control is based on the laws of justice."[100] In this section, Bāqir cautioned that if rulers were unable to combine reward and punishment, kindness and reprisal, the days of their power would be numbered. He urged that "the rulers should display the mercy of God toward the virtuous and the reformers (*muṣliḥān*) and the wrath of God toward the evildoers and the seditious."[101]

Consultation and Planning: Bāqir was sensitive to the importance of advisers in administration. While a group of his co-religionists in Iran regarded the Ṣafavid rulers as both spiritual and temporal leaders, Bāqir neither considered the emperor to be superhuman nor viewed him as divinely inspired.[102] He urged Jahāngīr to consult his advisers before making any decisions and referred to the Qur'ānic verse "Consult them in affairs"[103] in support of his argument. Being himself a member of the polity, Bāqir wrote in detail about the virtues of consultation and listed the qualities of the ideal adviser. He emphasized experience, sagacity, honesty, and integrity more than piety or religious affiliations.[104]

The Ruling Elite: Because the *manṣabdārs* were a creation of Mughal emperors, they could not be considered the emperor's equal, as they were during the reigns of certain Saljūq sultans in Iran or in the early Sultanate period in India. Bāqir, nonetheless, considered the nobility the most important instrument for implementing the ruler's policies. Thus, in the *Mau'iẓah,* he focused primarily on the nobility rather than on society in general. As a member of the noble class, Bāqir presents the aspirations and frustrations of the ruling elite from within.

He called the ruling class "pillars of the citadel of empire" (*qā'imah-i qaṣr-i salṭanat*) and divided them into four categories: people of the sword; people of the pen; the *qāḍīs;* and honest reporters and revenue collectors.[105] The people of the pen, in Bāqir's view, were more crucial to the stability of the state than the people of the sword because the latter could challenge the authority of the ruler and incite revolt against him. He also made specific reference to the importance of recruiting honest revenue collectors (*'āmils* and *amīns*), in order to ensure the well-being of the peasantry and economic prosperity. He proposed harsh punishments for corrupt officials because "to do good to depraved people is like doing bad to good people. To keep tyrants alive is akin to killing the pious."[106]

Patronage: Bāqir admonished the ruler to be extremely careful about recruiting among the nobility. Like a physician, the ruler should make a thorough diagnosis before extending his patronage to an individual and placing confidence in him. Clarity of thinking and soundness of judgment on the part of the ruler were integral to this process. The necessary attributes to qualify for the imperial service were: wisdom, rectitude, knowledge, continence, fidelity, honesty, piety, dutifulness, loyalty, and (above all) purity of lineage and highmindedness.[107] For social mobility and for becoming an adviser to the emperor, purity of lineage was particularly significant. He explained his position as follows:

> [The emperor] should consider worthy of patronage only an individual of pure essence and should refrain from encouraging the wicked person of mean origin—not every stone becomes a gem and and not every crimson fluid is turned into the finest musk. A despicable person of mean disposition and nasty mind does not think of or revere honesty and integrity. When honesty and integrity—the quintessence of purity—dissipate, one can expect every possible vice from that individual. A peevish man can by no means be led into rectitude, nor can a lowly and ill-mannered person, by forcing himself, [acquire] laudable disposition and pure-mindedness.[108]

Once the process of screening was complete, the emperor should gradually promote an individual through the ranks in order to establish his reputation and dignity firmly in the hearts of people.[109] When an individual was exalted to a position of authority, the ruler should lend his full support to safeguard his security and protect him from the conspiracy of rival factions. "Quick exaltation and rapid abasement damage the majesty of empire. [Sovereigns] should not banish their retainers and relations on mere suspicion. . . . In accepting the word of a selfish person and committing a disagreeable act, they would ruin their edifice of wisdom," Bāqir states.[110] At the same time, he cautioned the rulers that they should not "make a noble equal to themselves in rank, prestige, wealth and grandeur."[111]

Bāqir's discussion of conspirators could be interpreted as a reference to the party politics and various factions within the Mughal nobility. He stated categorically that the majority were serving the ruler simply for reasons of employment and that only a dedicated few put their heart and soul into their service. It was this loyal core which should be appreciated and encouraged by the ruler. The majority would strive to undermine them out of jealousy for the disparities in rank and prestige. If the emperor accepted the reports of conspirators without independent verification, the loyal core would be disheartened, thus weakening the state.[112] The author also listed five types of individuals who should never be appointed to the Advisory Council.[113]

As the nobility had special rights, so, too, did it have certain important responsibilities. After cautioning his fellow nobles of the perils of imperial service, Bāqir emphasized that every high-ranking noble must serve his master with the utmost sincerity, conviction, and goodwill. "Had he a thousand lives, he must sacrifice them for one moment of his lord's peace of mind. He must throw himself in the most perilous situation for requital of the favors of his patron and for leaving his name [inscribed] on the record of Time in recognition of his devotion [to his master]."[114] Honesty, integrity, and righteousness were key to the faithfulness and loyalty of an official, and under no circumstances should he compromise them. Bāqir urged nobles in advisory positions to be discreetly candid in expressing their opinions about the ruler's words and deeds, so as to promote consistency in his dispensation of justice, fairness in his administrative policies, and the maintenance of his good reputation. He admonished the nobility that their power and proximity to the ruler should not make them arrogant; rather, he advised that they extend beneficence to both high and low.[115]

Army: Hodgson called the later Islamic empires (the Ottomans, the Ṣafavids, and the Mughals) "Gun Powder Empires."[116] However, there is little mention of the army in the *Mau'iẓah* and other Mirrors of the Mughal period. From Abū'l Fażl's *Ā'in-i Akbarī*, we know that the army was an important element in Akbar's administrative reforms.[117]

The role of the army, according to Bāqir, was to suppress rebellion —a quite limited, if important, function. Bāqir did not echo the views of his predecessors, Kaykā'ūs, Niẓām al-Mulk, and al-Ghazālī, who considered a strong army to be a prerequisite for stable government and for the support of the masses.[118] In the *Mau'izah*, he reiterated the official policy of the Mughals, urging the ruler to assign appropriate *manṣab* and *jāgīr* to every noble to maintain a certain number of troops. Bāqir also suggested annual inspection of the army and its equipment to ensure its readiness. He concluded his military discussion by admonishing the ruler and nobility that instead of accumulating wealth, they should continually enlarge their armies; otherwise, he warned, "they will be bewildered at a time of need when boxes filled with gold will be of no use."[119] Bāqir did not imitate Kaykā'ūs and other writers before him in outlining the responsibilities and code of conduct for commanders of the armed forces—perhaps because the high-ranking *manṣabdārs* were performing both civil and military functions.[120]

The Sovereign and Society

As indicated earlier, Bāqir's focus of attention in his treatise is the ruling elite rather than society in general. There are, however, scattered remarks in various sections indicating his views on maintaining a social hierarchy. He believed that social groups should be kept in their designated places to sustain social equilibrium. He made a distinction between the high-born (*ashrāf*) and low-born (*arẕāl*), and he reiterated the views of previous writers on this issue:

> Rulers should not place incompetent and low-born people on the same footing with a high-born [person] and prudent persons of pure extraction. They should regard the maintenance of this hierarchy as a true principle in the laws of the empire and the covenants of kingship. If the distinction of ranks is abolished and the low-born boast of equality with the people of the middle class (*ausāṭ*), and the middle class of equality with the high-born, the grandeur of kingship will be damaged and total confusion will occur among the nobility.[121]

Unlike Baranī, Bāqir did not specify various strata (*ṭabaqāt*) of Indo-Islamic society on the basis of race or religion; he did not regard the Iranis and Turanis as the high-born and the indigenous Indian Muslim as the low-born, nor did he carry over aristocratic privileges into religious life.[122] However, like Baranī, Niẓām al-Mulk, and others, Bāqir was against universal education. For adopting this position, he offered the following rationale:

> Past rulers did not let the ignoble and ill-bred people learn calligraphy, the precepts of revenue accounts, and the rules of arithmetic. When this tradition [of permitting education] gains permanence, and when artisans join the ranks of the grandees of the state, its impairment spreads, and the economic resources of the noble and plebeian alike are disturbed.[123]

But Bāqir was concerned about the people excluded from the ranks of nobility because of their lower social status. Such people, he thought, should live between fear and hope, between apprehension and expectation, regarding their chances of promotion to the imperial service: "Just as riches make these people independent, causing rebellion and transgression, so does despair make them fearless, resulting in the defeat of rulers."[124] Furthermore, the ruler should not limit his benefactions to certain individuals or groups, because only through the collective efforts of both the nobility and the masses could a ruler engage himself in successful campaigns and provide stable rule.[125]

Unlike the author of *Qābūs Nāmah,* who suggested that the ruler should appear in public only rarely,[126] Bāqir strongly urged the ruler to be accessible to his people. In this regard, he was in agreement with the anonymous author of a twelfth-century Iranian Mirror, *Baḥr al-Fawā'id.*[127] To ensure the welfare of the masses, it was absolutely necessary for the rulers to maintain contact with them. Bāqir elaborated this point as follows:

> They must not consider it ignominious to speak with peasants, the elderly, the weak, and the poor. Having listened to the petitioners for justice, the rulers should . . . affectionately turn their attention toward resolving their problems. They should not be irritated by their [the petitioners'] loquacity. Indeed, the emperor is like a physician and the petitioner like a patient. If the patient does not fully explain his condition, the physician cannot apprehend his disease. How can he diagnose an unknown illness?[128]

Religion and State

Bāqir considered the role of religion in governmental policies to be theoretically important, supporting the view of al-Ghazālī and others that religion and politics were as twins. He considered "the [governmental] discipline to be an adornment of the state and community and an expedient for the welfare of religion and empire. Without the rulers' regulation of discipline," he continued, "the decrees of *Sharī'ah* will not be promulgated, nor is the basis of empire strengthened."[129] He agreed with the previous writers of Mirrors that after the Prophet Muḥammad, responsibility for the propagation of Islam rested with the rulers.[130] In a similar vein, he suggested that rulers should "pattern their policies after the advice, counsel, and judgment of the *'ulamā'* to adorn the head of the [Muslim] community with magnificence of religion."[131] These ideas, however, occur as isolated statements in the *Mau'iẓah* and do not form the main thrust of the treatise.

Rebellion (Fitnah)

Rebellion against government was a challenge to the authority of a ruler and a threat to sociopolitical stability, resulting in the ruin of the peasantry and the suffering of the weak and poor. Thus, it should never be tolerated.[132] Anyone in defiance of the imperial authority—a traitor or slanderer, no matter how weak and small—was an enemy. Without distinguishing between a Hindu or a Muslim, a prince or a commoner, Bāqir suggested drastic action (namely, execution) to deal with insurgents, traitors, and those harmful to other people.[133] Bāqir justified the harshness of this policy thus:

> Although scholars of religion and mystics of the highest order have greatly stressed the virtues of forgiveness and the glory of beneficence, punishment is far better than forgiveness in matters that would result in violence in the world and damage to the very foundation of the human race. In such cases, there should be no room for amnesty and indulgence. The punishment for and chastisement of seditious persons should be considered obligatory.[134]

It was only in the context of rebellion that Bāqir recommended the most severe punitive measures. In the second section of the first chapter, while discussing generosity, valor, and magnanimity, the author reveres the value of human life and warns the ruler to be absolutely certain of an individual's guilt before pronouncing the death sentence. If an innocent person is put to death, "the blood and [the burden of this] crime will be on [the ruler's] neck until eternity."[135]

The sections dealing with poverty and wealth represent two parallel world-views which are possibly connected to the affluence and prosperity of Jahāngīr's period on the one hand, and to the Naqshbandiyyah ascendancy on the other. Among contemporary writers of the Mirrors, Bāqir was the only one who vehemently condemned poverty and forcefully argued that wealth represented power and was crucial to success in life. In his view, "One could, with the help of wealth, achieve any level of ascendancy. A needy person, deprived of such pleasure in this world, would also be denied high rank in the hereafter."[148] To support his argument, he quoted the Prophetic *ḥadīth* in its exoteric sense, "Poverty is a disgrace on one's face in both worlds." He elaborated this view by citing situations in which a needy person, despite his intelligence and resourcefulness, was ignored and rejected by society. According to Bāqir, "Every quality for which the wealthy are admired and praised evoked condemnation and ridicule in the impoverished." For example, "Bravery is considered impetuousness, generosity prodigality, and affability meekness and spiritlessness. If he is inclined to calm and quietude, [the pauper] is deemed lazy and indolent. If he displays eloquence . . . he is labeled talkative. If he seeks refuge in silence, he is likened to a water-worm. . . ."[149] Bāqir discussed many more situations in which a destitute was misunderstood by his peers and concluded that "It is easier to put one's hand in the mouth of a snake in order to extract deadly poison or to snatch a morsel from a hungry lion or to dine with an enraged panther than to be needy—a condition that shatters one's ego. Death is better."[150]

The next logical step toward changing one's circumstances was to take risks and strive, although one could not achieve success without God's help and one could not "climb the ladder of dignity without struggle." Bāqir emphasized the importance of dignity and respectability in human endeavors because "the individual who stoops to abjectness and baseness has no value in the eyes of judicious people and is not taken into account."[151] If one could not find opportunities in one's own homeland, one should travel to other countries. The author (who himself came to India from Iran) poignantly depicts the agonies and ecstasies of an immigrant:

> Travel is a tree that bears only the fruit of separation. Leaving one's homeland is like a cloud that drops only the rain of grief. . . . When one is deprived of the bliss of visitation of one's parents, peers,

> friends, it is apparent that this agony is not remedied by delights [of the pleasant milieu]. . . . The pain of separation from one's friends and the affliction of parting from one's well-wishers are the most intense of all pains and the most agonizing of all tortures. Despite affluence and leisure, despite a life of extreme luxury, [an immigrant] in a foreign country [finds] the fountainhead of his comfort diverted and the vision of his good fortune clouded by separation from his most dear friends and spiritual companions.[152]

A major problem in a foreign land, according to Bāqir, was finding sincere friends. Friendship in a new environment with new people was usually based on worldly gains and ulterior motives. In a time of adversity, "the group that adorned his company like the Pleiades wither away like the constellation of the Bear."[153] But despite all the agonies and frustrations, Bāqir highly recommends emigration, because "travel takes an individual from the pit of obscurity to the heights of honor and glory." Experiences in a foreign land lead one to becoming refined and disciplined, and so contribute to success throughout life. As we have seen in his biographical sketch, Bāqir struggled to gain prominence in the administrations of Jahāngīr and Shāhjahān, and he served his masters with integrity and loyalty.

In the last, relatively short section, Bāqir covers a variety of themes such as the transient world, the omnipotence of God, the merits of striving for accomplishments, pleasing God, and seeking Divine approval of one's deeds. These topics have been dealt with in detail by earlier writers such as al-Ghazālī. In the *Iḥyā'*, for example, al-Ghazālī devotes one full chapter to each of these and to related topics. Bāqir, however, continues to be brief and lucid. Despite the religious and mystical orientation of the topics, he quotes only two verses from the Qur'ān to support his viewpoint. And like many mystical poets and religious writers, he saw human helplessness as controlling one's life and one's environment:

> Know that this harsh world is a mirage-like inn and a rough abode. In this tavern, the wine of pleasure is mixed with the blood of sorrow. . . . The Tailor of this workshop of antiquity has sewed the attire of all creatures with the embroidery of extinction. . . . Whom did He elevate and not throw down? Where did He grow a plant and not uproot it? Where is the one with whom He was extravagant without affliction?[154]

Like the well-known Persian poet Ḥāfiẓ (d. 1389), Bāqir personifies this world as a "husband-killing, decrepit woman . . . who has captured many men in her noose,"[155] and as a newly wed bride who enchants immature people "with her charming face . . . They remain unaware of her malevolent heart, perfidy, vile nature, and malicious character."[156] Nevertheless, life is a trust of borrowed time which everyone has to deposit. "Whoever steps into this universe has to sip the elixir of death," wrote Bāqir. "Moment by moment one traverses the path of nonexistence and, in a short time, the spring of life (which is youth) is transformed into the autumn of old age. Ultimately one has to undertake the long journey into the hereafter."[157] The advice he gave was based on the well-known religious admonishment: "Today, when one has the power and time to accumulate 'provisions for the road,' one should amass [them]."[158]

Other topics on which Bāqir wrote dealt with the significance of striving for accomplishments (*kamālāt*) and knowledge (*'ilm*). He did not, however, mean *kamālāt* in the context of mystical or religious knowledge. His treatment of the subject is in broad and general terms. He urges his readers to focus on "acquiring virtues, intellectual attainments, moral probity, and purification of the carnal soul and on amassing rewards for the next world [by doing good deeds in this]."[159] To please God, worshipping Him is of central importance—it is "a source of security in this world and a medium of salvation and honor in the next."[160]

Bāqir also states explicitly that all of his discussions are directed to thinking persons, the cream of creation rather than for "misguided individuals worse than cattle."[161] He concludes his work with an invocation for the stability of an ever-expanding empire and for perpetuity of the dominion of his master, benefactor, and the focus of his prayers—Jahāngīr. Bāqir repeats his praise for Jahāngīr's keen sense of justice and the purity of his royal lineage, and eulogizes him for being the most powerful ruler of his time. He dedicates the work to his patron by naming it *Mau'iẓah-i Jahāngīrī*.[162]

SOURCES OF THE *MAU'IẒAH*

Bāqir does not specify the sources he used for compiling his work. Major themes can be found in one form or other in earlier didactic literature and in contemporary works. However, a comparative study with al-Ghazālī's *Naṣīḥat al-Mulūk,* Niẓām al-Mulk's *Siyāsat Nāmah,* Wā'iẓ Kāshifī's *Akhlāq-i Muḥsinī,* Naṣīr al-Dīn Ṭūsī's *Akhlāq-i Muḥtashamī,* and Sa'dī's *Gulistān* shows that Bāqir mentioned some ideas found in these works but that his textual borrowing did not exceed a few phrases. For example, Bāqir quotes the following well-known Tradition: "On a pair of scales, one hour of justice outweighs sixty years of worship."[163] Al-Ghazālī had written earlier that one day of justice was better than sixty years of worship.[164] Kāshifī also quoted this statement.[165] Other phrases drawn from *Akhlāq-i Muḥsinī* are in quotes: The blemish on all virtues is avarice and "the virtue that conceals all defects is generosity;"[166] as goes the dictum, "Valor is like a sword, and advice and planning are akin to a strong hand which uses it;"[167] and to those who seek an empire, "the best dress is a coat of mail, the best crown is a helmet, the most pleasant lodging is the battlefield, the tastiest wine is the enemies' blood," and the charming beloved is the sword.[168] In the first section of chapter 1 (about justice and discipline), Bāqir borrowed with some changes from the *Akhlāq:* "If [governmental] control and discipline are not effective, enterprises will be in disarray. If punishment and chastisement are nonexistent, [state] affairs will be in ruin."[169]

Bāqir repeats the advice of Niẓām al-Mulk that two portfolios should not be given to one individual.[170] The first section of chapter 2 of the *Mau'iẓah* (about friendship and socializing) contains some ideas from chapters 34 and 35 of Ṭūsī's *Akhlāq-i Muḥtashamī* dealing with the virtues of associating with the *'ulamā'* and good men (*akhyār*) and of avoiding the company of seditious (*al-ashrār*) and ignorant people (*al-juhhāl*).[171]

In the second section of chapter 2 (concerning the evils of poverty), Bāqir quotes a *ḥadīth* in its exoteric meaning: "Poverty is a disgrace on one's face in both worlds."[172] In the seventh chapter of *Gulistān,* Sa'dī also discusses conflicting views about wealth and poverty in the form of a debate between a dervish and Sa'dī himself, and he quotes the above *ḥadīth* and another ("Poverty is my pride") to represent the opposite viewpoint.[173] It is difficult to say whether Bāqir was inspired to write his section on the virtues of wealth by Sa'dī's discussion. The conclusions reached by Bāqir are different, and the language and mode of presentation are much more effective than Sa'dī's.

Then too, it is quite possible that Bāqir borrowed from other works which are not available to this writer; but on the basis of the present comparison, it can be said that *Mau'iẓah* is an original work.

CONCLUDING REMARKS

Three questions arise out of viewing the *Mau'iẓah* from a broader perspective: Should we consider the *Mau'iẓah* and other contemporary Mirrors as a subtle protest against Jahāngīr's policies? What is the significance of the *Mau'iẓah* and other Indo-Islamic Mirrors as sources of sociopolitical and intellectual history? And do biographical, professional, and educational factors affect the perceptions of writers and the orientation of their literary productions?

At the beginning of this introduction, I referred to Dankoff's view that because they embody a conservative tradition, the Mirrors as a genre are useful during a time of internal crisis or external threat.[174] In one of her articles, Lambton wrote that the works in this genre were written to uphold an ideal, to edify a person in authority, or to "protest against the evils of contemporary society and its failure to reach that ideal. Mirrors, thus, in some measure, aimed at the remedy of contemporary political evils."[175] The view of a group of historians who consider the accession of Jahāngīr a victory for conservatism and the claim of some that there was a "Naqshbandiyyah reaction" to the policies of Akbar give credence to the arguments of Lambton and Dankoff. The fact that three extant manuals were written during Jahāngīr's period whereas not a single work in this genre was written for his father Akbar, for his son Shāhjahān, or for his grandson Awrangzēb perhaps reflects the desire of the intelligentsia to create an ideal Islamic government.

While discussion of the controversy over Jahāngīr's accession to the throne is beyond the scope of this introduction, I have suggested in another study that it was a split in the nobility, resulting in the success of a particular faction—and not any ideological considerations —which led to Jahāngīr's crowning.[176] If the objective of the Mirrors had been to protest the policies of Akbar and to steer Jahāngīr away from them, Bāqir and other writers would have presented their views on statecraft in terms of the *Sharī'ah*. Instead, as discussed above, theocratic orientation of the administration was not Bāqir's major concern. It was only in the Introduction that he used a 'religious veneer.'

That there are only four extant works in the genre of Mirrors from the Mughal period, while three were written during Jahāngīr's reign, may be accidental. It is possible that such manuals were also written for Jahāngīr's predecessors and successors but have either perished or not yet been discovered. There is another equally plausible reason. In the Introduction of *Javīdān Khirad* (the Persian translation of Ibn Miskawayh's didactic work in Arabic, *al-Ḥikmat al-Khālidah*), Taqī al-Dīn Muḥammad Shūshtarī, the translator, recorded that Jahāngīr had commissioned him to make this work available to the ruling polity and the general public.[177] Jahāngīr's interest in this type of literature is thus evident and doubtless provided an impetus to other writers to compose treatises for presentation to the emperor.

The next, and more important, question concerns the significance of the Mirrors as sources of sociocultural and intellectual history for a given period. In a broad context, this genre, while it contains elements of universalism and includes wisdom and advice that transcend the barriers of time and space, does not provide factual historical information. Nevertheless, the perceptions and remarks of writers, when considered in a general historical and political context, can sometimes help us better understand the events, campaigns, and personalities recorded in the historical chronicles. For example, if we look at Baranī's *Fatāwā-i Jahāndārī*, it reflects the ambitions of the polity who identified themselves with the *ummah* beyond the frontiers of India and cherished a desire to Islamize India, the land of infidels. By contrast, works written during Jahāngīr's period reflect the harmony which had developed between the communities during the intervening centuries and are free of communal bias. (This attitude can also be attributed to movements such as Bhaktī and the general eclectic trends of the period). Baranī and Mudabbir, because of the mood of their respective periods, differed from each other in the importance they attached to *jihād*, imposition of *jizyah*, and *kharāj*. By Jahāngīr's era, the Indo-Islamic civilization had evolved to a point where Bāqir, Khāqāni, and 'Abd al-Ḥaqq no longer considered the Hindus or any other community a threat to Islam and felt no need to discuss the concept of *jihād* or *ghazw* in unprovoked violence against non-Muslims. 'Abd al-Ḥaqq mentioned the imposition of *jizyah* in passing and urged the ruler not to use coercion and oppression to realize this tax.[178]

Writers of the Sultanate period also emphasized the personal piety of rulers. According to Baranī, an un-Islamic courtly code of behavior could become legitimate if the ruler were to be aware of his deviations, repent, and use his authority to enhance the cause of Islam.[179] By the time of the Mughals, the Muslim sovereign had become representative of a composite culture. The writers of Jahāngīr's period were not overly concerned about the personal piety and Islamic behavior of the ruler. They were not looking for ways to justify adoption of the Sasanid or non-Islamic court etiquette. This is the time when the terms *imām, pādshāh,* and *khalīfah* become synonyms.

Looking specifically at the *Mau'iẓah* for Jahāngīr's period, we do find some direct references to Jahāngīr's keen sense of justice, his place as supreme ruler amongst contemporary rulers, and his legitimate right to power because of his lineage (although this was never in question). In these sections, Bāqir simply acknowledges his indebtedness to his patron by praising him. However, following the norms of didactic literature, Bāqir's tone sometimes becomes prescriptive. He alludes to the difficulties of a government if the ruler is weak and indecisive, and he suggests remedies.

His remarks could be considered especially relevant to Jahāngīr's period. Among the factors which (according to Bāqir) could lead to catastrophe for the empire were "sensuality (that is, passionate desire for women), fondness for hunting, preoccupation with wine (drinking), and inclination toward amusement."[180] Again, this general statement could be taken as advice to his patron. Jahāngīr, as we know, was fond of hunting and drinking. Bāqir's discussion of nobility, party politics, mutual rivalries, and how the ruler should deal with these issues could be interpreted as Bāqir's views on Mughal nobility. Knowing that Bāqir was a Shī'ī, one is tempted to think that his discussion of forgiveness and of restraint in taking a human life was prompted by the Jahāngīr's orders to put to death the well-known Shī'ī theologian Nūr-Allāh Shūshtarī.[181] Both 'Abd al-Ḥaqq [182] and Baqir[183] complain about the conceit and selfishness of their contemporaries, and such statements are important in that they reveal the behavior and ethics of the Mughal elite.

What is the significance of the didactic stories quoted in the Mirrors? As we know, Mirror writings are based on realism as well as idealism. Although created for the edification of rulers, they are filled with stories for the enjoyment of the general reader. The Indo-Islamic Mirrors represent a literary tradition which attempts to integrate Persian and Islamic ideals. Stories from pre-Islamic Iranian, Islamic, and Indian traditions are drawn on freely by the writers to substantiate and strengthen their arguments. A study of the stories in the works discussed in this introduction strongly suggests that they reflect the intellectual preferences of the readership—and supports Janet Wolff's observation that the nature of any work of art (including literature) is determined by the general trends of the time in which it was produced.[184] The academic and familial background of the writers of Mirrors are other factors that also need to be taken into account.

The stories in the Mirrors tell the reader about the heroes and villains of earlier times, transcending geographical and historical boundaries and chosen by the writers to appeal to their contemporaries. If we look at the stories dealing with one topic—say, justice—we find a wide range in the authors' choices that to some extent illustrates their orientation. Amongst the writers of the Sultanate period, Mudabbir quotes three stories from the Sasanid Iran, one from the *khāqān* of China, nine about the caliphs, and three from Biblical tradition. Baranī did not rely heavily on examples from the past to illustrate his point. He narrates one story about Maḥmūd of Ghazna (his ideal ruler), two about caliphs, and one from the Sasanid Iran. Hamadānī quotes ten examples, all of them from the *ḥadīth* literature.[185] With the exception of Bāqir, who does not mention a single story, others in the Mughal period frequently quote stories to support their viewpoints. In *Akhlāq-i Ḥakīmī*, Munshī quotes three *ḥadīth*, two stories about the caliphs, two each about the Ghaznawids and the Sāmānids, one from the Īlkhānid Iran, and three from the Sasanids. 'Abd al-Ḥaqq quotes numerous stories on *siyāsah* but only two on justice: one about Najjāshī (a contemporary of the Prophet Muḥammad, the ruler of Ḥabshah) and the other a general story without reference to a specific person or era. Given Jahāngīr's proverbial sense of justice, Abd al-Ḥaqq probably did not feel it necessary to cite examples from history on this topic. Khāqānī narrates more stories in the *Akhlāq* than his contemporaries: three *ḥadīth*, eleven from classical Islamic history, twelve from pre-Islamic Iran, eleven from post-Islamic Iranian history, and one from the *khāqāns* of China.

In *Akhlāq-i Ḥakīmī* and *Akhlāq-i Jahāngīrī*, there are stories from Indo-Islamic history and society. For example, in his discussion of generosity, Munshī narrates the story of Sultan Jūnā (father of Sultan Muḥammad bin Tughluq)[186] and an eyewitness account of the generosity of two leading nobles of Akbar's period, Bairam Khān (killed in 1561) and Pīr Muḥammad Sharwānī.[187] *Akhlāq-i Jahāngīrī* is the most voluminous Mirror of the Mughal period. Its author drew many examples from Islamic, pre-Islamic, and Indo-Islamic history. He also made use of hagiographical literature. In his discussion of *siyāsah*, for example, he tells an interesting story of a Hindu who was seeking the help of Ṣūfī Shaykh Sharaf Pānīpatī (also known as Bū 'Alī Shāh Qalandar—d. 1324) to serve as an intermediary; Khāqānī includes the text of the Shaykh's letter to Sultan 'Alā' al-Dīn Khaljī.[188]

The transmission of stories, their historical accuracy, their use by writers, and their intended impact on readers could form the topic of another study. Suffice here to conclude that stories in the Mirrors reveal a great deal about the intellectual trends and interests of the readership in Islamic India.

The last point requiring discussion is the influence of the writer's familial, academic, and professional background in the way he formulates his perceptions and presents his ideas. Bāqir, Khāqānī, and 'Abd al-Ḥaqq, as is apparent from their biographical sketches, had quite diverse backgrounds. The juristical and theological orientations of Khāqānī and 'Abd al-Ḥaqq are evident in their writings. For example, administration based on *Sharī'ah* (*siyāsah Sharī'ah*) was a favorite topic of the jurist Khāqānī, who devoted an entire chapter to the subject. He unequivocally states that the ruler should use his power for the propagation of Islam (*tarwīj-i Islām*), integration of the community of the leader of humanity, i.e., the Prophet Muḥammad (*tansīq-i millat-i Ḥazrat-i Sayyid-al anām*), and elimination of the enemies of the faith.[189] In this discussion, Khāqānī makes no reference to Hindus. He also urged the ruler to curtail the power of his nobility so that they might treat the Muslims with respect and justice. He portrays Jahāngīr as a champion of Islam.[190] In the *Akhlāq*, he also quotes extensively from the Qur'ān and *ḥadīth*. 'Abd al-Ḥaqq, a reputable *'ālim* writing in his short *Risālah-i Nūriyyah*, does not portray Jahāngīr's administration as *Sharī'ah*-oriented. Nevertheless, 'Abd al-Ḥaqq's juristical background is reflected in his quotations from the Qur'ān and *ḥadīth* and especially in his frequent mention of the hereafter. He advises the ruler to spend his nights in prayer.[191] Bāqir, on the contrary, is not preoccupied with the hereafter and quotes from the Qur'ān and *ḥadīth* sparingly; there are only eight references to the Qur'ān and fewer still to the *ḥadīth* in his entire text.

In view of the *Mau'iẓah*'s idiom and style, absence of didactic stories, and general tenor, it will be fair to state that if Abū'l Fażl 'secularized' the art of writing history in premodern India,[192] Bāqir 'secularized' the genre of Mirrors for Princes. This orientation was obviously forged out of his background and experiences. Coming from a family of high-level administrators and holding various important positions himself, Bāqir developed a practical and pragmatic approach to political issues. A skilled administrator, an accomplished writer who was fond of belles-lettres, a keen musician and listener to music, and an inventor of *nān-i Bāqir Khānī*[193] (a delicious type of bread still popular all over India and Pakistan), Bāqir displayed his versatility in the *Mau'iẓah.* He did not become the spokesman of a certain school of thought. Unlike his contemporaries, he did not take it upon himself to influence his ruler's religious convictions. He simply produced a manual on the art of government which, based on in its content and form, is a fine piece of literature and an important source for understanding the social and intellectual history of Jahāngīr's India.

EDITING AND TRANSLATION OF THE TEXT

EDITING

There are only three known manuscript copies of *Mau'iẓah-i Jahāngīrī.* Two are preserved in the India Office Library, and one in the Salarjung Museum, Hyderabad, India.*

Description of the Manuscripts Used:

Ms. O. (India Office Persian Manuscript 1666). As this copy is the older of the two, it is taken as the basic text. It is written in clear and distinct *nasta'līq* script, contains 72 folios, is 10½" x 6½", and was written in 1028 A.H./1619 A.D. during the lifetime of Bāqir. The section on political ethics finishes on folio 62a; the remaining folios not included in the accompanying text contain a philosophical tract and a eulogy for the deceased emperor Akbar, ending with a short poem in praise of Bāqir's friend and contemporary, the poet 'Itābī.

Ms. K. (India Office Persian Manuscript 1330). This is the *Kulliyāt* of Bāqir, comprising all of his prose and poetry, including the *Mau'iẓah,* fols. 276b-312a. It is in *nasta'līq* script (but is not as clear as Ms. O.), is 10" x 5½", and was written in 1063 A.H./1653 A.D.

I collated the two copies to identify textual variations and establish an authoritative text, explained the Persian and Arabic words and terms wherever necessary, and gave references to the Qur'ānic verses.

---

*Despite my efforts, I was unable to get a copy of the Salarjung manuscript.

TRANSLATION

I translated into English the entire text of the *Mau'iẓah* dealing with the political ethics. I attempted to remain as close to the original text as possible, but—at the same time—not to be so literal as to make it incomprehensible to a Western reader. I made every effort to capture and transmit the concepts, images, and cultural connotations of the original Persian. For rendering the translation into smooth English, I switched clauses around and inserted phrases or words for this purpose in square brackets [ ]. For insertions for completing sentences and explaining certain metaphors or religious allusions, I used rounded brackets ( ).

TRANSLATION

PREFACE

Thanks and praise to (God) the All-Wise who, with (fol. 2a) prudence and flawless artistry, without assistance of an associate or partner, without resorting to tools or instruments, and without stooping for aid and assistance, with penetrating wisdom brought this multifarious cosmos from invisibility of nonexistence into existence by the mere utterance of two letters: *kāf* and *nūn*.[1] With the pen of omnipotence He clearly inscribed creation on the folios of the universe; He perfected the creating of the macrocosm by bringing into being the human body. By firmly establishing and confirming man at the center, He thus adorned the orbit of existence. Man is, however, the fountainhead of both good and evil. (fol. 2b)

God led those lost in the wilderness of aberration and the abyss of deviation to the destination of wisdom and insight under the leadership of (Muḥammad), who is the guide to *Sharī'at* and the right path. He is the chief of prophets and the seal of the messengers; he is the first fruit in the garden of the universe, the index to all creations; he is the initiate to the secret chamber of divine intimacy and munificence; he is the sun in the celestial sphere of prophethood and spiritual guidance.

Verse

Intellect is like the dirt [on his feet] to Aḥmad, the messenger.
Both worlds are tied to his saddle-straps.

May God bless him, his house, his executor ('Alī),[2] and his progeny.

It will not remain concealed from people of insight, whose minds are alight with sagacity and illuminated with the rays of wisdom and knowledge, that in this material world, which mirrors the spiritual world, no other jewel is more beautiful than good discourse. With the alchemy of speech, adulterated copper (an individual's heart) can be wholly transformed into gold of purest assay. In particular, words on didactic issues will be effective, as will those containing the blessing of advice. (fol. 3a)

Verse[s]

The first stroke the pen made
Kindled the first letter of discourse.

When the pen began its movement to and fro,
It opened the eyes of the world with discourse.

On the lifting of the first veil,
The first manifestation was made with words.[3]

Indeed, speech does not by itself reveal its mysteries
To a person of limited intellect.[4]

We have envisioned that discourse.
[Therefore], we will live and die for it.

So long as the word lasts, may it remain illustrious.
May my soul and heart abound with speech.

A wise and learned person (*khiradmand-i farzānah*) is, therefore, the one who devotes the prime of his life and choicest of his time to studying peerless discussions and pleasurable writings, and one who regards this activity as the essence of every admonition and source of every benefit. However, it is as apparent as the sun that darkened hearts will not be brightened by the flame of advice. And the darkness of ignorance and deviation, which has been intermingled in the human personality (fol. 3b), will not dissipate in the light of admonition. Advice to an egotistic person is like a soft voice to the ears of a person born deaf, or like the foot of an ant striking a solid rock. But perhaps once, such a person may be rescued from the devouring gulf of aberration of his egotism which is a source of his undesirable conduct. Nonetheless, a stubborn steed can be brought under control only by the whip of sagacity, and arrogant personalities can be reformed only by good advice.

Indeed, this miserable, ignorant Muḥammad Bāqir Najm-i Ṣānī, out of infinitely Divine guidance, was always inclined to listen to didactic tales and eager to study exhortative writings. Whenever he had some leisure and managed, like a dazzling flash of lightning, to escape the straits of the company of casual friends—socializing with most of them is more venomous than with a serpent and more arduous than laying down one's life (fol. 4a)—he (Bāqir), considering [reading didactic literature] a felicitous activity, became engaged in self-purification. He spent his precious time reading marvelous discourses and rare sayings and filled the treasury of his heart with the jewels of admonishing expressions. Wherever he found a sentence or text which served as nutrient to the heart and comfort to the soul, he inscribed it on the tablet of the mind with the pen of imagination. He wanted to write it down but, because of multifarious activities, from which to a certain extent an individual cannot escape, this wish never materialized.[5] [Despite] a strong urge, this desire was not realized. Indeed, without peace of mind the fulfillment of this objective was difficult, and procuring privacy—the source of physical and spiritual tranquility—was impossible.

Now, through unexpected good fortune, he (Bāqir) found himself in full control of the situation for two or three days; it occurred to him—him with the languid soul—that (fol. 4b) he should arrange on the thread of writing the sparkling pearls which have been formed in the shell of his mind, and not keep those beautiful jewels concealed in the casket of his mind any more. Thus, he began to jot down eloquent words with his broken pen, and directed the thread of narration to composition. He strung those lustrous pearls, with a few potsherds of his own, together in accordance with the theme of this hemistich:

> Leaves are made part of a bouquet of flowers.

In order to grasp the essence of good and bad, he adorned the pages of this book with the jewels of admonishing texts and with the flowers of wisdom-inspiring words. It contains discussions on the multiplicity of the benefits of knowledge and the virtues of advice, and is beautified just like a setting of gold and gems. He named it *Mau'iẓah-i Jahāngīrī* and organized it in two chapters and ten sections. Indeed, this dervish deserves condemnation because of this arduous undertaking; all the same, he hopes (fol. 5a) that even if cruel friends do not care to condone his shortcomings, fair-minded people would contrive to overlook them.

Verse

The eyes of a connoisseur will view my work favorably;
What does it matter, if an unsophisticated person finds flaws?

Note: Some Persian text has been omitted from the TRANSLATION section because it is already included in the CONTENTS, p. vii. This is done to avoid interruption in the flow of the text. The omissions are:

1. Persian text, fols. 5a-b, p. 142, covering the topics of the *Mau'iẓah*.

2. Ibid., fol. 5b, p. 143. The phrase in italics in the title of Chapter I. On Exhortation of the Emperors, *comprising an Introduction and six sections.*

3. Ibid., fol. 41b, p. 183. The sentence in italics in the title of Chapter II. The Admonition of the Subordinates and Peers. *This chapter comprises four sections.*

CHAPTER I

On Exhortation (naṣīḥat) *of the Emperors*

INTRODUCTION

Verily, the human race is divided into various types according to inherent, distinctive potentials and innate, divergent faculties. Not everyone is capable of making higher advances through personal striving and of attaining his objective of Divine gnosis. Yet, if the skeptical intellect alone is his guide, an individual does not tread the path of salvation (fol. 6a) to gain honor [of Divine gnosis].[6] Moreover, to maintain order in the affairs of the world and to carry out the business of the human race,[7] law is needed. With that law [people] would live together and none would be afflicted and oppressed. Consequently, the Lord, the Preserver, the Exalted—great are His favors and all-embracing are His blessings—raised from among humans the prophets and the apostles. Each of them is a pearl in the ocean of purity and a doorway to the tower of the right path. Each is imbued with love of the world and of seclusion, and is endowed with vigilance and isolation so that in their seclusion and isolation they may be directly blessed with Divine grace and, in this world of association and surveillance, they may in turn guide the wanderers in the desert of aberration and the thirsty in the valley of deviation to the goal of salvation and to the fountainhead of Divine bounty. These prophets leave [with man] the law called *Sharī'at*—the individual faithful on the path of its rulings will be immune from the overpowering wrath of God and favored with perpetual blessings and pleasures. Any who (fol. 6b) deviates from that right way is overtaken by the indignation of the Almighty

Avenger and is afflicted with painful chastisement. Thus, the prophets' call [to the right path] came forth successively for a period of time until the breeze of compassion blew from the vent of beneficence and blissful dawn appeared in the sky of sublimity. The bright, full moon ascended above the horizon of dignity, and the sun of Muḥammad's prophethood rose in the sky of Baṭḥā' (valley of Mecca). The light of Aḥmad's prophecy glowed from east of the Mother of Cities (Mecca).

And after the Prophet—the last of the prophets and seal of the apostles—there ought to be no alternative but to have a prudent and powerful ruler with exalted authority maintaining order and strengthening the pillars of the true religion, regulating activities and conveniences for mankind, and achieving the blessings of peace and security. His (the ruler's) amiable person should be adorned with justice and rectitude; he should restrain himself from mercurial irascibility (fol. 7a), and from [extremism] in all sensual and carnal instincts as well. [Such a person in authority] would ensure that people do not neglect their affairs, are not overpowered by their whims and desires, and do not get involved in wanton pastimes, prohibited things, and corruption, and would ensure that all classes of people lead prosperous and comfortable lives in a cradle of peace and tranquility.

Therefore, it is necessarily incumbent upon the Almighty's chosen creation, whom they call an emperor (*pādshāh*), to inculcate in himself the morals of the custodian of the *Sharī'ah* (Prophet Muḥammad).[8] Waging his campaigns and conducting the business of his dominion (*mulk*) and sovereignty (*dawlat*)[9] according to the injunctions of Islamic law, the ruler should develop in himself qualities that beautify the attire of power. Directing all his energies to understanding the counsel of the sages and to comprehending the intimations of the *'ulamā,'*[10] he should pattern his policies after their advice, counsel, and judgment, so that the head of the [Muslim] community (*millat*)[11] would be adorned with the crown of sovereignty, and the vesture (fol. 7b) of the dominion would be embellished with the magnificence of religion. Every prudent ruler who is distinguished by these qualities and adorned with these laudable moral jewels will find his country (*mamlakat*) prosperous and his subjects contented and happy. The hearts of the people will come together in the bond of his loyalty and obedience, and the garden of his empire (*salṭanat*) will

flourish. For many years, innumerable decades, his name will remain inscribed on the pages of Time because of his goodness.

Therefore, not since the greatest illuminator (the sun) began dispensing bounties to the world have the eyes of times seen the emperor's like, a sovereign with the grandeur of Farīdūn, the auspicious reigning monarch of the Īlkhānid Court, the illuminator of (Amir Timūr) Gūrgān's lamp, the supporter of the pillars of the Caliphate and of prosperity, the strengthener of the foundations of power and success, the ascender to heights of magnificence and glory, the exalter of the levels of greatness and prestige. The force of Time has never before installed on the throne of power and sovereignty such an emperor (fol. 8a), an emperor with the dignity of Jamshīd, the refuge of the world, with a huge army (like countless stars)[12].

Hemistich: the pure water of the fountain of emperor
Akbar's deepest hope,
Abū al-Muẓaffar Nūr al-Dīn Muḥammad Jahāngīr *pādshāh.*[13]

[The emperor], in his attempt to enforce the precepts of sovereignty, to dispense the obligations of the empire, to spread the rulings of illustrious *Sharī'at,* and to consolidate the foundations of the Muslim community (*millat-i bayżā'*), has opened to the masses the doors of kindness and beneficence with hands[14] of immeasurable benevolence. He has embraced the inhabited quarter of the world with justice and favors. He has shaded the heads of people with his affection so that recognition of his justice and power has spread to all parts of the world. His greatness and dominance shine like the sun at noon. In the felicity of his justice, the magnet has abandoned attracting iron, the yellow amber (fol. 8b) has ceased oppressing the straw, the sheep and the wolf have taken a vow of sisterhood, and the lion has pledged fraternity with the deer.

Verse

The lamb and wolf stroll together—
The deer and lion delight in each other

In the period of [Jahāngīr's] eternal reign, the deer have no fear of the panther's claws; nor has a quail fear of the eagle's talons;

the fierce wind dares defile none with dust; the high-flying falcon has no courage to even think of preying on a pigeon. During his ever-expanding empire, all creatures have come from the darkness of tyranny and oppression to the fountain of equity and justice. All classes of people (*ṭabaqāt-i umam*) rest in meadows of peace and security and in gardens of repose and affluence. Therefore, famous sovereigns have willingly submitted to his authority and emperors with exalted powers have heartily accepted servitude to him.[15] Certainly in the bliss of these laudable actions and praiseworthy qualities, the masses of people will remain wrapped in tranquility and comfort in his seemingly eternal and divine empire[16] for many years to come, and the foundations of his empire will remain strong. (fol. 9a) Reverent mention of him will forever remain inscribed on the folios of Time and on the tablets of day and night, until the world's disintegration.

May the Holy and Almighty God guard and sustain this august emperor[17] in his empire, his sovereignty, and his power, and grant victory according to his desires and aspirations. May He grant all humanity enjoyment and benefit,

Hemistich: As long as the sky is in orbit and the earth
is stationary,

from the bliss of justice and equity of this victorious, world-conquering emperor.

[Verses]

So long as the earth has a north and a south,
So long as the moon is in orbit and moves,

May his throne be the lofty sky,
May his crown be the full moon,

May the liver of his enemy be ruptured by a dagger, and
May the face of his adversary be cut as a yellow dying leaf.

The angels in heaven have said "amen" to this prayer.

SECTION 1: ON JUSTICE (*'ADĀLAT*) AND DISCIPLINE (*SIYĀSAT*)[18]

Know that the empire and kingship constitute exalted rank and high station. With endeavor alone one cannot reach that level of aspiration. One may attain the position [of sovereignty] only with divine assistance, perpetual felicity, strength of power, and intercession of good luck. When in unexpected good fortune (fol. 9b) such a situation becomes possible and Almighty God, Praise be unto Him, bestows favor upon one of His servants by putting a crown of authority on his head, he in turn must hold the empire dear and venerable. In systematizing rules and in maintaining their procedures, he must exert the utmost care to achieve justice and impartiality. If the judge (*shahnah-i 'adl*) (ruler) does not regulate the affairs of the people, a clandestine rebel, abetted by tyranny, will destroy the lives of the nobility (*khāṣ*) and plebeian (*'ām*) alike. If the light from the candle of justice does not illuminate the somber cell of the afflicted, the darkness of cruelty will blacken the entire country[19] just as it does the hearts of tyrants.

Because rulers are but the reflections of the Creator, without the sun of their justice the expanse of the world is not illuminated. For people, repose in cradles of peace and security can develop only in the shade of their [rulers'] compassion and benevolence. A just ruler is a refuge to the oppressed and a protector of fallen. In the Tradition (*khabar*) (it says] that "on a pair of scales, one hour of justice outweighs sixty years of worship." Indeed the benefit of praying is limited to the worshipper (fol. 10a), [whereas] the benefit of justice reaches to the public in general, from high to low. The sages have said that justice is not of virtue but is virtue; and tyranny, which is its opposite, is not a part of vileness but is all vileness. Among the virtues of justice is that the earth does not decompose a sultan's body [in the grave]; and if this just sultan is a Muslim as well, the fire of hell will also not affect him.

Indeed, rulers conquer the dominion of the hereafter only by helping the oppressed and redressing [the wrongs of] the afflicted. For every prudent ruler who establishes his administration on the law of justice and does not deviate from the path of impartiality, the religious and ruling institutions (*qawā'id-i dīn wa dawlat*) [as well as] the foundations of the dominion and the community remain firm and structured. If, however, he transgresses from the way of justice, the base of his empire will be destroyed and the foundations of his power will soon be shaken.

Wise men have enunciated that five types of persons should quit aspiring for five things, abandoning hope of their attainment: first, a tyrant ruler for the stability of the country (fol. 10b) and preservation of the empire; second, an arrogant and haughty person for people's praise; third, an ill-tempered person for many friends; fourth, a shameless and rude person for glory and a rank of dignity; fifth, a miser for a good name.

Certainly, the cable of security for the world's inhabitants is tied to the person of all-powerful emperors and rulers. Their commands have sway over people's lives and possessions; their mandates are like the descending decree, enacted and carried out to solve and resolve (*ḥall-o-'aqd*) problems. Therefore, rulers must consider that they occupy the throne in order to dispense justice, not to lead a life filled with pleasure. They must consider justice and equity as the means to survival of their rule, permanence of their fame, and reward in the hereafter (*ākhirat*). To them, nothing should be more binding than pursuit of the people's[20] welfare. They must not consider it ignominious to speak with peasantry (*ra'āyā*), the elderly, the weak, and the poor. Having listened to the petitioners for justice, the rulers themselves should probe the affairs of the oppressed and affectionately turn their attention toward resolving their problems. They should not be irritated by their [the petitioners'] loquacity. Indeed, the emperor is like a physician and the petitioner like a patient. If the patient does not fully explain his condition (fol. 11a), the physician cannot apprehend his disease. How can he diagnose an unknown illness?

One must, however, know that the roots of the tree of justice are invigorated and watered by showers from the clouds of discipline, because [governmental] control is based on the laws of justice. It is said that an empire is like a young plant and that control is akin to water. Therefore, to reap the fruit of peace and security, the roots of the empire must be kept refreshed by the water of discipline. If [governmental] regulation and discipline are not effective, enterprises will be in disarray. If punishment and chastisement are nonexistent, [state] affairs will be in ruin. [Imperial] control is the adornment of the country and community and an expedient for the welfare of religion and empire. Without the rulers' regulation of control, the decrees of the *Sharī'ah* will not be promulgated, nor is the basis of the power strengthened. If the sword of retribution is not drawn from the scabbard of vengeance, the roots of rebellion are not eradicated and the basis of oppression is not undermined. If the debris of tyranny is not burnt in the fire of [imperial] wrath, the seedling of repose will not flourish in the garden of hope. Popular insurgents, having witnessed the fire of punishment blaze, slip away. [However], if there is even a little intimidation discernible in the [state] control (fol. 11b), there will be uprisings everywhere and diverse disturbances will develop. Therefore, rulers should display the mercy of God toward the virtuous and the reformers (*muṣliḥān*), and the wrath of God toward the evildoers and the seditious. Rulers should dip the lancet of their rage in the honey of kindness and mix the poison of their majesty with the sugar of compassion. They should combine [their] control with justice in order to keep the meadow of righteous people's aspirations lush with the sprinkles of benevolence, and to uproot the foundation of the lives of the wicked with discipline's stormy winds.

SECTION 2: ON GENEROSITY, (*SAKHĀWAT*), BRAVERY (*SHUJĀ'AT*), AND FORBEARANCE (*ḤILM*)[21]

Know that there are no better qualities, especially for the nobility (*ashrāf*) and the rulers, than benevolence (*jūd*) and generosity. The blemish on all virtues is avarice and the virtue that conceals all defects is generosity. Religious and worldly bliss is attained through benevolence and munificence. Regarding religious felicity, God, the Most Exalted, has said, "He who does good shall have tenfold to his credit."[22] As for worldly blessedness, the bird of the people's heart can be captured through munificence. It is [rightly] said that a wild bird can be tamed in a net and man can be captured through reward and beneficence (*iḥsān*).

Generosity (fol. 12a) and beneficence result in fame, prosperity, and ultimate success. God, the Most Exalted, Glory be unto Him, loves high-minded people. Seeds of kindness bear no fruit other than felicity in this world and bounty in the hereafter. Venerable exaltation is conjoined with high-mindedness (*himmat-i buland*) so that their separation is impossible. The first master (Aristotle) is quoted as having said that the most virtuous characteristic of God, the Most Exalted, is His attribute as Benefactor (*Jawwād*), because His beneficence encompasses the entire universe and envelops all creatures. The master of supreme prophethood (Muḥammad), May God's blessings be upon him, remarked that benefaction was a young plant grown in the garden of paradise and nurtured on the bank of the river Kauṣar,[23] and that "generosity is a tree in paradise."

To rulers, high-mindedness (*himmat-i 'ālī*) is an efficacious helper and sincere deputy.[24] The more magnanimous they are, the loftier in power. However, valor should be given precedence over generosity because from gallantry emanates altruism. Once one masters the endurance of mortal danger, spending one's wealth, a [relatively] trivial matter, does not bother him at all. Although generosity encourages various qualities, it is uncommon to see a combination of bravery and magnanimity. (fol. 12b) A ruler not endowed with heroism is like a cloud without rain. Wise men have said that permanence of a country and stability of a ruler's power are not possible without [the following] four things:

First, perfect vigilance (*ḥazm-i kāmil*) [so that the ruler is] able to envision the face of tomorrow in the mirror of today.

Second, firm resolve (*'azm-i rāsikh*) [so that] infirmity and default will not interfere with his determination.

Third, sound judgment (*rāy-i ṣā'ib*) [so that he will] not deviate from the course of moderation into error and confusion.

Fourth, a sharp sword to ignite the harvest of his opponent's life as incendiary lightning.

It is a fact that the garden of power and glory does not become verdant and does not flourish except by the sword of victory. The seedling which is security and hope does not bear fruit which is success unless nurtured by *żaymorān*[25] which is the sword. To have a [state] like paradise, peace and security must be assured by the swords of the emperors. Indeed, the loftiest heaven is indebted to the swords of just rulers. [It has been said], "Paradise is under the shade of swords." The eye seeking world conquest perceives the beauty of its objective only when it uses the dust of battlefield as collyrium [to enhance its vision]. The hand that desires (fol. 13a) powerful rule can capture the bride of its purpose only by flirting with the countenance of an upright lance. To those who seek an empire, the best dress is a coat of mail and the best crown is a helmet, the most pleasant lodging is the battlefield, the tastiest wine is the enemies' blood, and the charming beloved is the sword.

Verse

Only that person who kisses the lip of the sword
Can embrace in a leap the bride of dominion.

Victorious emperors satisfy their driving passion for the virgin lady of sovereign rule only when the glare of their flaming sword has erased from life's tablet the name of their malicious enemy. Famous rulers raise the goblet of their desire to the lips of repose only when they have shattered their enemy's cup of aspirations with the stone of victory. Indeed, delight of power lies in three things:

First, to afflict and frustrate enemies.
Second, to exalt friends and well-wishers.
Third, to fulfill the needs of the oppressed and bestow favors on the destitute.

The ruler who disregards, on the day of combat, the aftermath of [this fierce battle to preserve his] fame and honor considers life and property to be [at that moment] worthless, insignificant, and awkward. (fol. 13b) He prefers to fight rather than have [his] name and grace obliterated. And indeed, he will embrace the beloved of victory. Although the sword is double-edged and the wind might blow from either direction, God, the Most Exalted, Glory be unto Him, loves the brave and is their Protector and Helper. Have you not observed that timid and cowardly people are usually slain in combat, and that fearlessly daring and dauntless fighters come out safe? The person who has smelled the fragrance from the garden of heroism prefers the affliction of a thousand wounds to dying in the bed of sickness like a decrepit old man.

Remember, nonetheless, that the sages have considered generosity, heroism, and magnanimity to be interdependent. Most of them have preferred magnanimity, combined with perseverance and prudence, over generosity and daring. They assert that valor is not helpful at all times—in a lifetime one needs it but rarely. There is a greater need for munificence and affability. Furthermore, the benefits of generosity are limited to a certain group, and only a special category of people (fol. 14a) profit from conferral of benefactions. But both small and large, both base (*waẓīʿ*) and noble, are in need of forbearance. Among the beneficiaries of affability are nobles and commoners, and soldiers (*sipāhī*) and peasants alike. [The imperial] ordinances govern the lives, possessions, properties, and honor of the people; [similarly], royal edicts and prohibitions are evenly enforced on the low-born (*asāfil*) and high-born (*aʿālī*), on commoners (*aṣāghir*) and grandees (*akābir*). [Therefore] if the rulers do not grace their days with altruism and perseverance, do not capitalize on these qualities, and do not distinguish their conduct with magnanimity and affability, in a fit of rage they might disturb and inflict suffering on their subjects and cause property and lives of many to perish. Even an emperor [who rivals] Ḥātim and Isfandiyār in generosity and bravery, [to an extent that he] obliterates their names from the records of Time, without magnanimity and perseverance will blacken the fount of generosity with a single tyrannical act, and in one dispute stir up countless[26] mortal enemies. [On the other hand], although a ruler might never have smelled the fragrance from the garden of benevolence and gallantry, he can [still] please and gratify the peasantry and army (*lashkarī*) with benignity, affability, and congeniality (fol. 14b), and can draw his subjects into bonds of loyalty and affection.

It is said that magnanimity is from the morals of prophets and anger is the inspiration of the satan. The chief of prophets (Muḥammad), blessings and peace be upon him, remarked that the bliss of this world and [fulfillment] of desires in the hereafter originate in magnanimity and congeniality. It is recognized by philosophers that unless a person overcomes his rage, he cannot reach the level of faithful witness to the Truth. A certain wise man has noted that relinquishing anger amasses all virtues of ethics and merits of character, and that reverting to it results in the rendezvous of all evil actions and shameful deeds. The sages have commented that an individual's strength can be judged [by his capacity] to extinguish the flame of his fury and to subdue the blaze of his rage at the instant ignited. Indeed, there is no taste more pleasant to the palate of wisdom than the syrup mixed with poison of magnanimity and perseverance, because the elegance of magnanimity and the virtue of dignity are the most laudable qualities with which God, the Most

Exalted, has adorned man. A magnanimous person is the darling of hearts.

Nevertheless, for rulers, opportune anger is far better than ill-timed and inappropriate forbearance. (fol. 15a) Indeed, to show leniency when there is need for sternness would cause embarrassment and destroy the edifice of their empire. However, rulers must be well aware of the appropriate [use] of these [moods]. Since man is not free of inadvertence and error, to punish him for every crime he commits would result in total disarray [in the ranks of] the pillars of the country (*arkān-i mamlakat*) (nobility). The [ruler] who is illuminated by the light of intellect, adorned by the ornament of wisdom, and distinguished by Eternal bounty attempts to extinguish flames of rage. At his farthest limits, he pours the water of clemency over the fire of rage. He well knows that although gulping the sherbet of forgiveness is bitter, it contains sweetness. Notwithstanding, enduring the drudgery of clemency and perseverance is as poison; it also constitutes an antidote made of grace.

In any case, rulers, [in order to show] their gratitude for having the power to inflict retribution, should bless a guilty criminal with the joyful tidings of forgiveness. Indeed, had there been no crime they would have been unable to dispense the best of virtues, forgiveness. [Rulers must] show restraint in all their actions, especially in spilling blood. If the execution [of an individual] is absolutely necessary, there will [always] be time to complete it. (fol. 15b) However, if in a hasty action, may God avert it, an innocent person is put to death, and it is later revealed that he should not have been executed, reparation for the action is impossible. The blood and [the burden of this] crime will be on [the rulers'] necks until eternity. Spilling [human] blood is arduous; destroying the very basis of human life is difficult; [but] bringing the past back and reviving the dead is beyond the power of a human being. Therefore, emperors and rulers should distinguish themselves by the qualities of magnanimity and patience, should cheerfully sip the unpleasant syrup of anger, and should always give precedence to the relish of forgiveness over the bitterness of punishment. No matter how great the crime, they should consider forgiveness even greater.

Recompense being inherent in the nature of this world, it is inconceivable that someone who imbibed from the goblet of tyranny would not languish in misery, or that he who sowed a seedling of injustice in the garden of his deeds would not harvest the fruit of chastisement and torture. [The rulers], to the extent of their power, must not unjustly torment anyone. What they do not like for themselves, their children, and relatives (fol. 16a), they should not consider for others. Thereupon, their enterprises and undertakings should be adorned, from beginning to end, with good fame and honorable mention. They must believe that a good deed is never lost and retribution to the evildoers is never suspended. There must be requital for every action. [However], some delay in it should not delude anyone, because deferral for a short time[27] is possible. The notion of not receiving punishment or reward is absurd. Every seed sown in the field of action, before long, bears fruit.

Wise men have compared this world, the abode of retaliation, to a mountain—whatever bad or good you say to it, it echoes back the same to you. The person who does evil should not expect goodness. The one wishing to have sugar cane should not sow wild gourd. To show gratitude to the Dispenser of Destiny for having elevated their imperial court and to the Controller of Fate for having vested in them an opportunity for power and rule, rulers should try to perform deeds resulting in the good name of the faith (Islam) and in salvation at various levels in the hereafter. They should feel duty-bound to improve their affairs and to concentrate on engaging themselves in laudable (fol. 16b) acts and deeds. They should shower the masses with their benevolence. The flowers of their aspirations will bloom in paradise—[according to the Qur'ān], "If ye did well, ye did well for yourself"[28]—and they will be rewarded in this world and the hereafter.

Verse[s]

If you do evil, do not expect goodness
For the wild gourd does not bear grapes.

Oh you who have sown barley in the autumn,
Do not expect to harvest wheat.[29]

The teacher (Aristotle?) said thus:
Do not be vicious because, Time will turn ugly on you.

The individual who is beneficent to humanity
Is blessed with both worlds.

SECTION 3: ON CONSULTATION (*MASHWARAT*) AND PLANNING (*TADBĪR*)[30]

You should know that the majority of wise men regard advice and deliberation as superior to bravery. They opine that what one can achieve through planning cannot be accomplished by sword and by arrow, as goes the dictum: "Valor is like a sword, and advice and planning are akin to a strong hand which uses it." A hand without the sword can perform all sorts of tasks, whereas a sword without a hand is useless, nonfunctional, and worthless. No matter how venturesome, audacious, and fearless a person is, he may equal ten (fol. 17a), twenty or, at the most, one hundred persons in combat. However, a wise person can destroy a country with one sound thought and break an army through contemplation. Specifically, rulers, through sound judgment and precise planning, can achieve objectives that are [normally]—despite immense treasures and riches and innumerable retinue and attendants—hard to attain.

Every prudent ruler endowed with the intellect's benediction bases his caliphate's ordinances and his empire's affairs on consultation and planning. Following the [Qur'ānic injunction] "Consult them in affairs,"[31] he does not meddle with the affairs of his country without seeking the advice and opinion of critical nobles [on a given matter]. Having tied the entire structure of his actions and ordinances to the planning of adept wazirs and prudent counselors, he seeks [further] support in the opinion of honest and trustworthy advisers. Indeed, [he acts] in accordance with this [statement]: "People do not consult each other unless God leads them; there is no Divine guidance in affairs which are conducted without consultation". Whatever emanates from the advisers is likely to be prudent and pertain to peace in the world and tranquillity for humanity. The empire [of a ruler with such consultants] will remain strong and his power solid. One who ignores the counsel of his advisers, despite their being harsh and unstinting (fol. 17b), [and] deviates from the policy of consultation and planning, is lacking in vigilance and farsightedness; he will be regarded as devoid of intellect and foresight. The end result of his undertakings will not be short of contrition. Nothing will remain in his control and under his power except regret and penitence. [Such a ruler] is like a patient who does not follow the advice of the physician, eats and drinks at his own whims, and [finds that], every moment, weakness and feebleness overpower him even more. One must be convinced that the planning of several minds will be more rightly directed and more advantageous than that of one mind. Accurate thinking is like game that cannot be brought down by one person but from a group of people cannot escape.

Thus, it is necessary that rulers regard contemplation and consultation as their aids and attempt to resolve every complex matter with the help of planning. They should manage their affairs by following the dictates of sound judgment and maintain extreme vigilance and care (fol. 18a) while attending to them. [As a matter of policy], they should envision, at the time of embarking upon an expedition, its end, and should evaluate in their minds its advantages and disadvantages. When rulers are faced with an issue, they should discuss its pros and cons with wise persons, experienced individuals, men with foresight, perceptive elders, and the group whose [keen] faculties of thinking the rulers should have previously measured. They should enact whatever is considered expedient and prudent. Should planning concur with Fate, the rulers will hold the throne of auspiciousness and success. If the situation is reversed, friends would excuse them and even slanderers would not dare to disparage [them]. The sages say that only such a [ruler], who envisions the end of every endeavor at the time of its start and thinks of the fruit even before planting the seedling, is [considered] wise. In every matter, he is well aware of possible failure of his effort and a [possibly] disastrous end to his expedition, so that he does not regret his action. [Consequently], his campaigns are usually joined with triumph and victory and [he] successfully achieves his objective. (fol. 18b)

He never hurries his actions and loves to be cautious and deliberate. Indeed, the risks in rashness are high and the advantages of forbearance and poise are innumerable. Discretion enhances [the effectiveness of] all endeavors, and restiveness damages many undertakings. Wise people have nothing to do with hastiness; sages have regarded it as the temptation of Satan. In any case, whoever makes haste master of his affairs ends his endeavors in regret, anguish, embarrassment, and penitence. But the ruler who bases his activities on patience and steadfastness, and who strengthens the roots of his campaigns with calmness and dignity, undoubtedly concludes his projects and operations in triumph and victory. The end result of haste is repentance and disgrace; a rash person is always denied fulfillment of his objectives. Patience remains the most agreeable and sanctioned quality; forbearance is the key to tranquility. The doorway to the abode of comfort cannot be opened without the key of endurance. No matter what befalls an individual, if he holds on firmly to the support of patience [and] follows the course of consultation and planning (fol. 19a), he will eventually see his desires come true. It happens quite often that the project that is initiated after considerable deliberation and caution often progresses as desired. The endeavor that is put together hastily and carelessly will most certainly not succeed properly. Carelessness is like an arrow shot from a bow; it cannot be recalled. Scrupulousness is akin to a sword in hand; if one wishes to use it, one may; otherwise, it does no harm.

Nevertheless, rulers should not traverse the course of consultation with all and sundry. They should not treat the secrets of the empire as public affairs and official transactions. Only after testing the piety, honesty, wisdom and sagacity of an individual several times should they discuss their secrets, because not every consulted person deserves to be trusted. The dictum is that the emperor's secrets are usually disclosed by those of his advisers who are not adorned with trustworthiness. [Therefore], whatever is gathered from consultations and deliberations and is agreed upon should be kept secret. There are two advantages accruing from concealing one's secret and hiding one's intent. (fol. 19b) First, the endeavor that is kept secret obtains success sooner. Second, if planning is not favored by Destiny and the intent is not realized through power, enemies and censurers will not be able to rejoice [over the failure]. Revealing secrets does not bear good results. The saying goes: "whoever discloses state secrets, risks his life."

Hemistich: If you wish to keep your head intact, guard
your secret.

For the rulers, it is absolutely imperative to safeguard secrets, especially from disappointed friends and frightened enemies. Wise men say that the emperor should not take the following seven [types of] people into confidence:

First, the one who languished as a result of his committing a crime or sin in the ruler's court, and whose suffering and affliction persisted for some time.

Second, the one who lost his wealth and integrity in the ruler's service, and saw his sources of livelihood dwindle.

Third, the individual dismissed from his post who has lost the hope of regaining the position.

Fourth, the perverse person instigating trouble who is not inclined toward security and peace.

Fifth, the culprit (fol. 20a) whose peers punished him and were excessive in [punishment].

Sixth, the individual who served the emperor commendably but was denied [recognition], while others [even] without working were patronized more than he.

Seventh, a person unacceptable in the emperor's court but admired by the enemy.

There are certain royal secrets that emperors should conceal even from themselves; that is, in safeguarding them such care should be taken as if they themselves did not know [the secrets]; still less should they share even a slight hint of them with someone else. Emperors should be their own confidants and should reveal their secrets to no one. Once they disclose their intent to someone, they should not be offended if that person talks about it to somebody else. If they could not conceal their secret and could not bear their own burden [of secrecy] despite their prudence, divine help, high-mindedness, and superb minds, how could others who are inferior in intellect and wisdom guard it? How could they bear the burden?

[Verse]

Do not disclose the secret to anyone;
Indeed, we have strolled the earth and found no confidant.

SECTION 4: GUARDING AGAINST ENEMIES (fol. 20b)

Know that there are two things of which even a small quantity should be considered large:

First is fire, a small amount of which has as much danger of burning as has a large fire.

Second is the enemy who, no matter how feeble and weak, follows his [hostile] course of action.

Wise men tell [us] that an antidote can be found for everything considered harmful except malevolence, which cannot be remedied by any possible means. For instance, a burning fire can be extinguished with water; but the flame of rancor and animosity cannot be smothered with the water of seven rivers. Although poison is fatal, its venom can be extracted from the body by an antidote; but no antidote can eliminate the poison of malevolence from the body. This is particularly true of personal hostility—no other enmity is as deep as personal malice. Consider that if temporary spite develops between two persons, it can be eliminated with little effort; however, if it develops into deep-seated animosity—and if old ill-will is combined with new animosity—its reversal (fol. 21a) is totally impossible. Its neutralization will be tied to the extinction of both individuals.

Verse

Hoping for new friendship from old enemies is
Like expecting [to find] a rose in a furnace.

Indeed, no fortress is stronger than vigilance and caution. Among the various aspects of vigilance is that of never trusting the enemy. Sages overly emphasize this aspect and remark that trusting an inexperienced friend is unwise, to say nothing of [trusting] a malevolent enemy.

Therefore, rulers should under no circumstances forsake the course of vigilance and should never consider the enemy small and feeble. Wise men have commented that the friendship of a thousand persons does not equal the enmity of one. Emperors must make their [enemies'] annihilation an important mission and must not be deceived by their show of kindness and adulation. No matter how much [the enemies] flatter and humble themselves, emperors should not trust them. They should not be fooled by false appearances and hypocritical tricks and should pay no attention to their powerful charm. The more kindness and affability the rulers observe in them, the more they should be skeptical (fol. 21b) and circumspect. To the same extent that the enemy makes advances in cordiality, the rulers should withdraw their approval, the maxim being that one should not be lured by the words of the enemy despite his benevolence, and that one should not believe the words of his adversary, no matter how much he exerts himself in cultivating friendship, because he is totally incapable of friendliness. The enemy, even though he emerges in a thousand [new] forms, will still have the taint of rivalry in his heart. The dictum states that malice in the hearts of one's opponent is like frozen charcoal: although it does not show its [inherent] quality at the moment, as the flame reaches it, it too catches the flames and the blaze of enmity flares up; it burns a world and its smoke dries up numerous minds and darkens countless eyes. Immunity to the hazards of animosity's blaze is impossible as long as even a speck of rancor's charcoal is in the heart's furnace.

No matter how small and weak the enemy is nor how large and powerful the emperors themselves are, they should consider it imperative to guard themselves against him. Once they have overpowered him and attained this heartfelt desire, they must not hesitate to extinguish the blaze of the enemy's life—since no other remedy works.[32] (fol. 22a) [If the rulers forgo this opportunity], no amount of regret will be of any avail. If rulers are negligent in dealing with the enemy and leave a loophole, the enemy looking for such an opportunity will, in a surprise ambush, shoot the arrow of planning into the target of this objective. At such a time, the power of reparation is diminished; regret and contrition are no help. Indeed, the ruler beguiled by the enemy's flattery and blandishment forsakes prudence, vigilance, and foresight, makes his life a target for the arrows of disaster, and kindles the fire of calamity; indeed, a wise enemy, in order to expedite his plans, manifests extreme benignity. Having ordered his external behavior, contrary to his inner motives, he subtly employs malignity and trickery. Meanwhile, he marshals all possible ideas and novel plans, and inflames the fire of finesse with excuses and pretense in such a way that no conceivable strategy[33] can extinguish that flame.

However, if the power, authority, and grandeur of the enemy is greater [than the emperor's], and if there is fear that violence from his [enemy's] dominance may spread to the territories, (fol. 22b) that the peasantry, the weak, and the poor may fall into the gulf of perdition and be killed, and that the rulers might not have the power to defend and resist, then war should be fought only out of necessity. If rulers are [in danger of being] ousted and know of no strategy to counter the enemy's plans, they should not initiate conflict. Instead, they should thwart the enemy's designs by tossing the dice of strategem with benevolence. They should turn their wealth into a shield [to protect] their country and the honor of the empire. Since on the dice-board of arrogance and pride the enemy's die predominates and the opponent's position is stronger, it would be imprudent to play hostility's chess game. The enemy can be routed faster with benignity and civility than with combat. By [analogy], when fire with all its ferocity strikes a tree, it can only burn what is above the ground; [whereas] water with its softness and smoothness can uproot even larger and stronger trees.

Undoubtedly, wishing without restraint or contemplation to wage war with the enemy for revenge would be like sleeping in the path of flood or like throwing a brick at the surface of flowing water. (fol. 23a) Relying on one's [physical] power and valor is far from prudent. Nonetheless, concern for caution is appropriate only to the extent that it furthers [the rulers'] action. They should not go to extremes in this because lowering one's self-respect increases the adversary's courage. [If rulers are overly cautious], they will close the avenues to thinking of strategies. If they observe that the enemy is bent upon taking their lives, they should, motivated by their sense of honor and integrity, set themselves up for a confrontation and fight. And they should open their hearts to the endless favors of the Causer of causes (God). Having renounced their lives, they should come to the battlefield maximally striving to their utmost; if they are negligent in their efforts, they will further [the risk of] spilling their own blood. Their effort [in the battlefield] can lead to two things: if they succeed, they will leave the imprint of their valor on the pages of Time; and if things do not work out, then too they will be considered to have not been lacking in manliness (*mardi*) and a sense of honor (*ḥamīyat*).

(fol. 23b) Since God, Praise be unto Him, the Most Exalted, loves valorous people and is their Protector and Helper, it has happened most often that the person who steps into the battlefield with a sense of virility and prowess, not caring for his life, embraces his cherished objective of triumph and victory. Indeed, audacity and bravery discourages the enemy, while fear and cowardice embolden the adversary. This is verified [in the Qur'ān], "How oft, by God's will, hath a small force vanquished a large one?"[34] The minority have overpowered the majority and the very weak have defeated the strong. No matter how strong and large a reed, it can be broken with a thin stick; and no matter how large and robust a crane, it can be seized by the talons of a weak falcon.

SECTION 5: ON NOT ACTING UPON THE ADVICE OF A SELFISH PERSON (*ṢĀḤIB-I GHARAŻ*) AND NOT PERMITTING A CONSPIRATOR (*SĀʿĪ*) AND CALUMNIATOR (*NAMĀM*) IN THE COUNCIL[35]

The emperor whose empire[36] is worthy of the crown of eminence and whose glory[37] deserves the seal of rulership (fol. 24a) should know what kind of people to associate with. He should listen to the advice of those whose counsel is [based on] good will and the welfare of the state. [He should also know] which group to shun and silence [on state matters]. Only a small group of employees in the royal court put their heart and soul into striving for their master to achieve a good name in this world and salvation in the hereafter. The majority of [the employees] remain in service for their own advantage or to avert hardship from themselves. When the aim of their activities is greed, these groups become jealous of each other because of the disparity of prestige and rank among them. When rancor and jealousy develop among themselves, they play various tricks and report incidents that never occurred.

If the emperor lacks caution, listens approvingly to their words, and does not care to inquire about and investigate the situation, various disruptions and dangers appear, and diverse evils develop. (fol. 24b) If the vigilant ruler shrewdly plumbs the depth of the matters, investigates them wholly and in part, isolates the brilliance of veracity from the darkness of a lie, and familiarizes himself with the truth and falsehood of every affair, the foundations of his empire will be immune from damage in this world and in the hereafter (*ʿuqbā*) he will be blessed with salvation and be elevated in [his] rank. If the ruler does not investigate truth and falsehood but listens to the accusation of this individual against that and the slander of that person against this, neither the emperor nor the pillars of the empire (nobility) can be trusted, since whenever they might wish to accuse a candid person, they would be able to. Innocent individuals would remain trapped in the whirlpool of annihilation while the culprits would lead lives of safety and security on the shore of freedom. The consequence of such a situation would be that those present would decline to accept an assignment and those absent would cease to serve. There would be a thousand kinds of confusion among the nobility and very soon the foundations of the empire would be destroyed. (fol. 25a) Sages opine that five groups [of people] should not be given access to the council.

First is an envious person: the poison of jealousy cannot be neutralized by any antidote. Rancor and jealousy are the vilest traits and most contemptible characteristics. Envy is considered a consequence of ignorance. A jealous person is forever tortured by [the sight of] others in comfort, and is grieved at their cheerfulness.[38]

Second are avaricious and parsimonious persons: they are outcast among people. Just as generosity hides defects, miserliness and parsimony conceal virtues.

Third are talkative persons: they are conceited and are very inattentive and mistaken in their discourse.

Fourth are traitors [and] ungrateful persons: they turn gratitude toward their benefactors into ingratitude through their failure to recognize that the rights [of their patron have been earned by] his favors.

Fifth are slanderers and calumniators: they incite violence and their activities [usually] end in major disaster. When they find access to the council meeting, they very tactfully conceal truth's elegance with the veil of falsehood; and with deceitful discourse (fol. 25b) they draw the ruler away from the path of generosity (*muruwat*) and then associate him with infidelity and perfidy. This contributes to depravity of the nobility and destruction of the empire's foundation.

Since the inherent worth of an individual depends on his excellence in clarity of judgment in every circumstance and occurrence, penetrating intellect and world-adorning thinking should characterize a just ruler and a perfect judge. Considering inquiry and investigation obligatory, the rulers should consistently practice caution and interrogation. They should deliberate over whatever reaches them and should with the bridle of patience prevent anger's steed from running wild. They should alleviate doubt's darkness with the light of intellect, should not lend [their] ears to the defamation of any slanderer, and should reject whatever others tell [them] of the faults of any individual. The rulers should interpret the evil spoken of others—whatever reaches them, whether it is small or big; they should [make sure to] close the avenue of talking about others. Until and unless they do witness manifest proof and clear argument [of what is said] (fol. 26a), they should ignore the idle talk of selfish people and should not act upon their words. When the rulers find out what these people say is independent and sincere, only then should they accept it.

When rulers exalt someone [by bringing him] close to them, they should not entertain the suggestion of others for his downfall. Indeed, whoever becomes close to the ruler will be envied by his peers and contemporaries and many will be jealous of him. When [rivals] see the ruler strongly favoring him, they will try to damage his honor by various tricks of diplomacy. [In pretense] of showing concern for the welfare of the state, they will transmit beguiling and deceitful words until they turn the ruler's heart from him—thus do they achieve their objective. Once they have learned this tactic,[39] most of the nobility will make the ruler miserable and frustrated. Total confusion will overpower the emperor and his endeavors will end in violence. The record of his happiness and exaltation will fall in the abyss[40] of extinction. If, however (fol. 26b), the rulers observe this trait in someone, they should extinguish, as soon as possible, the fire of his calumny by the luster of the sword, so that it does not blacken the surface of the world and blind the eye of Time.

Although scholars of religion and mystics of the highest order[41] have greatly stressed the virtues of forgiveness and the glory of beneficence, punishment is far better than forgiveness in matters that would result in violence in the world and damage to the very foundation of the human race. In such cases, there should be no room for amnesty and indulgence. The punishment for and chastisement of seditious persons should be considered obligatory.[42]

Verse

The individual who favors hurting people
Is the enemy of the country, and (the ruler) should
order his execution.

SECTION 6: ON TRAINING SERVANTS (*DAR TARBĪYAT-I MULĀZIMĀN*)

This section is divided into two subsections: (i) on the training of employees by rulers; and (ii) on the etiquette of serving emperors: on how to behave when one gains access to the imperial service.

Subsection (i): (fol. 27a) On the Training of Servants by Emperors

Know that emperors and rulers cannot do without pillars of the empire (nobility), eyes of the court (ministers), and other employees. There is an unquestionable need for emperors to have faithful advisers and honest officials (*'āmilan*) worthy of being confidants in [state] secrets and with ability and perseverance [to undertake] expeditions. It is said that the citadel of empire has four pillars and if one is missing, the foundation of [state] affairs cannot be strengthened. [The four pillars are]:

First, the great nobles (*umarā'-i 'uẓẓām*) who are the men of the sword (*aṣḥāb-i saif*) and who, having protected the frontiers of the state, divert the evil of enemies from the emperor and subjects; they are the pillar of the state and foundation of the empire.[43]

Second, the efficacious and competent ministers (*wuzarā'*) and honest revenue collectors (*'ummāl*);[44] they adorn the state and lead to the consolidation of the bases of the empire and to administration of the state affairs. The campaigns of the ruler of the empire are not successfully completed without the people of the pen (*arbāb-i qalam*).[45] Rather, this group has superiority over people of the sword for several reasons. First, the sword is useful against enemies (fol. 27b) but not for friends [whereas] the pen is used for the benefit of friends as well as in warding off enemies—the task that can be performed with a pen cannot be done with a sword; second, the notion of gaining sovereignty comes to the minds of the people of the sword, but the people of the pen would never behave in such a manner; third, the people of the sword empty the treasury whereas the people of the pen replenish it. [Indeed], the source of income is appreciated more than the source of expenditure.

Truly, the hand of failure would never find access to the glory, and the foot of disaster would not approach near the empire of the ruler who entrusts the reins of his affairs and his expeditions to a wise, prudent, virtuous, selfless, magnanimous, and upright minister (*wazīr*).[46] [However], if the situation is otherwise and a malevolent and iniquitous [person] is in charge of the state affairs, no matter how just, humane, and virtuous the emperor himself is, the peasantry and the people cease to benefit from his justice and compassion. (fol. 28a) Owing to fear of the *wazīr*, an account of the grief of afflicted people does not reach the emperor. [In analogy], if a person notices the face of an alligator in sweet and pure water, he can neither extend his hand [to get to the water] nor lower his foot into it, no matter how great his thirst.

Third, a magistrate (*ḥākim*)[47] representing the ruler, who investigates the affairs of people, punishes the powerful person on behalf of the weak, and thwarts and vanquishes adulterers and sinners.

Fourth, trustworthy reporters (*ṣaḥib-i khabrān-i amīn*)[48] who continuously make faithful and independent reports to the ruler after having probed the conditions of the country, the peformance of revenue collectors, and the state of the peasantry. When news of the country (India) and Iran (*wilāyat*) is concealed from the emperor and he remains unaware of the activities of friends and enemies, of virtuous and wicked persons, everyone is [free] to do as he wishes. When the ruler is uninformed, various kinds of disturbances arise all around and rock the foundations of the empire. Therefore, worthy rulers should train a group of people who are distinguished among their peers for being endowed with qualities such as wisdom, rectitude, knowledge (fol. 28b), righteousness, honesty, integrity, piety, dutifulness, and loyalty. The rulers should also assess the potential of each individual for a position according to his suitability, capacity of judgment, valor, level of intellect, sagacity, and resourcefulness.

[Rulers] should not assign two offices to one person because two assignments cannot be fittingly performed and managed. Every person is capable of doing one job and every individual is suited for one assignment.[49] The rulers should take it upon themselves to investigate the affairs of the *'āmils* and *amīns*[50] and [their handling of] the assignments entrusted to them. This will [help] the rulers know who among the chief *'āmils* is the sustainer of the peasantry and is righteous, and who is the oppressor and traitor. The official who is characterized by kindness to the peasantry and by honesty, who discharges his grave responsibilities in a fitting manner, the ruler should favor by strengthening his hand in the given position.

[On the other hand], that official who does not care for the subjects and who is negligent (fol. 29a) in performing the essentials of his assignment, who continues dishonesty and makes depravity his way of life, should have his name obliterated by the ruler from the record of employment and inscribed in the register of dismissal. [Indeed], destroying the roots of tyranny and chastising the corrupt people pleases the Creator and comforts [His] creation. To do good to depraved people is like doing bad to good people. To keep tyrants alive is akin to killing pious people.

It is said that the nurturing of employees should be founded in both kindness and severity. The rulers should treat employees sternly so that they do not become bold, and with kindness so that they do not despair. The kindness should be such that it shows no signs of weakness; and severity is appropriate only when it is free of the blemish of cruelty. Through such [policy], neither would loyal persons lose hope of the immense kindness [of the rulers], nor would seditious persons dare incite turmoil[51] for fear of discipline. In their mentorship and support [of the nobility], rulers should hold each noble in a special place and (fol. 29b) should not make any other grandee his partner or equal, so that hatred and jealousy do not develop among them. Moreover, rulers should encourage friendship and harmony among all of them and discourage discord. Concordance and candor [of the nobility] is extremely beneficial. Rulers should not listen with approval to the conversation of any noble against any other when it is prompted by pride and jealousy.[52]

Rulers should not place incompetent and low-born (*bad-gauhar*) people on the same footing with a high-born [person] (*aṣīl*) and prudent persons of pure extraction (*pāk-ṭīnat*). They should regard the maintenance of this hierarchy as a true principle in the laws of the empire and the covenants of kingship. If the distinction of ranks is abolished and the low-born (*arāẕil*) boast of equality with the people of the middle class (*ausāṭ*) and the middle class of equality with the high-born, the grandeur of kingship will be damaged and total confusion will occur among the nobility. For this reason, past rulers did not let the ignoble and ill-bred people learn calligraphy, the precepts of revenue accounts, and the rules of arithmetic. When this tradition [of permitting education] gains permanence, and when artisans (*arbāb-i ḥirfat*) (fol. 30a) join the ranks of the grandees of the state, undoubtedly, its impairment spreads and the economic resources of the noble and plebeian alike are disturbed.[53]

Since efficacious servants and skillful employees are the adornment and decoration of royal courts, since the grace of imperial servants lies in their intellect and competence, and since the elegance of this group lies in the knowledge and learning [of its members], it is necessary for rulers to evaluate the virtues of character, the depth of thought, the soundness of counsel, and the vivacity, skillfulness, honesty, integrity, sincerity, and loyalty of the servants and nobility, and to consider only those worthy of encouragement who have combined the honor of steadfastness with the dignity of eminence, honesty, and integrity. When they wish to patronize someone, [rulers] must at first probe and examine the affairs[54] of that individual to measure his judgment, knowledge, intellect, learning, and loyalty, and to look for [the following] three qualities in him.

First, honesty in actions. When employees of the imperial court are characterized (fol. 30b) by the quality of honesty, the foundations of the empire are more sound and the masses, too, are kept safe from their (the employees') oppressions. [However], if their demeanor is tarnished by dishonesty and they [also] have great influence over the ruler, they may afflict an innocent person with misfortune.

Second, truthfulness in speech. No fault is more glaring than falsehood and nothing is worse than telling a lie. If someone embodies all virtues but is a liar, he is not worthy of trust. The person whose tongue's sword lacks the luster of truthfulness will have no dignity in the eyes of people.

Third, purity of lineage (*aṣl-i pāk*) and high-mindedness. A lowly and stingy person does not recognize the worth of favors and honors, diverts the ruler from the path of generosity, and prevents him from bestowing beneficence and honors on anyone. Sages have opined that whoever is not of high birth is not destined to hope [for high office]. When an individual is distinguished by the qualities [of purity of lineage, etc.], he is graced by eminence and is free from lowly habits. (fol. 31a) Having combined inherent righteousness with acquired integrity, this individual exits from the rulers' aforesaid crucible faithful and candid. [The rulers, in turn,] should consider patronizing and nurturing him. They [thus] insure gain in their [own] affairs. [Sovereigns] should promote him gradually into the ranks of propinquity and authority so that his reputation and dignity are firmly established in people's eyes and hearts.

Sages have said that the emperor, [in his efforts] to be mentor for the employees, should be like an adept physician. The physician cannot initiate medical treatment and remedy unless he first makes a thorough investigation and categorical inquiry into the condition of the patient about the particulars of the disease, its causes and symptoms. Similarly, emperors, after making inquiries into the affairs of the employees and initiating their patronage, should not easily trust any individual. They should search for prudent and learned men, not opt for negligent and incompetent individuals over accomplished and skillful persons, and not appoint stupid people to positions belonging to wise individuals. It would be like tying a head ornament to the feet, or hanging footwear on the head. Wherever skillful people perish (fol. 31b) and ignorant and stupid people assume the reins of power, there complete confusion overtakes the nobility leading to disaster for the army and peasantry.

Verse

Tell the *hamā*[55] to never bless with its shadow
The land where parrots are fewer in number than crows.

[The emperor] should consider worthy of patronage only an individual of pure essence, and refrain from encouraging the wicked person of mean origin—not every stone becomes a gem and not every crimson fluid is turned into the finest musk. A despicable person of mean disposition and nasty mind does not think of or revere honesty and integrity. When honesty and integrity—the quintessence of purity—dissipate, one can expect every possible vice from that individual. A peevish man can by no means be led into rectitude, nor can a lowly and ill-mannered person, by forcing himself, [acquire] laudable disposition and pure-mindedness; [as an Arabic proverb says] "The vessel will give out whatever is in it."

[Another] maxim [states] that to nurture a sordid person is to disgrace oneself and shorten the life of one's pursuits. Efforts to civilize (fol. 32a) and sustain such people are like testing one's sword on stone or expecting the qualities of best treacle from deadly poison.

PROVERB

Can't teach an old dog new TRICKS

Qiṭ'ah (distich)

A person who is mean by nature,
Do not expect any goodness from
Because one can never make, no matter how one tries,
A white falcon from a black crow.

[The sovereigns] should not, however, deprive these people altogether of their benefaction, lest in despair they resign from the [imperial] service and turn to the enemy. Rather, [the attitude of the ruler should be such] that [these people] live between fear and hope, and are caught between promises and evasions and between apprehension and expectation. Just as riches make these people independent, causing rebellion and transgression, so does despair make them fearless, resulting in the defeat of rulers.

Verse

A desperate person can become bold and insolent,
O, my friend, do not do that which makes me dejected.

[Rulers] should not deny their benefactions to their subjects.[56] Just as they need the nobility and grandees of the court (fol. 32b) to successfully undertake campaigns, so they may need the help of their subjects in overcoming any emergency at the court.

Hemistich: [Yes], on this path (world), a fly is as useful as a peacock.

The work that a thin needle can perform cannot be done by an errect spear. A lustrous sword is at a loss to do what a thin pen-knife can. An [imperial] retainer, despite insignificance and powerlessness, has [the ability] to be of some benefit or to prevent some harm [to his master]. Dried wood, lying by ass-loads on the paths, may be of appropriate use one day. If it is suitable for nothing else, a toothpick [at least] can be made from it.

Verse

If we are incapable of making a bouquet of flowers,
We should be good enough to be wood for the caldron.

It is said that the position of an empire is that of beauty and elegance. The more lovers of a charming beloved there are, the more increased splendor there is in her appearance. [Similarly], the more servants sovereigns have, the more inclined they are to increase their retinue and retainers. (fol. 33a) Therefore, they [the sovereigns] must strive to increase the number of grandees, nobles, army chiefs, and court attendants through succor and kindness.

When [rulers] patronize someone, they should not humiliate him without the best of reasons; whomever they elevate, they should not disgrace unless he commits a grave mistake. Quick exaltation and rapid abasement damage the majesty of the empire. [Sovereigns] should not banish their retainers and relations on mere suspicion. Unless the suspicion is well-founded,[57] they should not attempt to annul their rights; and they should not become enraged on mere hearsay. Until they receive information on the truth of the matter, with convincing argument and evident proof, they should not sign any decree. [If they were to do so], it would mar their own work and deviate from the policy of generosity and truth. In accepting the word of a selfish person and committing a disagreeable act, they would ruin their edifice of wisdom. Any chastisement (fol. 33b) of the selfish calumniator for the sake of admonishing others [or done out of] repentance would be of no avail. Certainly, it is not always possible to find an employee who carries out enterprises successfully; and it is not easy to spot a servant worthy of confidence and patronage. Just as the rulers do not lend a receptive ear to the talk of others concerning that individual, they should likewise not hold other [employees] in indignity on [that individual's] comments [about them]. [Such policy] will prevent aversion of other employees and well-wishers toward that individual's service; and [with such policy] the benefits of their service and advantages of their counsel [to the rulers] would not cease. [Otherwise], such a situation could cause grave disasters.

It is said that any of the following three or four things could bring calamity to the country and danger to the empire:

First, depriving well-wishers of propinquity and holding prudent and experienced people in humiliation.

Second, sensuality, that is, passionate desire for women, fondness for (fol. 34a) hunting, preoccupation with wine [drinking], and inclination toward amusement.

Third, harshness, that is, excessive expression of anger and immoderation in punishment and discipline.

Fourth, foolishness, that is, taking up arms in a time of reconciliation and inclining toward peace when it is appropriate to fight, being contentious at a time requiring benignity, and opening the door of benevolence when wrath's barrier should be erected.

Thus, rulers should not censure and reproach retainers on minor faults. Sovereigns have always washed the stains of offenses from the records of ordinary people with the water of forgiveness and clemency and, in their compassion, they have disregarded the temerity and rudeness [of these individuals].[58] When [the royal] family and its employees commit a crime and are [in turn] comforted by the emperors' forgiveness and made succulent anew with the nectar of their benevolence, [these individuals] become embarrassed by the royal kindness. This sense of guilt (fol. 34b) is worse than any disciplinary [action].

Couplet

Why is it that water does not drown wood?
Because it is ashamed to swallow its own fosterling.

If rulers reprove and censure someone, then they should not grant favors shortly afterwards and they should never issue an absurd decree. In every enterprise they command and every word they utter, they should try, as far as possible, not to reverse themselves. All these things convey disrespect [of the emperors' position]. If there is no interlude between their anger and kindness, they will not appear credible.

When they patronize someone, they should not permit an overflow of their patronage and propinquity. When an individual sees his hand strong and absolute in issuing orders and counter-orders and finds himself controlling the destiny of the people,[59] the seeds of sedition are sown in his mind.[60] The desire for rebellion will creep into the core of his heart and ravage (fol. 35a) the foundations of the empire. Therefore, when [rulers] make one of their employees equal to themselves in rank, prestige, wealth, and grandeur, they must rectify it before the opportunity escapes them. Otherwise they will be regretfully bewildered,[61] which will be of no help [to them]. Indeed, it is an error to forgive people who pose a threat to one's survival and it is a prudent act to imprison them in a cell.

Despite a man's long association with teeth, the extraction of the tooth is the only way to get relief from the pain of a toothache. Food helps prolong life, but when it turns bad in the stomach, its evacuation is the only means of relief from its harm. A finger is an adornment for the hand and a tool [used] to close and open; however, if a snake bites it, it is severed to protect the rest of the body, and the pain [of its removal] is considered an assurance [of recovery]. On this topic, sages have opined that there are three groups of people; the perfectly prudent; the half-prudent; and the ill-advised, indolent.

The perfectly prudent is a person who makes farsightedness (fol. 35b) his habit, always contemplates the end of affairs, and recognizes the nature of danger before its occurrence. What others learn upon the termination of affairs, he, with his penetrating intellect, visualizes at the outset. He plans the conclusion of [his] undertakings at the beginning. Such a person can deliver himself on the shore of safety even before falling into the whirlpool of annihilation and calamity.

The half-prudent is an individual who keeps his heart intact and does not let himself be stupified and terrified when confronted with disaster. The path of reason and the method of planning will not [in such a situation] remain concealed from this person.

An ill-advised, indolent person is one who is confounded, disturbed, and distressed by a looming episode and by the occurrence of a disaster, and [who] cannot rescue himself from the gulf of affliction and calamity.

Since this world is the abode of misfortunes, no one knows at what moment a disaster might occur and from which direction a rebellion might ensue (fol. 36a). It [therefore] behooves rulers to consider the organization of the army their prime duty, arrange the army, and always be ready and equipped for a war. They should concentrate on and emphasize [the importance] of this matter to the grandees, ministers, and nobility. They must assign an appropriate *manṣab* and *jāgīr*[62] to every noble to maintain a certain number of troops. Every year they should inspect their own army and that of the nobles in a parade.[63] They should pay [special] attention to the readiness of its weapons and other equipment of war.[64]

If the rulers and nobility preoccupy themselves in accumulating treasures and wealth and do not enlarge the army, they will be bewildered at the time of need and, at that moment, boxes filled with gold will be of no use. No matter how great their regret,[65] it will be of no help.

Subsection (ii): On the Etiquette of Royal Service (dar ādāb-i khidmat-i mulūk)

Know that imperial service is perilous and demanding. Sages have compared the rulers (fol. 36b) to a lofty mountain; although there be in it a mine of precious gems, it is arduous to pass over and difficult to stay atop. [The wise men] have also likened royal service to an ocean [and the employee] to a merchant embarking on a voyage—[the merchant] either accrues immense profit or becomes trapped in a whirlpool of annihilation. [Savants] have stated that in this world five things will not be without five [consequences]: imperial service without peril; worldly wealth without pride; harmony without effort; company of women without disaster; and association with scoundrels without disgrace. None joins the service of rulers and returns safely from the fatal precipice. Who takes a draught from the wine vault of the world (worldly wealth and fame) and does not become intoxicated, emboldened, and [thus] contumacious?[66] None traverses the path of sensuality and does not fall to temptation. No man associates with a woman and is not carried away (fol. 37a) by diverse temptations. [It is hard] to find a person who socializes with ignoble, mischievous, and seditious individuals and is not in the end disgraced, humiliated, and abandoned.

Philosophers have compared rulers to burning fires. Indeed, with the light of their favor, they illuminate the dark cell of candidates [for imperial service]; with the flame of chastisement, however, they also burn the harvest of employees' past [service and dismiss them]. All agree[67] that whoever is closer to fire is more [exposed] to danger. Nonetheless, people who have viewed the glow of fire from a distance are unaware of its burning [quality]. [Those aspiring for government position] imagine the pleasure, speculate about the benefits, and yearn for propinquity to the rulers. Such is not, however, the situation. If they became aware of the royal control and the imperial awe and terror, they would realize that favors of a thousand years do not equal discipline of one moment. Savants remark that helpless is he who serves the rulers. Because the thread of their promise (fol. 37b) is weak and the foundation of their fidelity shaky, they bruise civility's face with wickedness and fill the fountain of generosity with the dirt of perfidy. They have no respect for sincerity and friendship, no regard for previous service to them, and no esteem for and appreciation of prior employment.

It is said that associating with one who does not appreciate the worth of it and serving one who does not recognize the value of it is like sowing seeds in marshy land in the hope of a harvest or like writing unique and refreshing *ghazals* in the surface of flowing water.

Couplet

From this dinner table, none eats a morsel
Without feeling a small stone under the teeth.

The saying is that a royal employee, in his fear, [sense of] danger, apprehension, and terror, is like one sleeping with a panther or like one dwelling with a lion. Although the panther sleeps and the lion hides, in time one [of these beasts] will rise and the other will open its mouth [to attack].

Verse

Join not the service of an emperor. I fear
(fol. 38a) It may turn unexpectedly into the interplay
of a stone and an ewer.

The majority of a ruler's friends and enemies turn against the individual who is in imperial service and who gains closeness to the ruler—friends, from jealousy of his exaltation and his rank, enemies from his sincerity in [handling] state and community affairs. He cannot live happily and securely when most of the community assumes hostility; he cannot [then] save his neck even if he reaches Saturn's heights. [The Arabic dictum that] "Sincere people are in great danger" comes from observing that contemplative people recline against a wall of peace and serenity. Turning away from the transitory world, they choose worship of the Creator, not service of His creatures. In the divine court of exaltation, there is not room for inadvertancy, error, and negligence; oppression and tyranny are not permitted; rewarding good with evil and recompensing obedience with punishment do not hold here. In the ordinances of the Sovereign of sovereigns (God), there is no regression from justice.

Indeed, most deeds of creatures, contrary to the nature of the Creator (fol. 38b), are blemished by diverse disagreements and altercations and have deviated from harmony and from sensitivity to the rights of others. Thus, criminals deserving punishment are sometimes bestowed with rewards due loyal individuals of pure intentions; on occasion, well-wishers worthy of patronage are degradingly tormented—[treatment appropriate for] traitors. [The behavior of rulers is so unpredictable that sometimes] they show not an iota of gratitude to an individual, even one who has surrendered the riches of the earth to the ruler's treasurer and [sometimes the ruler] exalts an individual to the highest rank of honor on that person's swearing.[68]

Couplet

Guard yourself against want and show contentment
Whether you be a singer or a hired mourner.

When an individual gains intimacy with the rulers and when, with benedictions of their favors [showered on him] as on their kin, he gains fame and honor in the shade of their power and service, and when he supersedes his peers and contemporaries in glory, he must never ignore the dues for these bounties and favors [granted to him]. He must concentrate his energies on showing them allegiance and he must serve them with utmost sincerity, conviction (fol. 39a), and good will. He must not neglect in any matter the well-being of his benefactor. Had he a thousand lives, he must sacrifice them for one moment of his lord's peace of mind. He must throw himself in the most perilous situation for requital of the favors of his patron and for leaving his name [inscribed] on the record of Time for his devotion [to his master]. Despite [such spirit of sacrifice] he will not be able to return even one of the favors of [his benefactor].

Basing his operations on honesty, integrity, and righteousness, he should not let the glow of the flame of bribery dazzle his vision of uprightness. The seditious greed and enchanting avarice should not overpower his guiding intellect, making him indulge in rapaciousness. [He should make sure] that by following [the maxim] "honored is the contented and humbled is the greedy," he does not let the attire of his dignity transform into rags of humiliation, and does not allow the dust of baseness aroused by somber greed to settle over his affairs. The savants enunciate that honesty is the greatest pillar of laudable (fol. 39b) morals and integrity is the stronghold of esteemed ethics. Honesty and integrity are taken as symbols of faith. Honesty is a quality that makes even lowly people venerable and dishonesty degrades respected people. Therefore, one should not deviate from the path of uprightness in any situation and should keep his disposition in a manner that will bring fame to his master, prosperity to the country, and happiness to the masses. Having denied himself comfort and luxury, he should strive to be always present [in the court]. He must abstain from telling a lie which is the most abominable of deeds and, by the same token, he should avoid praising the ruler in a blatant show of flattery.

Having observed the devoirs of counseling [the ruler], he should speak politely and with courtesy. Instead of being harsh and rude, he should be inclined towards kindness and softness. He should strive to observe respect [for the ruler] and should shun boldness and rudeness. If [the employee] observes disparity between the words and deed of the ruler (fol. 40a) or [finds that] the ruler intends to concentrate on a matter that is likely to have a noxious end, a disastrous finale that could hurt his master, he should, in gentle language and absolute courtesy, relate the hazard involved. With humility, he should warn him [of the consequences]. During his discourse, quoting pleasing and interesting proverbs, he should point out the faults of others. By revealing whatever he thinks is appropriate, he should caution him about the disastrous end [of the ruler's intended plan]. He should make the cause of the depravity clear, [and] so long as the ruler's opinion and planning is not rectified, he (the noble) should not cease his efforts. [Indeed], he will be the ruler's enemy if he does not fulfill the stipulations of honesty and good counsel. Likewise, if the ruler conducts a business that is prudent and pertains to expediency, the [noble] should highlight it, bringing the benefits and gains of [the undertaking] to the attention of the ruler. It will enhance the ruler's satisfaction over the excellence and veracity of his policy.

In an amiable way, [the employee] must (fol. 40b) convey to the ruler that tyranny is an abominable act and must make justice attractive to him through commendation and praise, so much so that if the ruler is inclined towards iniquity, [the noble] must not let his heart be tarnished with selfishness but must make requisition for justice. He must observe rectitude and draw the ruler's attention to it. He must communicate with the ruler whatever he considers favorable to the empire and must under no circumstances relinquish the rendering of sincere advice. [Furthermore], he should gather information on every [possible] servant [of the state] through all available means and transmit it to the sovereign. In this way, the emperor becomes well-acquainted with his supporters and followers, and with the extent of their sincerity, discernment, judgment, and prudence. [With such background information], the ruler can [better] benefit from their services, and can patronize each of them according to their potential. However, to avoid embarrassment at a critical juncture, [the employee] should not recommend [an individual to his master] until and unless he has tested him several times and has full confidence and trust in him. (fol. 41a)

Closeness to rulers lacks permanence. Every action is followed by inaction and prosperity by adversity. [Likewise] in a short time, success and good fortune are overridden by dejection. Therefore, an individual in power must not be arrogant in his might and authority, and must not lean on respect and reverence [shown to him]. He must not be irritated by the appeals of the people and the anxieties of the masses. While meeting with the [less fortunate], he must not be short-tempered. [In his position of authority] he must [instead] strive to be good to the people, and to serve his subordinates in the manner he would like them to serve him. The advantage of having intimate contact with and access to the imperial court is that one may pass on the benefits of benevolence to nobles and plebeians alike, and may oblige both the high and low with beneficence and goodness. [Indeed], whoever does good deeds himself, and whoever (fol. 41b) in himself embodies the abovementioned characteristics will be blessed by the Exalted God with all worthy and propitious things in this world and the next. The ruler, in turn, will continuously strive to elevate the prestige of and seek intimacy with such an individual, and will be inclined to share in his company. By virtue of such characteristics, his good name, worthy of commemoration, will remain inscribed on the pages of Time, year after year, and decade after decade. He will be loved and acknowledged by the Creator and the created [alike].[69]

Poem

If you do good, the people in turn will be good to you.
If you do bad, however, they will treat you in a worse manner.

Today, you are oblivious to the good and bad [in your actions].
However, there will be a day when you will be apprised of your bad and good deeds.

CHAPTER II

The Admonition of Subordinates and Peers

SECTION 1: ASSOCIATING AND INTERMINGLING WITH FRIENDS

Know that a majority of the sages have preferred association with others over solitude. In their opinion, association with a virtuous person is better than being alone. However, when one is (fol. 42a) unable to find an affectionate companion and a caring friend, isolation is better than socializing. Indeed, loneliness is hard and difficult [to endure] and a policy of isolation and alienation from one's comrades is arduous to practice. No one in this world can do without a suitable companion or shun a congenial friend. Friendship is a delight and can have unique rewards.

In this world, the company of amicable friends and affectionate associates exceeds [all other pleasures], and the stature of devoted companions stands above all else. If one could manage this, it is to one's advantage to have as many friends as possible—[to have] one thousand friends is to have one. However, to have even one enemy is to have many. Therefore, in the view of adept, learned men and sages with laudable qualities, no wealth is more precious than the existence of sincere confidants and visitation by true friends. Wise men, [who constitute] the true essence of people and (fol. 42b) the cream of humanity,[70] associate with each other, initiate affection, and [thereafter] bring it to fruition with sincere intentions and pure hearts. The benefits [of such association] become discernible in the lives of each of them. In the support of help from their peers, they convey an intense sense of true friendship, and affiliate both in times of prosperity and adversity, affluence and impoverishment.

Through adversities in fortune and calamities of Time, they stand by each other, sincere in helping to facilitate their [return to] successful, prosperous, and affluent positions in society. Indeed, the ingot of such a group's affection is transformed into a coin, embellished with faithfulness in sincerity's mint. And it is the seedling of their friendship that is nurtured in an exclusive meadow with the gentle rain of harmony. They are a solace for the soul, an aid to bounty and munificence. There can be no experience more delightful than the honor of their company (fol. 43a), and no affliction worse than their separation. However, it should be kept in mind that every one is not worthy of friendship.

The philosophers, having gauged [the concept of] friendship, opine that it is appropriate to make friends with any of the following three groups: first, people of knowledge and ingenuity—by virtue of their company, one attains happiness in this world and the next; second, people of virtuous character who will cover up the errors of their friend and will not hesitate to counsel him; third, selfless people who base their friendship on truth and sincerity. Friendship with these three groups only is appropriate. Similarly, abstaining from three other types of people is essential: first, immoral individuals and fornicators, whose energies will be totally confined to carnal desires—association with them will ensue neither repose in this world nor bliss in the next; second, liars and hypocrites—interaction with them is akin to intense torture and association with them is a great affliction. (fol. 43b) They incessantly tell untruthful stories about you and transmit them to other people. Regarding others, they disclose damaging and terrifying reports, quite contrary to truth. Third, foolish and stupid people—one could rely on them neither to make gains nor avert losses. Quite frequently, it happens that what they consider to be beneficial and advantageous turns out to be harmful and damaging.

Hemistich: A wise enemy is preferable to a foolish friend.

The main point of this saying is that an enemy graced with wisdom always makes use of [his] sense of anticipation and strikes his [opponent] only at the most opportune time. Thus, one could defend oneself by observing signs of vengeance in the enemy's movements, pauses, behavior, and words. However, a friend deprived of wisdom's wealth will be counterproductive in assisting in the management of affairs and expeditions no matter how much he tries. Chances are that because of the inadequate planning and unsound advice of [such a friend], a person could be trapped in a dangerous situation. Sages further add that (fol. 44a) people who claim friendship can be divided into three types. Some of them are like food that one cannot do without and in their absence discourse appears to be unilluminated.[71] Others are like medication, needed from time to time. And [yet] others are like pain, of no help—they are lipservers and hypocrites. One can neither trust their friendship nor their enmity.

Indeed, prudent is the individual who in his short life[72] does not withdraw from the company of the learned people, who considers his association with them a source of felicity and prestige and their admonitions as guidelines for his actions and as a medium to achieving a distinguished position. The company of virtuous people (*akhyar*) and intimacy of pious individuals (*abrar*) must be regarded as a means of acquiring virtues and knowledge. Associating socially with them should be given exalted and supreme stature. (fol. 44b) The benefits of their association are innumerable and the advantages of their company countless. Fellowship with the righteous is an alchemy of felicity, and association with the virtuous is [akin] to having an eternal guide. One must strive to acquire an affectionate friend and avoid enemies with pretensions of friendship. He must persist [in his association] with real friends and like-minded comrades, must initiate friendship with intellectuals, and must distance[73] [himself] from the company of illiterates. By avoiding impure, ignoble, and debased people, he will not place the precious gem of his fine stature on the string of the lowly, vile, ignoble, and hypocritical people. While keeping company with virtuous and pious people holds enormous benefits, association with inept and mischievous people can be devastating. If fellowship with righteous individuals is essential, avoiding socializing with seditious people is also obligatory. [Peer] influence is certainly very effective.[74] (fol. 45a) Undoubtedly, the company of moral people is a source of increase in prestige and exhileration. However, camaraderie with vicious individuals can as well cause deviation and degradation. [It appears that] association with the latter is the more persuasive and that its negative effects are discernible in a rather short time. Indeed, whoever does not shun associating with the ignoble has his boat of life plunging into a whirlpool, and even a prudent boatman is humbled in its rescue. The thread of his life is cut so short that the fingers of strategem are bewildered in their attempt to tie it back together. The maxim [that applies here] is: "Living with a poisonous snake is better than staring at a worthless friend in despair." No experience could be more tormenting than the company of an ignoble.

It is true that one cannot trust the friendship of most of one's peers. A true friend has become [a rare thing] like alchemy, and selfless love has nestled into nonexistence like [the fabulous bird] "'*anqā*." Looking for a like-minded friend and an affectionate consort is like hammering cold iron, or sailing a boat on land, or galloping a horse (fol. 45b) on the surface of the ocean. Expecting people to keep their word is like joining the star Canopus with the Pleiades. To hope for faithfulness from the people is akin to planting a rose shrub in the fire of a furnace.

The [sages] opine that the unpredictable character of love and the malice of the people of this world is similar to the intimacy of rulers, the beauty of a beloved, the fidelity of women, the love of the insane, the generosity of intoxicated people, and the deception of enemies—one can trust none of them nor count on their permanence. Fidelity is a preparation rare in the tray of the world's perfumers, and keeping one's word is a nonexistent gem in the earth's treasury. Faithfulness is the second mythical bird, the griffin, which exists only in name on this planet. Abiding by one's promise is akin to alchemy with an unknown chemistry. Whosoever strives in this regard and trusts the veracity of his contemporaries, putting his faith in the companionship and cooperation of his peers, fools himself (fol. 46a) and exposes his ignorance to prudent people. Nevertheless, whoever is endowed with [the following] six attributes is worthy of befriending and his friendship will have no flaws.

First, if this individual becomes aware of shortcomings in you, he attempts to point those out to you and to persuade you to agree to their elimination.

Second, if he becomes aware of some virtues or skills in you, he highlights them repeatedly.[75]

Third, if he incidentally does you a favor, he does not remember it.

Fourth, if he notices some favor and support from you, he does not forget it.

Fifth, if he sees an omission or mistake on your part, he does not drift away [from you] nor sever his relationship with you, and he accepts your apology [for] "to err is human."

Sixth, laudable character and meritorious qualities are so ingrained in his disposition that the basis of his friendship and harmony is founded in selflessness and truthfulness.

The company of such an individual with sincere motives and a pure heart is one of the privileges of life. Indeed, the pleasure of his association wipes the dust (46b) of anguish from the mirror of the heart. In the light of his presence, affliction's darkness is lifted from one's bosom. In short, in the civilities of socialization and companionship, according to the belief of the compiler of this treatise, fidelity, sincerity, and steadfastness [are the basic ingredients] of friendship. The individual who has not smelled the fragrance of fidelity holds no share in the aroma of the odoriferous herbs [of friendship].[76] And the eyes of a heart unexposed to the hues of fidelity are deprived of the rays of the excellencies of character.

Faithfulness is the waiting-maid of the bride of excellence and a black mole on the cheek of beauty and elegance [enhancing its charm]. Never would the bird of the heart chirp on the twigs of love in a garden where the seedling of faithfulness is not nurtured. However, signs of hypocrisy and infidelity are the scars of insolence discernible in the personalities of wretched persons.[77] The mark of having broken one's promise is like a degrading inscription on the foreheads of the low-born.[78] The official whose countenance is beautified with the black dot of sincerity is loved by everyone.[79] No person with insight, [on the other hand], would care for an individual who lacks (fol. 47a) faithfulness; no courageous man would desire the company of a person noted for making excuses and for hypocrisy; the person stigmatized for breaking promises and for insincerity will be approved by none. Rather, people will consider it imperative to abstain from his agreements and refute his deeds and words.

Verse

The person whose intentions differ from his words
Should be struck in the heart by a sword.

Keeping their promise and fealty is the practice of manly and accomplished individuals. This is the reason that high-minded persons become friends easily and become adversaries only with difficulty—just as it is hard to break a golden cup but easy to reshape it. The low-minded, [on the other hand], take a long time to develop a friendship and the basis of their friendship is fragile—just as it is easy to break earthenware but hard to repair it.

Savants opine that friends are of two types: first, individuals attracted to love and friendship with complete and intense desire, with absolute sincerity (fol. 47b), and with spontaneity, lacking any semblance of self-interest and hypocrisy. Their friendship will not be for timely convenience, temporary expediency, or worldly power and wealth. In the second [group] are those who display affection for ulterior motives.

The first group open the doors of love with pure intentions and sincere motives, and are therefore worthy of trust in all situations; one could feel secure with them at all times. Every expression of their love rises from the bottom of their hearts. [However], the behavior of those who base their friendship on selfishness will not be consistent: at a joyous moment, they receive their friend cheerfully;[80] in time of danger and terror, they view their friend with indifference. A wise person does not attach himself emotionally to such friends.

It is said that the person who maintains friendship for timely convenience and opportune expediency (fol. 48a) is like a hunter who spreads grain for his benefit and not to feed the birds. Since such friendship is contaminated with selfishness, it could well end in rivalry. Therefore, when you find great generosity (*futūwwat*), fidelity, well-wishing, and affection in a friend, when you know that his love is free of hypocrisy and that you are benefitting from the fruits of friendship and affection, you must fully focus your attention on his friendship and love and must fulfill all social duties. Having established a bond of unity, under no circumstances should you lose contact with [your friend; it would] be sad to easily lose a friend who was won with [great] effort.

The person who wins a friend after great effort and loses him easily denies himself the fruits of friendship. His other friends also become disappointed and sever their friendship with him. [Therefore], when you are able to find an affectionate friend and have strengthened the bases of affection, (fol. 48b) you should [yourself] earnestly seek out your own shortcomings. Following an extended period of association and friendship, ask him about your drawbacks. In this probe, exercise extreme diligence and importunity. No matter how many times he says, "I see no shortcomings in you," do not accept it. Showing your disgust, repeat your question. When he mentions your faults to you, consider that a gesture of his deep concern for you, express your happiness, and endeavor to eradicate that shortcoming. Consider this a favor to you, and show your indebtedness to him. Your [high] expectation and trust [should be matched] by an equally [high] display of faithfulness, friendship, and concord.

It is said that five things symbolize stupidity: first, the hope of friendship from deceitful persons and the expectation that they will honor the privilege of friendship; second, [attempting to] learn the intricacies of science in ease and comfort [without working hard]; third, courting women with harshness and severity; four, expecting a reward in the hereafter without austerity [here]; and fifth, considering one' gains in other people's losses. (fol. 49a) A resolution to mutually maintain sincerity in good intentions and purity of heart should be such that if you find a contradiction between the eyes and the tongue—the sentinel of the body and the representative of the heart—[resolve this contradiction immediately].[81] Be friend to a friend and an enemy to each other's enemy. The dictum is that he who endears the friend of an opponent and intermingles with the enemy of a friend will be invariably ranked amongst the enemies.

The sages suggest that there are three categories of friends: a real friend, the friend of a friend, and the enemy of an enemy. [Similarly], there are three groups of enemies as well: an apparent enemy, the adversary of a friend, and the ally of an enemy. You should consider the associate of your friend as your friend, and regard the individual who strives for the goodwill of your friend as your friend. [Likewise] it is incumbent upon an individual who is close to your friend to befriend you. Even when there are many [mere] acquaintances and one of them deserts yur friend, it is imperative for you to sever [your contacts] with him. If all of them are kindred relatives, . . . ? [lacuna]. (fol. 49b)

Verse

The advice of the sage is total accuracy and complete goodness.

Indeed, who listens to [this advice] with
acquiescence is blessed.

SECTION 2: IN CONDEMNATION OF POVERTY, AND ON ENDEAVORS FOR THE ACQUISITION OF WEALTH

Know that the people of this world seek one of the following positions: first, abundance of wealth and convenience of resources—this is the goal of those whose aspirations center on drinking, fine clothing, and carnal pleasures; second, elevation of position, advancement in rank and exaltation in dignity—this group has grandeur and rank, and one can not achieve [either of] these two categories without wealth; third, receipt of rewards in the hereafter and attainment of levels of veneration—people in this group attain salvation and ascendancy. This position could be achieved as well through lawful wealth. [As the Arabic saying goes], "Wonderful is legitimate wealth owned by virtuous person." In short, wealth can be an asset in [both] this world and the next.

One could, with the help of wealth, achieve any level of ascendancy in this world. A needy person, deprived of such pleasure in this world, would also be denied high rank (fol. 50a) in the hereafter. This point is substantiated by the exoteric [meaning] of the Prophetic *ḥadīth:* "Poverty is a disgrace on one's face in both worlds." Since [a poor person] might resort to unlawful means of earning his living, this would ensure chastisement and punishment in the next. As he is restricted by the affliction of poverty in this world, so he will be incarcerated in eternal disgrace in the next. It is said that the individual lacking wealth is like a bird without feathers and wings.

Money is a resource for boldness, a furbisher of opinion, and an ornamentation of and support to power. A person without money is without friends. No task initiated by an empty-handed pauper reaches completion. No desire that germinates in his heart is destined for fruition. As the savants say, whoever is without a brother is like a stranger wherever he goes. Whoever is without a son will find his name and memory erased from the pages of Time. And whoever is penniless, neither does he enjoy his life nor does he benefit his friends. Apparent destitution and privation are the root cause of all sorts of disaster. [Destitution] is linked to the animosity of the people, abrogates the mask of shame (*ḥayā'*), disrupts the basis of politeness, assembles evil and calamity (fol. 50b), severs vigor and ardor, and initiates disgrace and degradation. Whoever is restrained in the trap of need has no alternative but to remove the mask of shame. When the inscription "modesty is part of faith" has been erased from the folio of his situation, his life is rendered melancholy, and he suffers torture and affliction. Happiness folds up [and exits] his heart and the army of dejection overpowers his mind's core. Protest's candle lies unkindled. His mind, ingenuity, understanding, and sagacity falter. Correct planning, [normally] beneficial, proves in this case to be [further] damaging. Despite uprightness, he becomes the target of accusation and dishonesty. The favorable opinion of people about him is reversed. If someone else commits a sin, blame is directed to him. Every quality for which the wealthy are admired and praised evokes condemnation and ridicule in the case of the impoverished. Bravery is considered impetuousness, generosity prodigality, and affability meekness and spiritlessness. If inclined to repose (fol. 51a), [the pauper] is deemed lazy and indolent. If displaying eloquence and expressiveness, he is labeled talkative. If seeking refuge in silence, he is likened to a water-worm. If choosing for himself a corner of isolation, he is called crazy. If he greets others cheerfully and sociably, his [behavior] is considered facetious and buffoonery. If he discriminates in food and clothing, he is called self-indulgent. If he manages with a [mere] cloak and little food, he is seen as afflicted and indigent. If he settles in one place, he is branded a slave [to that place] and deemed ignorant of the world. If he resolves to travel, he is seen as stupified, vagrant, and unfortunate. If he opts for celibacy, he is accused of abandoning the *sunnah* [of the Prophet]. If he marries, he is called sensual and lustful.

In summation, a needy person is rejected and condemned by his peers. And if under these circumstances, God avert! [his peers] perceive covetousness in him, opposition to him overpowers their hearts and they estrange themselves from him, fulfilling none of his needs. Greed is the source of every degradation. (fol. 51b) "He who is content [with what he has] is honored and respected, and he who is avaricious is despised and degraded," (so goes the Arabic saying). In short, it is easier to endure an incapacitating terminal illness or to undertake a journey with no return and no settling down than [suffer] destitution. It is easier to put one's hand in the mouth of a snake in order to extract deadly poison or to snatch a morsel from a hungry lion or to dine with an enraged panther than to be needy—a condition that shatters one's ego. Death is better than such a situation.

The divine system works in such a manner that most of this world's events are tied to a cause. God Almighty, Praise be to Him, has situated this world's orbit on factors and means. Although His power could yield success without means, Divine wisdom nevertheless requires that undertakings and their completion [be tied] to factors. Because of this, a system of benefitting from and utilization of [resources] was introduced. Thus, where someone can benefit others is better (fol. 52a) than the tapping of another resource for himself. (As goes an Arabic maxim), "The best among humans is he who is useful and helpful to people."

Verse

> Be like an eagle eating prey and feeding others [with the leavings of your prey].
> Do not be a feast-hunter like the featherless and wingless crow.

What a pity if a person of power possessing the ability to benefit others should become lazy and seek advantage from others! What a shame to see one wandering in the pit of avarice and baseness, a failure, who could reach the zenith of his goals fulfilling his heart's desire! What a gross mistake to step into afflictions' thorny place when one could enjoy the flower of pleasure in the garden of luxury. But one must remember that through striving an individual is led to his intended destination. Traversing with exertion the desert of endeavor brings into view the beauty of one's [desired] goals. Whoever raises the banner of struggle in the field of courage and in enduring afflictions eases his grip over physical comfort and leisure, reaches his destination sooner. Without intense struggle, none sees the sun of his desires rise from beyond the horizon of hope, and without exhaustive searching, (fol. 52b) hope's introduction never leads to the attainment of one's objectives.

Verse

> A ruler understands very well the position of a rose in a garden.
> Indeed, a rose despite its tenderness, reclines on thorns.

True, whatever has been apportioned to an individual reveals itself from [within] the concealed place of the Invisible, and for whatever has not been allotted [to that person] all effort is expended in vain. Without God's favor and Eternal blessing, the arrow of good fortune misses the target that is its goal. However, "struggle" is a big factor. A person seeking oblivious repose will remain in the corner of degradation and failure, while another individual, fearless of the thorny place and habitat of difficulties, will pluck the flower of his goal in a short time and will sit on the throne of felicity in the garden of honor. The rose of mirth cannot be picked without the thorns of hardship, and the treasure door of one's wishes cannot be opened without the key of toil. Lust for luxury shows baseness and degradation, [while] exposing oneself to risks points to [imminent] wealth and respect. (fol. 53a) It is not possible to drink of glory and affluence without the stinging from affliction and drudgery. No one can achieve his objective and drink the wine of his goal from the goblet of his desire without enduring immeasurable suffering and tasting unpleasant dregs. [Indeed], he can be called a "man" who rises to seek his objective, tying around his waist the girdle of striving. By keeping his aspiration high, he rejects base actions. By rejecting the goals of petty and lowly people, he does not stoop to trivial things like decrepit women. Despite a roselike short life, the person reaching high status achieves, according to the sages, long life because he is well remembered [by posterity]. [However], despite a long life, like the leaves of pomegranate, the individual who stoops to abjectness and baseness has no value in the eyes of judicious people and is not taken into account. One must know that climbing the ladder of dignity is possible only after great struggle, [yet] the fall from respectability can happen with little trouble—just as a heavy stone is lifted from the ground with difficulty (fol. 53b) [yet] can be hurled back easily. It is for this reason that only an individual with lofty aspirations is inclined toward eminence.

Verse

The person fearful of the throes of returning sobriety
Is [refused] a drink from the cup of his goal's wine.

If there is no possibility of ascendancy in one's own homeland, one should consider travel to achieve preeminence, in either physical or spiritual dimension. He should venture out in accordance with [the Qur'anic injunction], "Say: go ye through the earth . . ."[82]

Couplet

O you who are wounded by your home country, seek its dressing by departing from there.
Know, however, that in the case of your death, there will be none to mourn you.

Travel is a tree that bears only the fruit of separation. Leaving one's homeland is a cloud that drops only the rain of grief. According to [an Arabic saying], "Absence from one's homeland is agony, and separation [from loved ones] is a burning torture." The delight of [travel] in various parts of the world and visual enjoyment of a heavenly garden is [possible] only in the company of intimate companions and confidants. When one is deprived of the bliss of visitation of one's parents, peers and friends, it is apparent that this agony is not remedied by delights [of the pleasant milieu]. (fol. 54a) How much relief from such pain can one expect from a [delightful] view? The pain of separation from one's friends and the affliction of parting from one's well-wishers are the most intense of all pains and the most agonizing of all tortures. Despite affluence and leisure, despite a life of extreme luxury, [an immigrant] in a foreign country [finds] the fountainhead of his comfort diverted and the vision of his good fortune clouded by separation from his most dear friends and spiritual companions. When he achieves an orderly life, wealth, and riches, others will broadcast their friendship and boast of harmony and concord with him. But when he becomes destitute, may God avert [such a calamity]!, the dust of adversity clouds the sight of his fortune, and the group that adorned his company like the Pleiades wither away like the constellation of the Bear, because the friendship of worldly people and the love of persons with temporal concerns is limited to their ulterior motives and worldly gains.

[Verses]

As long as you have worldly materials, they listen to you.
Like a bee, they hum[83] around you.

When the village becomes desolate, (fol. 54b)
[And] the goblet becomes [empty] like the head of a reback,

Then they cease associating with and caring for you.
Consider them as if they were never your friends.

The reason that the wrist of the ruler is made the resting place of the eagle is that it does not lower its head into a nest. And the owl remains behind the wall of degradation because it does not detach itself from desolated places.

Couplet

Move fast like the eagle and ride for pleasure.
How long can you stay behind a wall like the owl?

When someone in a foreign land falls into the whirlpool of toiling, he, besides [acquiring] wealth, becomes disciplined and refined. He gains experiences from which he benefits throughout his life. The hardships of travel mature him. In short, no overly cautious person rides the steed of hope over the ground of his goal. Travel takes an individual from the pit of obscurity to the heights of honor and glory. Through travel, [opportunities] for advancement become available. As is said (in Arabic), "Travel is a means to triumph [in life]." Unless the sword is pulled out of the scabbard, it can not gain honor in combat with brave men. The sky (fol. 55a) is the highest of all because it is constantly in motion while the earth, being static, is trampled upon by all, both high and low. Don't you see that a pawn achieves the position of queen (in chess) after traveling six positions? And a fast-moving moon moves from the position of new moon to full moon over fourteen nights.

Distich

One should look at the mass of the earth and that of sky [to understand]
Where this [earth] is as a result of its inaction,
and where that [sky] is as a result of its movement.

Travel is [like a] patron to an individual, and is a threshold of glory.
It is a treasure of wealth and a teacher of skills.

If a tree could move from place to place,
It would have suffered neither the affliction of a saw nor the oppression of an axe.

In sum, toiling is the vocation of valiant men and the occupation of the valorous. Only that individual can be considered a "man" who, renouncing his life, steps into the arena of "quest" and, not deterred by hard work, performs to expected and achievable levels of striving and endeavor. The situation will not be beyond two things: if he succeeds, [all is] well and good;[84] if not, his excuse will be acceptable to wise men. (fol. 55b) His high-mindedess in search of glory and exaltation will be unequivocal in the minds of others.[85]

[Verses]

Why submit to the arrogance of the world?
Why aspire to minor achievements?

Disregarding the ocean and mountain,
We cross them like griffin, bringing under our wings the seas and land.

Either we step over the sky to achieve our goal,
Or we submit to the struggle like a "man."

SECTION 3: SUBMITTING TO THE DIVINE WILL (*QAŻĀ-I ILĀHĪ*), CONTENTMENT (*QANĀ'AT*) AND SOLITUDE (*'UZLAT*)

[Verses]

If change in the affairs of people is not pre-ordained,
Why do things happen contrary to their wishes?

Indeed, destiny holds the reins of good and bad for people.
That is why the plans of all are nullified.

Thousands of patterns emerge in this world,
But not even one of them materializes as we imagine.

The screens of the imagination of insightful people portray all existences as related to the Divine decree, and Eternity and the origin of everything as Divine will and the command of the Eternal. All good and bad, all benefits and disasters are tied to the injunctions of Divine decree existing from eternity. (fol. 56a) In the bureau of Eternity, whatever the Scribe of design (God) has set down with the pen of will on the pages, which are the lives of the creations, manifests itself in the span of one's existence. Attempting to shun or escape it is of no avail. The means and intermediary links [to achieving one's goals] are futile if Divine will thus determines. One cannot undo the knot of Fate with fingers of deliberation, because the journey from the desert of planning to destiny is long. There is an immense and limitless traverse between the plain of reflection and the frontier of Divine will. When the Creator, the most exalted, glory be to Him, wishes to put an ordinance into effect, He blurs the insight of visionaries with the bodkin of negligence. Neither remains there light in the eyes of insight, nor is the contrivance of wisdom beneficial. When the Controller and Implementor of the injunctions of destiny puts into motion the chain of will, He bounces into midair the fish from the depth of the ocean and pulls to the earth's center the bird from the height of the sky. Without support of the Divine will, every line drawn by a colorful thought (fol. 56b) on the slate of imagination turns, in the end, into a bad image; every spell conjured up by an enchanter of contrivance, takes on in the end, the coloring of a fictitious tale. None can escape the bonds of destiny and Fate's incarceration; no human can challenge the Eternal decrees and Divine will; and no creature can but submit and resign to the ordinances of Eternity. Except for an individual to prostrate himself before God's order and Divine decree, there is no other right way and no other straight path.

No matter how accomplished an individual is in learning and other virtues, he will see no fruition nor reward from his progress toward achievement unless God's will is in his favor. [We know that] many erudite persons deserving wealth have been denied food for even one day, and many inept, ignorant individuals have been seated in honor and glory. Indeed, this situation is brought about only by God's order and Divine command. Perpetually, it is recognized that the true agent is the Exalted God and when He wills it (fol. 57a), one's objective can be achieved without hardship and struggle. Nevertheless, if God does not intend its realization, struggle in any form will be futile. Thus, if the particle of potential existence (human being) in the court of actual existence (God) does anything other than show consent and happiness, it will seem to be a sign of ingratitude. Whatever emanates from Him should be considered, without any doubt, a glimpse of mercy and the essence of benediction. Although an individual cannot perceive its essence nor its mysterious implications [in a cursory fashion], nonetheless, when he ponders upon it, he would certainly find his well-being in it. [An analogy would be] that even when an incompetent physician whose treatment is dubious prescribes bitter medication, people take that cheerfully and show their gratitude as well. [Therefore], how and why could things consigned by the Dispenser of Justice and the Creator of the World cause pain?

[Verse]

Do not concern yourself with dregs or with clear
wine, drink well.
Because whatever our cup-bearer (God) serves is
indeed a favor.

Wise is the person who does not rebel against Divine decrees but develops affinity with the dictates of Destiny. He accepts all predestined afflictions and distresses cheerfully and willingly [*Kulliyāt*, fol. 308b],[86] and leads his life lightheartedly and happily. He is not caught, like a silly child, between being happy [at one moment] and [*Kulliyāt*, fol.309a] angry [the next], between crying and laughing—if others amuse the child and trill for him, he laughs and is happy; if he is disciplined and treated harshly, he cries and is enraged. [A wise] person quietly accepts the lot assigned to him by God.[87] He does not label abominable greed to be a high level of endeavor, nor does he consider mean avarice an introduction to greatness. Having rejected baseless, empty talk as a means to achievement, he is not attracted by transitory, worldly wealth and grandeur. He believes that his wealth is that which he sends before him, and his assets are such as he deposits in the hereafter.

Good speech, laudable actions, virtuous character, and good manners are territory immune from the catastrophies of fortune and reversions of Time. Such an individual takes the fruit of contentment from the branch of acquiescence, (*riżā*) abstaining from the greed of the carnal soul (*nafs*), the lust of wealth, and the desire of glory. The sages opine that the person who is not content with the sufficiency of worldly goods but seeks more is like the person who passed over a mountain of diamonds—time after time, he saw a larger piece, and [always] desiring more he soon reached his objective. However, the return was impossible. Small pieces of diamond scratched and injured his feet while that heedless one, absorbed by greed, remained unaware of his condition. Overwhelmed with grief, he died on the mountain and, in the end, settled in the stomachs of birds.

[Verse]

The desire for more hinders your mission.
If you desire profit, do not seek to exceed the limits.

The Cupbearer of divine benedictions has given to each a goblet according to his capacity, and has denied no one the elixir of kindness and fount of benevolence. [Therefore], one should be happy with whatever has been bestowed by the Eternal Exchequer and should not in vain desire more [*Kulliyāt*, fol. 309b], for whatever emerges from the receptacle of desire cannot be realized according to one's wishes. Many individuals, in their desire for wealth, instigated by greed and avarice, have been swept into the whirlpool of drudgery and affliction, and in their [hope for] enormous profit are entrapped by the precipice of loss. A neck tied with the chain of covetousness is, in the end, severed by the sword of embarrassment. And a head occupied in the craze for greed is ultimately rubbed against the dirt of degradation.

Verse

If you [try to] get more than one skull from your
head,
[I swear] by the dust of the feet of your
inexperience that you will be a cause of trouble.[88]

It is not befitting that wise men express great delight[89] on their wearing a robe of honor and shed tears of grief on their taking a gulp of affliction, that they be joyous of their excessive wealth and disconsolate on the lack of it. [Nor is it befitting if] they be unaware that the luxuries of this world are transitory like a flash of lightning and its troubles temporary like the darkness of clouds. Learned people have said that one should not expect permanence and durability in five things: first, the shade of the cloud that passes while you view it; second, friendship based on selfishness, which becomes extinct in a short time like a flash of lightning; third, the love of women, which robs one's peace of mind for trivial causes; fourth, the charm of handsome individuals, which fades away in the end; fifth, worldly goods, which traverse the path of faithfulness with their master but are destroyed in the end.

How unfortunate are the people who acquire worldly wealth after great trouble and pass away in the end with intense sadness. One wonders at individuals who seek solace in amassing a great deal of wealth and know not that one could get comfort from having little of it. They consider "richness" to be the accumulation of material things; they do not know that one can attain high stature with very little. The individual who gallops his steed of courage in the field of contentment should be considered a "man." He is neither exhilarated on having material things[90] (*Kulliyāt*, fol. 310a), nor expresses regrets on their loss. He does not imprint the leaf of his heart with

[Verse]

The fascination of short-lived phantom,
By stupid persons, called property and wealth.

He spends his life in acquiring the means of renouncing the world and abandoning the requisites of association [with worldly goods]. [*Mau'iẓah,* fol. 57b] He sews the impudent eye of greed with the needle of contentment, and dissociates himself from material things. Most people of this world, by following their tyrant carnal soul, have manifested such vicious characteristics as rancor, jealousy, cruelty, conceit, deceit, arrogance, hypocrisy, and so forth. Their company is more venomous than deadly poison, and associating with them is more difficult than the ordeal of laying down one's life. [A worthy person] should seek repose in solitude and comfort in isolation by closing off the avenue to the company of others. By reclining against solitude,[91] he should cancel the epistle of desire and greed as absurdity. Indeed, the benefits of seclusion are greater than those of association with people. The sages who have spent prolonged periods of time in the corner of a cave or at the bottom of a well had this fact in mind.

Quatrain

Rise up and run away, wherever you can,
From the upheavals of this world.
If you do not have the power to run (fol. 58a),
Try to hold on to solitude.

(Prayer in Arabic): O God! Please rid us of psychical fears and misgivings and from devilish insinuations. Please confer honor upon us with the dignity of attainment and lead us to the world of reason.

SECTION 4: STRIVING FOR ACCOMPLISHMENTS (*KAMĀLĀT*) AND DIVINE CONSENT

Know that this harsh world is a mirage-like inn and a rough abode. In this tavern, the wine of pleasure is mixed with the blood of sorrow. The foundations of this picture gallery (world) are raised with the water and soil of annihilation. The intoxication of this banquet is followed by sluggishness. This craze ends in anguish. Whither is the heart without grief and whither is the eye without bloody tears? This mound of dirt is transient and deserves to be relinquished. This dark pit (life, earth) is to be leveled and filled. All relations are to be severed and deaths to be endured.[92] The

Imperial Scribe of Eternity has not inscribed an everlasting existence in the portfolio of life of any creature. The Portrayer of the images of creatures has depicted on the screens of possible creations (fol. 58b) only these strokes: "Every thing (that exists) will perish except His own face"[93]. The Tailor of this workshop of antiquity has sewed the attire of all creatures with the embroidery of extinction. The Chamberlain of this prison of nature has lighted the candle of leisure [to be blown off with] the swift wind of labor. Whom did He elevate and not thow down? Where did He grow a plant and not uproot it? Where is the one with whom He was extravagant without afflictions? For whom did He open the door of wealth without following with countless sufferings?

This husband-killing, decrepit woman named the World is a wicked woman who has captured many men in her noose. She is the traitor Zāl[94] who has thrown many Tuhmatans[95] into the well of affliction, like Bizhan.[96] She displays herself to the people in the garb of newly-wed brides and entraps the hearts of unwise and haughty individuals with her short-lived charm and ephemeral adornments. Whoever brought her in wedlock could not fulfill his desire. Whoever brought her in the bond of unity could not bring her to consummation for one night. There are many devotees (fol. 59a) disillusioned for not attaining their objective and many lovers thwarted [by her love]. Immature people, because of their stupidity, become enchanted with her charming face and fall into the trap of misfortunes. They remain unaware of her malevolent heart, perfidy, vile nature, and malicious character. The person whose mental perception is illuminated with wisdom and insight, however, is not attracted by her transitory deceptions and does not involve his heart in the love [of the world]. An insightful and perceptive person discerns that the beam of the scale of life is inclined more towards finiteness than eternity.

Whoever came into existence from the hideout of nonexistence has to return to that state of nothingness. Although death is an unpopular sleep and unwanted repose, no one can escape the ring of annihilation and death. Whoever steps into this universe of existence has to sip the elixir of death and must wear the dress of destruction. Moment by moment one traverses the path of non-existence and, in a short time, the spring of life (fol. 59b), which is youth, is transformed into the autumn of old age. Ultimately one has to undertake the long journey into the hereafter. There is no option but to deposit the trust of a borrowed life. There is an end to every beginning and a conclusion destined to every introduction. No one has smelled the fragrance of faithfulness in this garden [of life], and no one has tasted the syrup of repose from the hands of Time. In the end, it is imperative to tread the precarious roadway of the other world and to sleep in the dreadful place of the grave. The message of death arrives unexpectedly; there is no fixed time nor allotted period for the trust of life. When the life span ends and the moment of death approaches, there is no respite, not even for a blink of the eye. Thus, when this reality becomes manifest, wisdom demands that the bird of love for this world should not be allowed in the territory of one's heart. One should not be enchanted with its snakelike, embellished looks, its softness and tenderness. One must not trust life, which declines quickly like the summer cloud, fragrance of a garden, beauty of comely faces, and the fidelity of women (fol. 60a).

Life flashing like lightning and transient as a wave should be considered an invaluable jewel. One should treasure every moment of it and recognize its worth, because whatever is gone from life is impossible to bring back and whatever is left is hidden behind the veil of the 'unknown.' Between the past and future, there is a time called the 'present'—that is the time one should consider to be one's life, and one should not waste it in trivial pursuits. Having awakened from the slumber of negligence and having regained sobriety after the intoxication of the wine of ignorance, one should not be perplexed nor wander in the wilderness of deviation and the gulf of eccentricities. Every moment of life inappropriately expended should be counted as death's time. Today, when one has the power and time to accumulate provisions for the road, one should amass [them]. As long as the destroyer of delight (death) has not grabbed the collar of life, one should not submit to the dictates of the carnal soul (fol. 60b), nor lose his control over wisdom nor let the opportunity of attaining accomplishments escape him; for these are the sources of deliverance from the torment and chastisement of the hereafter. An individual must focus his efforts on acquiring virtues, intellectual attainments, and moral probity, on purifying the carnal soul and on amassing rewards for the next world [by doing good deeds in this], because one cannot accrue the benefits of life and its rewards [without these aforementioned activities]. He should not consume the poisonous morsel of this world but take up the brackish water of austerity, which tastes like honey to the palate of the intellect, instead of the syrup that soothes the carnal soul or the elixir of lust.

Taking advantage of life, one should learn to traverse the wilderness of annihilation and death, and deem the attainment of virtues, perfections, and God's pleasure as the means of felicity and salvation in this world and the next. He should adorn the page of his affairs with the inscription of worship—a source of security in this world and a medium of salvation and honor in the next—and tread the path of submission and worship through austerity.[97] (fol. 61a) He should keep himself busy day and night to remedy the time already lost and make penitence and repentance the "provision of the road to hereafter." Vowing to seek God's pleasure and approval, he should not let his desires interfere with this endeavor. Carnal desires, indeed, destroy spiritual deeds. It is said that a human being has two parts: One is angelic, which leads him to knowledge and its application, and the second is bestial, which [stirs] a craving in him for unlawful things. Thus, the characteristic of unique intellect is to shun bestial inclinations as far as possible. This short life of two or three days should not be made the captive of carnal delights. The span of one's life[98] should be regarded as capital for gains in the hereafter and the field of this life prepared for harvest in the next. As a traveler on the path of spirituality, one should not consider this world and its material resources and wealth [symbols] of power and dignity, and should be indifferent to all these attractions. Thus, (according to this Arabic saying), "No one unites with the whole (God) unless he severs with all," you may reach the whole. You may ascend the ladder of elevation with dignity (in accordance with the Qur'ānic verse) "We (fol. 61b) have honored the sons of Adam,"[99] and you will not be trapped in extreme degradation, (as is in the Qur'ān: "They are like cattle), nay more misguided."[100] When the time of depositing the trust of the soul arrives, it will be easier for you to traverse the path to the hereafter.

Hemistich: This act is an act of triumph now—whosoever avails of it now.

CONCLUSION

Oh God! The compiler of these pages is intangled in the strife of this world and its evils, bless him with the anguish of Thy search, and with Thy eternal blessings and interminable guidance, relieve him of insensitivity. Let not his desires determine his plans. Guide him according to Thy will. This manual of regulations for vigilant and wise people has become too long, and these extremely valuable pearls have been strung in order. Therefore, sincerity and servitude demand that it be concluded with an invocation for the stability of ever-expanding empire, and for perpetuity of the perdurable dominion of my master, benefactor, and real focus of my prayers:

Verses

The ruler of the countries of the world,
Because of his justice and banner of power,
(fol. 62a) Bestows crowns upon the rulers ascending the throne;
Under his sovereignty are the East and West.

The Turks and the Dailamites are his slaves
Caesar is among his warders.

All of his ancestors with fortunate dispositions
The masters of the crown and throne since Adam.

It is, indeed, rude for the pen to repeat his famous and honorable name. (Therefore, this treatise) ends (with a reference to him).

Verse[s]

As long as with the radiance of the sun,
The highest levels of the sky are illuminated

May the surface of this earth be an envy of [all] Paradise
Because of the justice of the clear-headed emperor.

The date of the completion of *Mau'iẓah-i Jahāngīrī* is as follows:

When this epistle was completed
With the power of penetrating genius,

For its chronogram, I was searching
In the world of imagination.

All of sudden, from the invisible guardian angel
Echoed a voice in my heart:

"O thou, the bird of the soul of the people of knowledge,
Flying in the garden of your ingenuity,

In resurrecting mental images,
Indeed, you have performed a miracle like the Christ

(fol. 62b) O ye, distinguished in the art of poetry and prose,
You have named it the *Mau'iẓah.*

For the sake of conformity,
Write *Mau'iẓah*, as its chronogram,"
(1021 A.H./1612A.D.)

Written on the 10th of Rabi' al-Thānī 1028 A.H./1618 A.D. The scribe is the sinner 'Abd-Allāh Shihābī. May Allāh forgive his sins.

INTRODUCTION NOTES:
Pages 1-34

1. In all standard secondary works on Muslim rule in India, the treatment of the subject is meager and sometimes entirely superficial. Articles by Aziz Ahmad and Peter Hardy are of an introductory nature and survey the sources without going into detail. See Aziz Ahmad, "Trends in the Political Thought of Medieval Muslim India," *Studia Islamica* 17(1962): 121-30, and Peter Hardy, "The Muslim Ruler in India," in *Sources of Indian Tradition*, edited by William Theodore De Bary (New York: Columbia University Press, 1958), vol. 1, pp. 455-500. However, more substantial analysis is available in the Introduction to Żiyā al-Dīn Baranī, *Fatāwā-i Jahāndārī* (*Rulings on Temporal Government*), edited by A. Saleem Khan (Lahore: Research Society of Pakistan, University of the Punjab, 1972). The following articles are limited to the fourteenth century: Peter Hardy, "Unity and Variety in Indo-Islamic and Perso-Islamic Civilization: Some Ethical and Political Ideas of Ḍiyā' al-Dīn Baranī of Delhi, of al-Ghazālī and of Naṣīr al-Dīn Tusī Compared," *Iran* 16(1978): 127-35; Khaliq Ahmad Nizami, "Aspects of Muslim Political Thought in India during the Fourteenth Century," *Islamic Culture* 52(1978): 213-40.
2. Ibn Khaldūn's views on the 'Mirrors' are based on his comments about Abū Bakr al-Ṭarṭūshī's *Kitāb Sirāj al-Mulūk:* Abū Bakr "did not exhaust the problems and did not bring clear proofs . . . he tells a great number of stories and traditions and he reports scattered remarks by Persian sages such as Buzurjmihr and Mobedhan. . . . He does not verify his statements or clarify them with the help of natural arguments." *The Muqaddimah: An Introduction to History*, translated by Franz Rosenthal (Princeton, NJ: Princeton University Press, 1967), vol. 1, p. 83.
3. E. I. J. Rosenthal, *Political Thought in Medieval Islam: An Introductory*

Outline (Cambridge, England: Cambridge University Press, 1968), pp. 68-9.

4. Ann K. S. Lambton, in her recent work *State and Government in Medieval Islam: An Introduction to the Study of Islamic Political Theory: The Jurists* (New York: Oxford University Press, 1981), cited only al-Ghāzālī's *Naṣīḥat al-Mulūk* from amongst the Mirrors.
5. Yūsuf Khāṣṣ Ḥājib, *Wisdom of Royal Glory (Kutadgu Bilig): A Turko-Islamic Mirror for Princes,* translated by Robert Dankoff (Chicago, IL: University of Chicago Press, 1983), p. 4.
6. A genre that became popular among the eighteenth-century Indian poets, who, writing in Urdu and Persian, focused on sociopolitical disintegration. Thus, this genre may also be called the literature of crisis.
7. The tradition of historiography changed in eighteenth-century India. The historians, unlike their predecessors, criticized the shortcomings of the government and named their works *'Ibrat Nāmahs.* Notable among these historians are: Muḥammad b. Mu'tamad Khān, Sayyid Muḥammad Qāsim Ḥusaynī, and Maulawī Khayr al-Dīn.
8. See note 9.
9. For a comprehensive study of Niẓām al-Mulk's political career, see Murtada Hasan al-Naqib, "Niẓām al-Mulk: An Analytical Study of His Career and Contribution to the Development of Political and Religious Institutions Under the Great Saljuqs." Unpublished Ph.D. dissertation, McGill University, 1978. For *Siyāsat Nāmah,* see ibid., pp. 18-37. For al-Ghazālī, see Abdul Hakim H. O. M. Dawood, "A Comparative Study of Arabic and Persian Mirrors for Princes from the Second to the Sixth Century A. H." Unpublished Ph.D. dissertation, University of London, 1965, p. 244-51. For further discussion of al-Ghazālī's views on statecraft, see Lambton, *State and Government*, pp. 107-29; Lambton, "The Theory of Kingship in the *Naṣīḥat ul-Mulūk* of Ghazālī," *Islamic Quarterly* 1(1954): 47-55; and L. Binder, "Al-Ghazālī's Theory of Government," *The Muslim World* 45, no. 3 (1955): 229-41. For a general discussion, see Lambton, "Islamic Mirrors for Princes," *La Persia nel medioevo* (1971): 419-42 [Accademia Nazionale dei Lincei, quaderno 160]. Dawood's thesis is a comprehensive study of the Mirrors in Arabic and Persian during their formative phase. Louise Marlow's unpublished Ph.D.

dissertation "Theories of Social Stratification in Islamic Literature until the End of the Mongol Period," Princeton University, 1987, is a major contribution to the study of this genre in the thirteenth and fourteenth centuries. These studies, however, do not include Indo-Islamic Mirrors.

10. Muḥammad bin Manṣūr Mubārak-shāh Fakhr-i Mudabbir, *Ādāb al-Ḥarb wa al-Shujā'at*, edited by Aḥmad Suhailī Khawānsārī (Tehran: Iqbal Press, 1346 H.S.).
11. We have little biographical information on Mudabbir. He claims to have taken great pains in compiling this unique manual in order to impress the Sulṭān with the versatility of his knowledge (*Ādāb al-Ḥarb*, p. 23). The language of this work has religious overtones, with frequent quotations from the Qur'ān and *ḥadīth* and with anecdotes taken liberally from Islamic history.
12. *Fatāwā*, Introduction, p. 28.
13. Ibid., pp. 19-20.
14. Among writers of the Mirrors of the Sultanate period, Baranī (coming from a family of high officials) is the only one who very strongly believed in nobility of birth; indeed, he was obsessed with this notion. The class character of the *Fatāwā* could be an indication of the power struggle between the Turks and the indigenous Muslims, the rising economic influence of the Hindus, and Baranī's personal financial difficulties.
15. Sayyid 'Alī Hamadānī, *Ẕakhīrat al-Mulūk*, edited by Sayyid Maḥmūd Anwari (Tabriz: Dānishkadah-i Adabiyāt wa 'Ulūm-i Insānī, Mu'assasah-i Tārīkh wa Farhang-i Irān, 1358 H.S.), p. 2. Sayyid 'Ali Hamadānī was born in Hamadān of a notable family of Sayyids, whose chain of initiation traced back to 'Alā' al-Dawlah al-Simnānī and through him to Najm al-Dīn Kubrā. Leading the life of a dervish, he is said to have visited the Kashmir valley three times—in 1372, 1379, and 1383—and is credited with the Islamization of that region. *Encyclopaedia of Islam*[2], edited by H. A. R. Gibb, *et al* (Leiden: E. J. Brill, 1960), vol. 1, s.v. "'Alī bin Shihāb al-Dīn Hamadānī".
16. For details about al-Mawardi's views on the Islamic state, see D. P. Little, "A New Look at *al-Aḥkām al-Sulṭāniyya*," *The Muslim World* 64, no. 1 (January 1974): 1-15; Qamaruddin Khan, *Al-Māwardī's Theory of the State* (Lahore: Bazm-i Iqbāl, n.d.); and John Mikhail,

"Māwardī: A Study in Islamic Political Thought," unpublished Ph.D. dissertation, Harvard University, 1968.

17. For references to al-Ghazālī, see note 9, above. The responses of other thinkers, such as Ibn Taymiyyah (d. 1328) and Ibn Khaldūn (d. 1406), who wrote after the extinction of the Caliphate, were different. Ibn Taymiyyah considered the role of *Sharī'ah* to be of fundamental importance in his plan for an Islamic government, and Ibn Khaldūn extolled the mechanism of *'aṣabiyyah* as a new basis for the stability and endurance of a given political power. For further discussion on the writings and thought of Ibn Taymiyyah, see Lambton, *State and Government*, pp. 143-51; Qamaruddin Khan, "Ibn Taymiyyah's Views on the Prophetic State," *Islamic Studies* 3(1964): 521-30; and various writings of H. Laoust. See *Encyclopaedia of Islam*[2], edited by B. Lewis, *et al.* (Leiden: E. J. Brill, 1969), vol. 3, s.v. "Ibn Taymiyya." On Ibn Khaldūn, many scholarly works are available in European and Islamic languages. For Ibn Khaldūn's political thought and further bibliographic citations, refer to Muhammad Mahmoud Rabi', *The Political Theory of Ibn Khaldun* (Leiden: E. J. Brill, 1967).
18. *Fatāwā*, p. 140. In Baranī's opinion, "Three caliphs—'Umar, 'Uthmān, and 'Alī—were martyred by reckless devotees because of the caliphs' efforts to adhere to the *sunnah* of the Prophet." Ibid.
19. *Ẕakhīrah*, p. 254.
20. *Ādāb al-Ḥarb*, p. 283.
21. *Fatāwā*, pp. 3, 88.
22. *Ẕakhīrah*, p. 250.
23. Ibid., p. 256.
24. Muhammad Habib and Afsar S. Khan, *The Political Theory of the Delhi Sultanate* (Allahabad: Kitāb Maḥal, 1961), p. 3.
25. *Fatāwā*, p. 18.
26. Ibid., pp. 164-66.
27. Baranī expressed his views thus: "They are to be tolerated due to the sheer dint of necessity and as such bare social and economic survival are recommended for them. Social status must not be granted to them and they should constantly be reminded rather haunted by the consciousness of their social inferiority." Ibid., Introduction, p. 96.
28. *Ādāb al-Ḥarb*, pp. 15, 64, 65, 112.
29. *Ẕakhīrah*, pp. 285-87; al-Māwardī, *Al-Aḥkām al-Sulṭāniyyah*, Urdu

translation by Muḥammad Ibrāhīm (Hyderabad, Deccan: Osmania University Press, 1931), pp. 238-39.

30. *Ẕakhīrah*, pp. 218-26.
31. Peter Hardy has called the interaction of this group with the ruler "a partnership between pious professors and pious policemen" (*Sources of Indian Tradition*, p. 465). His use of the term "pious policeman" does not properly convey the image of the ruler in medieval times. The position of the ruler was more like that of a patriarch, and the people were like his family, as wrote Niẓām al-Mulk, *Siyar al-Mulūk, Siyāsat Nāmah*, edited by Hubert Darke (Tehran: Bungāh-i Tarjumah wa Nashr-i Kitāb, 1340 H.S.), p. 153; English translation by Hubert Darke (London: Routledge and Kegan Paul, 1960), p. 122. That there existed a partnership between the *'ulamā'* and the ruler is also open to question. We do know that the sultans of Delhi tried to accommodate the views and verdicts of the religious elite, but only to the extent that they considered it prudent. The extent of the *'ulamā'*'s influence fluctuated with the personality of the ruler.
32. *Ādāb al-Ḥarb*, pp. 434-35.
33. *Fatāwā*, pp. 10-11.
34. *Ẕakhīrah*, p. 350.
35. Ibid., p. 257.
36. Baranī conceives the Indo-Islamic society as comprising of two layers: the nobility or elite (*khawāṣ*) and the low-born (*arāẕil, asāfil*). He considers both religion and politics to be privileges of the aristocracy and categorically states that the low-born should not be taught how to read and write—because should they become literate, the balance of power and religion would be disrupted; they would aspire for high administrative positions for which they were unworthy (*Fatāwā*, p. 180). For more discussion on Baranī's views on society, see Habib, *Political Theory*, Introduction, pp. ii, v-x.
37. *Ādāb al-Ḥarb*, p. 456.
38. Ibid., p. 452.
39. *Ẕakhīrah*, p. 214.
40. To make his work look authentic and comprehensive to his patron, Mudabbir considered it necessary to provide specific details of a battlefield, such as the position of troops, weapons, horses, and armor in the field and various fighting strategies

(*Ādāb al-Ḥarb*, pp. 20-22).

41. Referring to Aristotle's description to Alexander of the qualities of a good commander, Baranī added such attributes as unconditional loyalty to the person of the ruler, nobility of birth, the commander's personal power and prestige in his own ethnic group, valor, righteousness, and sensitivity to the needs of troops (*Fatāwā*, pp. 98-99).
42. *Ādāb al-Ḥarb*, pp. 388, 399-400.
43. Mudabbir discussed various types of combat in his work and suggested that in the event of an attack by infidels, women and slaves could also engage in combat without the permission of their husbands and masters (Ibid., pp. 336-39; 399-400).
44. *Fatāwā*, p. 166.
45. Ibid., p. 18.
46. *Ẕakhīrah*, p. 468.
47. *Ādāb al-Ḥarb*, pp. 117-18; 121.
48. Habib, *Political Theory*, Introduction, p. xi. For more details of 'Alā' al-Dīn's economic policies, see Kishori Saran Lal, *History of the Khaljis: A.D. 1290-1320* (Allahabad: Indian Press, 1950), pp. 241-55, 269-94.
49. Marshall G. S. Hodgson, *The Venture of Islam* (Chicago, IL: University of Chicago Press, 1974), vol. III, p. 60.
50. J. F. Richards, "The Formulation of Imperial Authority under Akbar and Jahāngīr," in J. F. Richards, ed., *Kingship and Authority in South Asia* (Madison, WI: University of Wisconsin-Madison South Asian Publication Series, 1978), pp. 252-53.
51. Talcott Parsons, *Societies: Evolutionary and Comparative Perspectives* (Englewood Cliffs. NJ: Prentice-Hall, 1966), p. 17, quoted by M. N. Pearson, "Shivaji and the Decline of the Mughal Empire," *Journal of Asian Studies* 35(1976), p. 223. For further discussion of the Mughal nobility and state, see Pearson, ibid., pp. 223-26. It should be emphasized that the centrality of *manṣabdārs'* role in the Mughal administration has already received adequate scholarly attention. The most recent major work is M. Athar Ali, *The Apparatus of Empire: Awards of Ranks, Offices and Titles to the Mughal Nobility (1574-1658)* (New Delhi: Oxford University Press, 1985). This work provides information on awards of *manṣabs* in chronological order. The data concerning recruitment, racial composition of the nobility, patterns of promotion,

and the official titles in this work make it an indispensable reference tool for institutional, political, and social historians of Mughal India. An illustrated biographical dictionary of Shāhjahān's period is currenty being compiled under the joint authorship of Wayne Begley And Z. A. Desai and should be equally useful. For discussion of the *manṣabdārī* system, see the Translation, notes 52 and 63.

52. For discussion of the concept of *'aṣabīyyah,* see Ibn Khaldūn, *The Muqaddimah,* Introduction, pp. lxxviii-lxxxiii.
53. India Office Persian Manuscript 1684.
54. *Akhlāq-i Ḥakīmī,* fol. 6b.
55. Ibid., fols. 7a-b.
56. Some of the works referred to are: *Qābūs Nāmah* of Kaykā'ūs (fols. 17b, 89a, 90b); *'Ahad Nāmah-i Ardshīr* (fol. 21b); *Waṣāyā-i Niẓām al-Mulk* (fol. 48b); *Mathnawī-i Maulānā Rūm* (fol. 64b); *Jawām' al-Ḥikāyāt* of al-'Awfī (fols. 73a, 88a); *Tārīkh-i Mir'āt* of Mu'īn al-Dīn Asafzārī (fol. 75b); *Makāram al-Akhlāq* (fols. 79a, 104a,b, 105a); *Haqāyaq al-Īqān* (fol. 83a); *Ḥabīb al-Sayyar* of Khawānd Mīr (fol. 83b); *Al-'Ajāz fī al-Ījāz* (fl. 91a). The writer also quoted Sirāj al-Dīn Tūstarī (fol. 107b).
57. For details of Abū'l Fażl's life and works, see S. A. A. Rizvi, *Religious and Intellectual History of the Muslims in Akbar's Reign with special Reference to Abū'l Fażl, 1556-1605,* (New Delhi: Munshiram Manoharlal Publishers, 1975), pp. 90-103, 455-508; for his political philosophy, ibid., pp. 352-73.
58. India Office Persian Manuscript 1547.
59. *Risālah-i Nūriyyah-i Sulṭāniyyah,* edited by Muhammad Saleem Akhtar (Islamabad: Iran-Pakistan Institute of Persian Studies, 1985). Unlike *Mau'iẓah-i Jahāngīrī* and *Akhlāq-i Jahāngīrī, Risālah-i Nūriyyah* is named after the first name of Jahāngīr, i.e., Nūr-al Dīn.
60. *Akhlāq,* fol. 95b.
61. The title of the work is a chronogram for the completion of the work, viz. A.H. 1031/A.D. 1622. Ibid., fol. 3b. At the end (fols. 524b-25a), the author noted that he had finished the work in A.H. 1029/A.D. 1620. Khāqānī probably wrote the *muqaddimah* two years after the composition of the main work.
62. *Akhlāq,* fol. 3a.
63. Rizvi, *Religious and Intellectual History,* p. 197.
64. *Akhlāq,* fol. 434a.

65. Ibid., fol. 3b.
66. For a fuller account of 'Abd al-Ḥaqq's life and works, see Khalīq Aḥmad Niẓāmī, *Ḥayāt-i Shaykh 'Abd al-Ḥaqq Muḥaddith Dihlavī* (Delhi: Nadwat al-Muṣannafīn, 1964).
67. *Risālah-i Nūriyyah*, pp. 25-6. Jahāngīr, in his autobiography, recorded his meeting with the Shaykh to discuss religious issues. He praised the Shaykh's work *Akhbār-al Akhyār* (a biographical dictionary of religious personages) but did not mention the *Risālah* (Nūr al-Dīn Jahāngīr, *The Tūzuk-i Jahāngīrī or Memoirs of Jahāngīr*, 2nd edition, English translation by Alexander Rogers [Delhi: Munshiram Manoharlal Publishers, 1968], vol. II, p. 111).
68. Maḥmūd bin Amīr Walī Balkhī's travelogue is the only primary source in which the name of Bāqir's father is recorded (*Baḥr al-Asrār fī Manāqib al-Akhyār*, edited by Riazul Islam [Karachi: Institute of Central and West Asian Studies, University of Karachi, 1980], p. 66). Shaykh Farīd Bhakkarī, Bāqir's near contemporary, noted that Bāqir's father was employed for some time by the chancery (*diwān*) in Farāh, Khurasan (*Dhakhīrat al-Khawānīn*, edited by Syed Moinul Haq [Karachi: Pakistan Historical Society, 1970], vol. II, p. 254). Bāqir wrote the name of the place, Farāh, in a poem that he composed for his father and sent it with his poet friend, 'Itābī, who was returning to Iran. (Farāh is the name of a mountain and a river in Seistan, midway between Herat and Jalalabad—Sayyid Ḥasan 'Askarī, "Mirzā Muḥammad Bāqir Najm-i T̲h̲ānī," *'Arshī Presentation Volume*, eds. Malik Ram and M. D. Ahmad [New Delhi: Majlis-i Nazr-i 'Arshi, 1965], p. 104).
69. Shāhnawāz Khān speculates that Bāqir came to India either during the reign of Akbar (being given the rank of 300 *sawār*) or during the reign of Jahāngīr (being given the rank of 250 *sawār*—*Ma'āthir al-Umarā,'* Urdu translation by Muḥammad Ayūb Qādrī [Lahore: Markazī Urdu Board, 1968], vol. I, p. 406). Bhakkarī states that he received an initial appointment of 100 *sawār* in Jahāngīr's service. After serving the emperor in various capacities, during which he displayed great brilliance in subduing various tribes between Multan and Qandhar, he rose rapidly into the upper echelons of the Mughal *manṣabdārī* system (*Dhakhīrat*, vol. II, pp. 254-55).
70. Ibid., p. 255; 'Abd al-Hamīd Lāhawrī, *Bādshāh Nāmah*, edited by Kabīr al-Dīn Aḥmad and 'Abd al-Raḥīm (Calcutta: Royal Asiatic

Society of Bengal, 1867), vol. I, pp. 8, 72, 80, 87, and 125.

71. 'Askarī, "Mirzā Muḥammad Bāqir," p. 104.
72. *Ma'āthir*, op. cit., p. 407.
73. India Office Persian Manuscripts 1666 & 1330 respectively.
74. In two volumes: Pers. *Kalām*, 1409, 1409/1. This work is not recorded in any of the printed catalogues of Oriental manuscripts. During my library research trip to India in 1986, I located it in the Oriental Manuscripts Library, Research Institute, Hyderabad.
75. As discussed in note 69, Bāqir became a prominent Mughal *manṣabdār* by virtue of his prudence in political matters. For further details of his political appointments and distinctions, see 'Askarī, "Muḥammad Bāqir," pp. 106-14, and Nūr al-Dīn Jahāngīr, *Tūzuk-i Jahāngīrī*, Urdu translation by A'jāz al-Ḥaqq Quddūsī (Lahore: Majlis-i Taraqqī-i Adab, 1968), vol. II, pp. 7, 106, 112, 127, 151-52, 253, 273, 287, 295, and 334. It should be further noted that during the rebellion of Prince Khurram (later to become emperor Shāhjahān), Bāqir served his master, Jahāngīr, faithfully by opposing the rebellious prince (see ibid., pp. 350, 351, 353 and 360). However, after his coronation (and consistent with the Mughal tradition), Shāhjahān let Bāqir continue as the governor of Orissa ('Askarī, "Muḥammad Bāqir", p. 107). Furthermore, Bāqir did not let his Shī'ī religious persuasions interfere with his commitment to the Mughal imperial interests. In 1629, it was Muḥammad Bāqir who led the Mughal armies into the territories of Shī'ī rulers of Deccan, the Quṭub Shāhīs. Wālah Harawī, one of Bāqir's court poets, described in detail Bāqir's victory at Deccan. For a text of the *qaṣīdah* and its English translation, see ibid., pp. 113-14; also pp. 47-8 of my article, "Shī'ism in India During Jahāngīr's Reign: Some Reflections," *Journal of the Pakistan Historical Society* 27, no. 1 (1979): 39-65.
76. *Baḥr al-Asrār*, p. 66; *Ma'āthir*, op. cit., p. 408; and *Dhakhīrat*, op. cit., p. 254. One of Bāqir's recently located works—*Sirāj al-Manāhij* (see note 74), written by the author himself in beautiful *nasta'līq* —bears testimony to Bāqir's skills in calligraphy.
77. As an example of Bāqir's interest in prosody, philosophy, mathematics, and astronomy, see one of his published *qiṭ'ah* composed as a riddle (Alvi, "Shi'ism in India," pp. 50-65).

78. Bāqir patronized poet Wālah Harawī. A fairly detailed account of Bāqir's court in Katak (the provincial capital of Orissa) appears in Maḥmūd Balkhī's travelogue, *Baḥr al-Asrār*, pp. 66-8. It mentions Bāqir's patronage of literary figures and his own intellectual interests. Balkhī was traveling from Ceylon to China with some Europeans when his boat was caught in a storm and beached on the Coromondal coast. As spokesman for his fellow travellers, he was taken to Katak. To win Bāqir's favor, he composed a *risālah* in prose and poetry and presented it to him (for details, see ibid., Introduction, p. 7, text, p. 66-7). In this *risālah*, he praised Bāqir for his various literary and artistic skills. He also claimed that Bāqir wished to retain him in his court, desiring him to translate certain epistles on Practical Wisdom (*ḥikmat-i 'amalī*) from Arabic into Persian. Referring to a conversation between Bāqir and a certain Mirzā Ḥusain, Balkhī mentioned a large number of men of learning (*ahl-i fażl*) and artists (*arbāb-i hunar*) in Bāqir's court. Ibid., p. 68.
79. *Mau'iẓah*, fol. 62a.
80. Bāqir, according to his own words, always yearned to write a didactic treatise and struggled to find time for such an undertaking. Eventually, he wrote *Mau'iẓah-i Jahāngīrī* (*Mau'iẓah*, fols. 4a-b).
81. Ibid., fol. 6b.
82. Some of the earlier jurists discussed the concept of rulers as caliphs of God (*khalīfat-Allāh*) at length: for example, al-Māwardī, *Al-Aḥkām al-Sulṭāniyyah*, Urdu translation, pp. 3-41. A later jurist, Fażl-Allāh b. Ruzbihān Khunjī (d. 1521), addressed the issue of *khalīfat-Allāh* in his work *Sulūk al-Mulūk*. Written in 1514, this work shows great flexibility in dealing with various practical problems of running a government. However, Fażl-Allāh opined that a sultan could be called *khalīfah, imām, amīr al-mu'minīn*, or *khalīfah-i rasūl*, but not *khalīfat-Allāh* (*Sulūk al-Muluk*, edited by M. Nizamuddin [Hyderabad, Deccan: Ministry of Education, Government of India, Persian Manuscripts Society, 1966], p. 48). Commissioned by the Uzbek ruler 'Ubaid-Allāh Khān Uzbek (d. 1539?), this work indicates the continued desire of some Sunnī Muslim rulers to know the injunctions of *Sharī'ah* on statecraft. Among Bāqir's contemporaries, Khāqānī and 'Abd al-Ḥaqq considered the rulers to be successors to prophets,

caliphs of God, and shadows of God (*sāyah-i khudā*). *Akhlāq*, fol. 3a, and *Risālah*, p. 24.

83. For philosophical, juristical, and historical theories of an Islamic state, see Lambton, *State and Government in Medieval Islam*, and Rosenthal, *Political Thought in Islam*.
84. *Mau'iẓah*, fol. 8a.
85. Ibid., fols. 16a-b.
86. Ibid., fol. 7a.
87. For example, see W. F. Thompson, *Practical Philosophy of the Muhammadan People*, English translation of al-Dawwānī's *Akhlāq-i Jalālī* (London: Printed for the Oriental Translation Fund of Great Britain and Ireland, 1839), pp. 312-28, 365-76, and Fażl-Allāh, *Sulūk al-Mulūk*, pp. 40-7, 58-60. To a lesser degree, Niẓām al-Mulk (*Siyāsat Nāmah*, pp. 74-5) and al-Ghazālī (*Naṣīḥat al-Mulūk*, pp. 100, 106-7, 110) also tried to impress upon their Saljūq patrons the need for preserving religion in their state policies.
88. *Mau'iẓah*, fol. 6b. I concur with Lambton that it is difficult to distinguish between Shī'ī and Sunnī writers of the Mirrors in their theories of rulership ("Islamic Mirrors," p. 420). For the Shī'ī concept of *Imāmat*, see *Encyclopaedia of Islam*[2], edited by B. Lewis, *et al* (Leiden: E. J. Brill, 1971), vol. 3, s.v., "*Imama*"; J. Eliash, "The Ithnā 'asharī-Shī'ī Juristic Theory of Political and Legal Authority," *Studia Islamica* 29(1967): 17-30; and Lambton, *State and Government*, pp. 219-41. Within the theoretical framework of Persian rulership in Islamic political thought, the views of such jurists as al-Ghazalī are particularly significant—see *Naṣīḥat al-Mulūk*, p. 81. For additional references on al-Ghazālī's concept of kingship, see note 9.
89. *Mau'iẓah*, fol. 10b.
90. Ibid., fol. 9b.
91. For details of this complex issue of lineage moving from Semitic to Turco-Mongol race, see Abū'l Fażl, *Akbar Nāmah*, translated by H. Beveridge (Calcutta: Royal Asiatic Society of Bengal, 1897), vol. 1, pp. 143-54, 178-94, and 204-22.
92. *Mau'iẓah*, fol. 7b.
93. Ibid., fol. 8b.
94. Ibid., fol. 14a.
95. For more details, see A. K. S. Lambton, "Justice in the Medieval Theory of Kingship," *Studia Islamica* 17(1962): 91-119. Also

useful is Majid Khadduri, *Islamic Conception of Justice* (Baltimore, MD: John Hopkins University Press, 1984). In this work, the concept of justice is discussed from political, theological, philosophical, and ethical perspectives.

96. *Mau'iẓah*, fol. 9b; *Naṣīḥat al-Mulūk*, p. 124; and Ḥusayn Wā'iẓ Kāshifī, *Akhlāq-i Muḥsinī* (Lucknow: Munshī Nawal Kishawr, 1878), p. 23.
97. *Mau'iẓah*, fol. 10a.
98. Ibid., fol. 9b.
99. Jahāngīr, *Tūzuk-i Jahāngīrī*, translated by Alexander Rogers, vol. 1, p. 7. Jahāngīr's reputation as a just ruler must have been widespread during his reign. 'Uthmān, a Ṣūfī poet who lived in Ghazipur during the reign of Jahāngīr but was not associated with the court, heard about Jahāngīr's golden chain of justice and applauded him in his long poem *Chitravali* (B. K. Singh, "Some Glimpses of Society and Polity in Usman's *Chitravali*," *Proceedings of Indian History Congress* 25[1958], p. 336). For more discussion on the subject, see my forthcoming article "Religion and State during the Reign of Mughal Emperor Jahāngīr (1605-27): Nonjuristical Perspectives," *Studia Islamica*.
100. *Mau'iẓah*, fol. 11a.
101. Ibid., fol. 11b.
102. On the Iranian scene, Iskander Bēg Turkomān (in *Tārīkh-i 'Ālam ārā-i 'Abbāsī*, edited by Īraj Afshār [Tehran: Chāp-i Gulshan, 1350 H.S.], vol. 2, part 2, pp. 1100-1101), considered his patron, Shāh 'Abbās I, to be divinely inspired in his every action. According to Iskander Bēg, even when his counselors occasionally considered him wrong, he proved to be right because of divine guidance. Said Amir Arjomand argues that before the ascent of the Ṣafavids to power, the separation of religious and political spheres led to the secularization of political power and a more pragmatic approach to it ("Religion, Political Action and Legitimate Domination in Shi'ite Iran: Fourteenth to Eighteenth Centuries A.D.," *Archives Europeennes de Sociologie* 20, no. 1[1979], p. 69). However, it was only after the ascendancy of the Ṣafavids that issues related to the legitimacy and abuse of political power were raised, issues that were no longer of great concern in the Sunnī circles.
103. Qur'ān, 3:159; *Mau'iẓah*, fol. 17a. For a juristical discussion on

consultation and community, see Fazlur Rahman, "The Principle of *Shūra* and the Role of the *Umma* in Islam," *American Journal of Islamic Studies* 1, no. 1(1984): 1-9.

104. *Mau'iẓah*, fols. 16b-20a. A closer look at the Mughal central administration shows that the advisory councils were not restricted to ministers; high-ranking nobles, irrespective of their race and religion, were instrumental in making, as well as implementing, the state policies. For further details, see Ibn Hasan, *The Central Structure of the Mughal Empire* (New Delhi: Munshiram Manoharlal Publishers, 1970 reprint), pp. 296-301).
105. *Mau'iẓah*, fols. 27a-28a.
106. Ibid., fol. 29a.
107. Ibid., fols. 28a-b.
108. Ibid., fol. 31b.
109. Ibid., fol. 31a.
110. Ibid., fol. 33a.
111. Ibid., fol. 35a.
112. Ibid., fol. 24b.
113. For details, see ibid., fols. 25a-b.
114. Ibid., fols. 39a. For a discussion of the practical application of a Mughal noble's code of behavior, see John F. Richards, "Norms of Comportment among Imperial Mughal Officers," in *Moral Conduct and Authority: The Place of Adab in South Asian Islam*, edited by Barbara Daly Metcalf (Berkeley, CA: University of California Press, 1984), pp. 276-89.
115. *Mau'iẓah*, fols. 41a-b.
116. Marshall Hodgson has titled the third volume of his history of Islamic civilization *The Venture of Islam: The Gun Powder Empires and Modern Times* (Chicago, IL: University of Chicago Press, 1974).
117. I. H. Qureshi, *The Administration of the Mughul Empire* (Karachi: University of Karachi, 1966), pp. 114-39.
118. As discussed above, writers during the Sultanate period perceived the role of the army to be crucial in maintaining the sovereignty of the ruler and in securing the submission of the people and the suppression of insurgents.
119. *Mau'iẓah*, fol. 36a.
120. For more discussion, see the Translation, notes 62-3.
121. *Mau'iẓah*, fol. 29b.

122. Baranī divided the Muslims into grades and sub-grades. In his scheme, all high positions and privileges were to be the monopoly of the high-born Turks, not the Indian Muslims. Even in his interpretation of the famous Qur'ānic verse "Indeed, the pious amongst you are most honored by Allāh," he considered piety to be associated with noble birth (Habib, *Political Theory*, Introduction, p. ii). Baranī's views, as well as those of other medieval historians, have led to lively discussion among the sociologists and social anthropologists of Indian society. Louis Dumont, for example, considered social hierarchy in the Indo-Muslim community to be analogous to or a replica of the Hindu caste system (*Homo Hierarchicus: The Caste System and its Implications*, translated by Mark Sainsbury (Chicago, IL: University of Chicago Press, 1974), pp. 205-14. Imtiaz Ahmad has further discussed the question of high-born and low-born in his article "The *Ashrāf-Ajlāf* Dichotomy in Muslim Social Structure in India," *Indian Economic and Social History Review* 33(1966): 268-78. By contrast, the Muslim writers in medieval India, while writing on social hierarchy, were not influenced by the Hindu caste system. They continued to maintain the early Islamic tradition of stressing the importance of *ḥasab wa nasab* (acquired capacity and lineage) and classification of the social structure into various categories, known as *ṭabaqāt*. For more general discussion on the *ṭabaqāt* in early Islamic social context, see Roy P. Mottahedeh, *Loyalty and Leadership in Early Islamic Society* (Princeton, NJ: Princeton University Press, 1980), pp. 98-115.
123. *Mau'iẓah*, fols. 29b-30a.
124. Ibid., fol. 32a.
125. Ibid., fol. 32b.
126. Kai Kā'ūs Ibn Iskandar, *A Mirror for Princes: The Qābūs Nāma*, translated by Reuben Levy (Bristol, England: E. P. Dutton & Co. Inc., 1951), p. 223.
127. Edited by M. T. Dānish-Pazhūh, Tehran, 1966—quoted and discussed in detail by Lambton, "Islamic Mirrors," pp. 426-36. The author of the *Baḥr* included passages on seclusion. In one such passage, he gave three possible reasons for the seclusion of rulers: to conceal their sins against God; to hide their faults from the public; and because of their miserliness, to justify

their inability to fulfill the demands of the people (Ibid., p. 427).

128. *Mau'iẓah*, fols. 10b-11a.
129. Ibid., fol. 11a.
130. Ibid., fol. 6b.
131. Ibid., fol. 7a-b. For detailed discussion on the role of religion in Jahāngīr's state policies and of Bāqir's lukewarm approach in projecting Jahāngīr as the champion of Islam, see my forthcoming article, "State and Religion."
132. *Mau'iẓah*, fols. 22a-b. See also the Translation, Note 32.
133. Ibid., fol. 21b.
134. Ibid., fol. 26b.
135. Ibid., fol. 15b.
136. For details of al-Ghazālī's views, see Fazul-ul-Karim, *Imam Ghazzali's Ihya Ulum-id-Din* (Lahore: Sind Sagar Academy, n.d.), vol. 2, pp. 109-44.
137. *Mau'iẓah*, fol. 3a.
138. Ibid., fols. 42a-b.
139. Ibid., fol. 44a.
140. Ibid., fol. 44b-45a.
141. Ibid., fol. 45b.
142. *Akhlāq*, fols. 188a-200b and 428b-434a respectively.
143. *Akhlāq-i Ḥakīmī*, fols. 23b-28a.
144. Al-Ghazālī combined his discussion on *tawakkul* with *tawhid;* see *Imam Ghazzali's Ihya*, vol. 4, pp. 234-96.
145. *Mau'iẓah*, fols. 56a-b.
146. For al-Ghazālī's discussion on *'uzlah* and *mukhālaṭah*, see *Imam Ghazzali's Ihya*, vol. 2, pp. 172-87.
147. *Mau'iẓah*, fol. 57b.
148. Ibid., fols. 49b-50a.
149. Ibid., fols. 50b-51a.
150. Ibid., fol. 51b.
151. Ibid., fol. 53a.
152. Ibid., fols. 53b-54a.
153. Ibid., fol. 54a.
154. Ibid., fols. 58a-b.
155. Ḥāfiẓ called this world a "decrepit woman" who was "wife of a thousand grooms." For Persian text, see Khawājah Shams al-Dīn Ḥāfiẓ, *Diwān-i 'Aksī-i Ḥāfiẓ* (published by Muḥammad 'Alī 'Ilmī, n.d.), p. 27.

156. *Mau'iẓah*, fols. 58b, 59a. It is not only the world that the author likened to the infidelity of women. He suggested that the royal service involved peril just as the company of women involved disaster (fol. 36a). In another context, he compared the untrustworthy behavior of rulers to the infidelity of women (fol. 45b). On fol. 59b, he cautioned the reader not to "trust life, which declines quickly like a summer cloud, like the fragrance of a garden, and like the fidelity of women."
157. Ibid., fols. 59a, b.
158. Ibid., fol. 60a. In the Qur'ān, there are several verses on the subject: "(To what provision) he has sent forth for the morrow." 59:18; "(Deeds) which your (own) hands sent forth." 8:51; also see 22:10; and 28:47.
159. *Mau'iẓah*, fol. 60b.
160. Ibid.
161. Ibid., fols. 61a-b. In his categorization of individuals, Bāqir was referring to Qur'ānic verses: Qur'ān, 25:44, 7:179.
162. *Mau'iẓah*, fol. 62a.
163. Ibid., fol. 9b.
165. *Akhlāq-i Muḥsinī*, p. 23.
166. *Mau'iẓah*, fol. 11b; *Akhlāq-i Muḥsinī*, p. 45.
167. *Mau'iẓah*, fol. 16b; *Akhlāq-i Muḥsinī*, p. 68.
168. *Mau'iẓah*, fol. 13a; *Akhlāq-i Muḥsinī*, p. 75.
169. *Mau'iẓah*, fol. 11a; *Akhlāq-i Muḥsinī*, p. 83.
169. *Mau'iẓah*, fol. 11a; *Akhlāq-i Muḥsanī*, p. 83.
170. *Mau'iẓah*, fol. 28b; *Siyāsat Nāmah*, p. 201.
171. *Mau'iẓah*, fols. 41b-49b; Naṣīr al-Dīn Tūsī, *Akhlāq-i Muḥtashamī*, edited by Muḥammad Taqī Dānīsh-Pazhūh (Tehran: Dānish-gāh-i Tehran, 1339 H.S.), pp. 364-80.
172. *Mau'iẓah*, fol. 50a.
173. Muṣliḥ al-Dīn Sa'dī, *Gulistān*, edited by Sa'īd Nafīsī (Tehran: Kitāb-farūshī-i Farūghī, 1342 H.S.), pp. 207-17.
174. See above, note 5.
175. Lambton, "Islamic Mirrors," p. 420.
176. Alvi, "Religion and State," p. 1, note 2.
177. Aḥmad bin Muḥammad bin Miskawayh, *Jāvīdān Khirad*, translated by Taqī al-Dīn Muḥammad Shūshtarī, edited by Behrūz Thirvatian (Tehran: McGill University, Institute of Islamic Studies, Tehran Branch, 1976), pp. 2-4. For further discussion

on the work, see the English translation of W. B. Henning's article: M. S. Khan, "The Jāwidān Khirad of Miskawaih," *Islamic Culture* 35(1961): 238-43.

178. *Risālah*, p. 36.
179. *Fatāwā*, pp. 141-42.
180. *Mau'iẓah*, fols. 33b-34a.
181. For further discussion on Nūr-Allāh's execution, see my article, "Shi'ism in India."
182. 'Abd al-Ḥaqq found an escape by leaving for Hijaz (*Risālah*, pp. 25-6). 'Abd al-Qādir Badāyūnī, in his well-known work *Muntakhab al-Tawārīkh*, edited by Ahmad 'Ali (Calcutta: Asiatic Society of Bengal, 1869), vol. 3, p. 113, gave the same reason for his journey to Hijaz.
183. Bāqir took refuge in reading didactic literature. He used quite strong language in condemning his peers: "Whenever he [Bāqir] had some leisure and managed, like a dazzling flash of lightning, to escape the straits of the company of casual friends—socializing with most of them is more venomous than with a serpent and more arduous than laying down one's life—since he considered [reading didactic literature] a felicitous activity, he became engaged in self-purification." *Mau'iẓah*, fols. 3b-4a.
184. Janet Wolff, *The Social Production of Art* (New York: St. Martin's Press, 1980), pp. 26-66.
185. Muḥammad Sadīd al-Dīn al-'Awfī's *Jawām' al-Ḥikāyāt wa Lawām' al-Riwāyāt*, written in India during Iltutumish's period (1211-36), is not included in the works of the Sultanate period. Although it has many elements of Mirrors, it is not considered to be one. It is mentioned here because it is a great reservoir of stories and is used as a source by Baranī, Munshī, Khāqānī, and 'Abd al-Ḥaqq. The period in which 'Awfī lived is significant for two reasons: the Mongol invasion and its rich literary productions (both in Arabic and Persian prose). 'Awfī, an accomplished scholar and a native of Bukhara, wandered from court to court in Samarqand, Khawarzm, Jurjan, and Sijistan in search of patronage, and he witnessed the havoc wrought by the Mongol onslaught in Khurasan and other regions. He arrived in India around 1218-1219. As a literary figure, 'Awfī became the inheritor and transmitter of the

tradition which was to become lost to posterity as a result of the Mongol invasion. See Muhammad Nizā-mu'd-Din, *Introduction to the Jawāmi' u'l-Ḥikāyāt wa Lawāmi' u'r-Riwāyāt of Sadīdu'd-dīn Muḥammad al-'Awfī* (London: Luzac & Co., 1929), p. 23. Here, we are not concerned about the historical authenticity and accuracy of these stories (2,113 of them in 'Awfī's work), which represent a treasure encompassing every conceivable dimension of Islamic civilization.

186. *Akhlāq-i Ḥakīmī*, fol. 75b.
187. Ibid., fols. 79b-81a.
188. *Akhlāq-i Jahāngīrī*, fols. 387b-388a.
189. Ibid., fols. 385b-386a.
190. Ibid., fols. 139a, 160b.
191. *Risālah*, p. 48.
192. For more details, see Jagdish Narayan Sarkar, *History of History Writing in Medieval India: Contemporary Historians* (Calcutta: Ratna Prakashan, 1977), pp. 139-40; Harbans Mukhia, *Historians and Historiography During the Reign of Akbar* (New Delhi: Vikas Publishing House, 1976), pp. 86-7; Norman Ahmad Siddiqi, "Shaikh Abul Fazl," in *Historians of Medieval India*, edited by Mohibbul Hasan, (Meerut: Meenakshi Prakashan, 1968), p. 124; and Peter Hardy, "Abū'l Fażl's Portrait of the Perfect Padshah: A Political Philosophy for Mughal India—or a Personal Puff for a Pal?" in *Islam in India, Studies and Commentaries—* vol. 2, *Religion and Religious Education*, edited by Christian W. Troll (New Delhi: Vikas Publishing House, P V T Ltd., 1985), pp. 114-37.
193. Ibrāhīm Khān, in his *Tadhkirah Ṣuḥūf-i Ibrāhīmī*, recorded that *nān-i Bāqir Khānī* was Bāqir's invention (*mukhtra'āt*). Quoted by 'Askarī, "Mirzā Muḥammad Bāqir," p. 115.

TRANSLATION NOTES: Pages 37-101

1. A reference to the Qur'ānic verse, "To Him is due the primal origin of the heavens and the earth: When he decreeth a matter, He saith to it: 'Be' (*kun*), and it is (*fayakūn*)" (2:117). All translations of the Qur'ānic verses in the text are taken from 'Abdullah Yūsuf 'Alī, *The Holy Qur'ān, Text, Translation and Commentary* (Washington, DC: The American International Printing Company, 1946).
2. In the entire text of the *Mau'iẓah,* this is the only explicit reference to Bāqir's Shī'ī religious persuasions.
3. A reference to the transmission of knowledge to man: "And He taught Adam the nature of all things" (Qur'ān 2:31).
4. Perhaps the writer had this Qur'ānic verse in mind: "They have hearts wherewith they understand not, eyes wherewith they see not, and ears wherewith they hear not. They are like cattle —nay more misguided" (7:179).
5. Lit. (i.e., literal translation)—the bride of this wish did not manifest herself from behind the veil of purpose.
6. Lit.—to gain access to the pavilion of dignity.
7. Lit.—sons of Adam.
8. Part of this passage is translated by Peter Hardy in *Sources of Indian Tradition,* vol. 1, p. 462. Compare my translation with the following by Hardy: ". . . then there is no escaping, indeed it is necessary and unavoidable, that there shall exist that chosen being of creation whom we call a king. He, the king, being created with the morals of a doctor of holy law. . . ." In my view, Hardy has misunderstood the grammatical structure of the sentences—to the detriment of the acuracy of his translation.
9. In the text, the words for dominion and state are *mulk wa dawlat.* Bāqir has used *dawlat* in its concrete and modern sense of the

state and sovereignty rather than in its abstract meaning of "bliss" or "felicity." This is in line with usage of the term by the Mughal and Ṣafavid historians. For example: Abū'l Fażl, *Akbar Nāmah* (Lucknow, 1881), vol. 2, pp. 13, 17, 29. For a discussion of the use of this term in the Ṣafavid sources, see Roger Savory, "The Safavid State and Polity," *Iranian Studies* 7(1974), pp. 179-81; and *Cambridge History of Iran*, edited by Peter Jackson and Laurence Lockhart (Cambridge, England: Cambridge University Press, 1986), vol. 6, pp. 351-52.

10. Niẓām al-Mulk, in *Siyāsat Nāmah*, pp. 74-5, suggested to the Saljūq sultan a more structured plan which included holding weekly meetings with the *'ulamā'* to learn about Islam and which emphasized the virtues of learning. However, Bāqir's more sophisticated patron, Jahāngīr, did not need to have such contact with the *'ulamā'*; rather, he was urged to engage in independent exploration of the finer and more subtle aspects of religion. Even Khāqānī, not withstanding his position as a *qāḍī*, suggested only minimal role for the religious elite in so far as "Jahāngīr, because of his thorough training and education, was himself able to resolve the knottiest issues and problems of the state." Khāqānī, however, urged the *'ulamā'* to satisfy the religious inquisitiveness of the emperor (*Akhlāq-i Jahāngīrī*, fol. 65b). In recent times, religion and politics in Islam and the role of the *'ulamā'* in the political sphere have received increasing attention from scholars. For example, see Ishtiaq Husain Qureshi, *Ulema in Politics: A Study Relating to the Political Activities of the Ulema in the South Asian Subcontinent from 1556-1947* (Karachi: Ma'ref, 1972); Aziz Ahmad, "The Role of 'Ulemā' in Indo-Muslim History," *Studia Islamica* 31 (1970): 2-13; and W. C. Smith, "The 'Ulamā' in Indian Politics," in *Politics and Society in India*, edited by C. H. Philips (London: Allen and Unwin, 1963), pp. 39-51. (Scores of recent works on the Revolution in Iran and the Shī'ī *'ulamā'* are not cited here). I am inclined to agree with the viewpoint (Aziz Ahmad, p. 7) that the influence of the *'ulamā'* in political affairs, curtailed by Akbar, was never subsequently restored. For a detailed discussion of the role of the religious elite in state policies during Jahāngīr's period, see my forthcoming article, "Religion and State". This paper gives evidence that Bāqir's

suggestion—that the *'ulamā'* be granted powers to shape the state policies—was apparently not heeded.

11. The term *millat* is used here in the sense of religious community, its usual meaning in medieval writings such as those of Ibn Khaldūn (Rosenthal, *Political Thought*, p. 95).
12. If we read the phrase as *"sitārah-i sipāh"*, it means "the luminary of the army".
13. With the advent of the Mughal period, historians and political theorists no longer had any qualms about the legitimacy of the institution of monarchy. As discussed in the Introduction, in his hyperbolic description of Jahāngīr's grandeur, Bāqir compared him to Farīdūn and Jamshīd, the legendary heroes of pre-Islamic Iran, while simultaneously calling him the supporter of the Caliphate. By Bāqir's time, such terms as *khalīfah, imām, amīr al-mu'minīn, pādshāh,* and sultan were used interchangeably, stripped of all historical and religious connotations. For details, see Introduction, note 82.
14. Lit.—fingers . . .
15. Territorial expansion and display of might and power were basic elements in the political thought and ethics of the premodern period. Each Mughal emperor, from Bābur to Awrangzēb, tried to extend the boundaries of his dominion. Awrangzēb, for example, in a letter to his grandson Muḥammad Bedārbakht, wrote that his empire was a gift from Timūr and Akbar and efforts to stablize and extend it would make the names of subsequent rulers immortal in the pages of history. To realize that goal, "Winning the hearts of soldiers is the greatest part of success." *Ruka'āt-i 'Ālamgīrī, or Letters of Aurangzēb*, translated by Jamshid H. Bilimoria (Delhi: Idarah-i Adabiyat-Delli, 1972 reprint), pp. 81-82.
16. Lit.—shady garden of delight with a shadow of eternity. . . .
17. Lit.—this emperor with the grandeur of Jamshīd . . .
18. In the text, the term *siyāsah* is interchangeably translated as "discipline" or "control"—discipline and control in the management of state affairs or execution of state policies.
19. Lit.—all directions and corners of the country . . .
20. Lit.—servants of God . . .
21. In the text, the term *ḥilm* is interchangeably translated as "forbearance" or "magnanimity." For discussion of this virtue,

see Encyclopaedia of Islam[2], edited by B. Lewis, *et al* (Leiden: E. J. Brill, 1971), vol. 3, s.v. "ḥilm." All writers discussed in the Introduction devoted separate chapters to generosity, bravery, and magnanimity. To illustrate these topics, their writings, with the exception of the *Mau'iẓah,* contain stories from pre-Islamic and Islamic history and quotations from religious literature. For details, see *Akhlāq-i Jahāngīrī,* fols. 214b-264a, 302a-316a, and 372b-394b; *Akhlāq-i Ḥakīmī,* fols. 61b-82a, 50b-61b, and 106b-111a; and *Risālah-i Nūriyyah-i Sulṭāniyyah,* pp. 42-45 and 53-74.

22. Qur'ān, 6:160.
23. For the description of Kauṣar, refer to Qur'ān, 108:1-3.
24. Bāqir did not abide by the tradition of other writers in devoting a chapter to *futuwwa* (chivalry, highmindedness). Even this reference in the text is quite general. Another reference is on fol. 55b, where he enumerates the benefits of travel and emigration. In other Mirrors, the theme is discussed under various terms. For example, Kaykā'ūs devotes a full chapter in *Qābūs Nāmah* (Persian text, pp. 219-222) and clearly defines his understanding of *jawānmardī.* Al-Ghazālī uses the term *bulandhimmatī* in his chapter to discuss the topic (*Naṣīḥat al-Mulūk,* Persian text, pp. 197-219). Baranī devotes twenty-five pages to the virtues of *'uluw-i himmat* in successful rulership (*Fatāwā,* pp. 232-257). Bāqir's contemporaries, Munshī and Khāqānī, also consider the topic important enough to write a chapter on it (*Akhlāq-i Ḥakīmī,* fols. 17b-22a; *Akhlāq-i Jahāngīrī,* fols. 177a-188a). For further discussion in a broader context, and bibliographical references, see *Encyclopaedia of Islam,*[2] edited by B. Lewis, *et al* (Leiden: E. J. Brill, 1965), vol. 2, s.v. "Futuwwa."
25. Żaymorān or sipargham: Sweet basil, which adds to the fragrance of a garden and rejuvenates the human mind (*Ghiyāṣ al-Lughāt*).
26. Lit.—Thousand . . .
27. Lit.—for two to three days . . .
28. Qur'ān, 17:7.
29. Lit.—do not expect to reap wheat at harvest time.
30. All writers regard consultation to be an important element of statecraft. For details, see Baranī, pp. 26-49, Khāqānī, fols. 323b-333a, and Munshī, fols. 117a-122a. These writers discuss

the topic by quoting from biblical stories and pre-Islamic Arabian and classical Islamic history, and by making isolated references to Indian heritage.

31. Qur'ān, 3:159.
32. Violence and rebellion against the state or between individuals and groups is discussed in almost all significant primary sources of medieval Indian history. For further discussion, see Peter Hardy, "Force and Violence in Indo-Persian Writing on History and Government in Medieval South Asia," in *Islamic Society and Culture: Essays in Honour of Professor Aziz Ahmad*, edited by Milton Israel and N. K. Wagle (New Delhi: Manohar Publications, 1983), pp. 165-208. Satya Prakash Sangar's work, *Crime and Punishment in Mughal India* (Delhi: Sterling Publishers, 1967), is useful for an introductory study of law and its application during the Mughal period. The last chapter, "Offences Against the Safety of the State," pp. 189-227, is especially relevant to our study. See also Muḥammad Basheer Aḥmad, *Judicial System of the Mughul Empire* (Karachi: Pakistan Historical Society, 1978); and Ibn Hasan, *Central Structure*, pp. 304-44.
33. Lit.—the water of strategy . . .
34. Qur'ān, 2:249.
35. In the central administration of the Mughals, there was no cabinet or well-defined advisory council. The *wazīrs/diwāns* (heads of various administrative departments) and *wazīr-i a'lā'* (see below, note 46) were consulted by the emperor on various administrative issues. Depending on the nature of issues, private meetings were held between the emperor and *diwāns* and high-ranking nobility. A private chamber designated for such meetings was called *diwān-i khāṣṣ* or *ghuslkhānah;* for details, see Qureshi, *Administration of the Mughul Empire*, pp. 49-50 and 70-72. Confidential meetings of the emperor, princes, and highest officials of the empire took place in a more exclusive place named *shāhburj;* for details, see Ibid., p. 50.
36. Lit.—the head of whose empire . . .
37. Lit.—the finger of whose glory . . .
38. Lit.—when anyone dances with happiness, the envious one slaps his head with hands of anguish.
39. Lit.—reality . . .
40. Lit.—into the niche of extinction.

41. Lit.—experts of the knowledge of truth . . .
42. Bāqir prescribed the death penalty for unfaithful nobles. In view of their close relationship with the emperor, the nobles were expected to offer up their lives for the name and honor of their master. The emperor, in turn, showered them with favors and took a keen interest in their welfare. A noble betraying his master was thus a grave offence. For an insightful discussion on this subject, see Richards, "Norms of Comportment among Imperial Mughal Officers," *Moral Conduct and Authority*, pp. 255-89.
43. For discussion on the Mughal nobility, see below, notes 52, 63, and the Introduction, notes 50-51.
44. See note 50.
45. "Pen and sword are supreme in everything," according to al-Ghazālī. "If there were no swords and pens, this world would fail to operate" (*Naṣīḥat al-Mulūk*, p. 189). Al-Ghazālī devoted a whole chapter to this topic. Almost all Mirror writers have written on it. Among the works which do not strictly fall in this category, Niẓāmī 'Arūżī Samarqandī's *Chahār Maqālah* (edited by Muḥammad Qazvīnī and Muḥammad Mu'īn [Tehran: Zawwar Bookshop, 1955-57], pp. 19-41), also include a discussion on the qualities desired in a *dabīr* (secretary, 'person of the pen') and his salient position in the state administration. That Bāqir and his contemporaries did not devote much space to the topic could be attributed to the fact that during the Mughal period, the distinction between 'people of the pen' and 'people of the sword' or high-ranking civil and military officials was not so clear-cut. We have the examples of 'Abd al-Raḥīm Khān-i Khānān, Abū'l Fażl, and Bāqir Najm-i Ṣānī, who were 'people of the pen' as well 'of the sword.' (A historical perspective on the conflict and dichotomy between these groups still awaits a study). It should be noted here that epistolary (*inshā'*) was a fully developed discipline by the time of the Mughal period. The employees of department of correspondence (*dār al-inshā'*), however, should not be confused with the scribes or administrative clerks (*kātibs*), who developed into a powerful administrative and cultural elite during the classical Islamic period. For more details, see *Encyclopaedia of Islam*[2] edited by E. van Donzel, *et al* (Leiden: E. J. Brill, 1978),

vol. 4, s.v.*"Kātib."* Also, for details on *inshā'* in the Indian environment, see Riazul Islam, *A Calendar of Documents on Indo-Persian Relations (1500-1750)* (Karachi: Iranian Culture Foundation, Tehran, and Institute of Central and West Asian Studies, 1979), vol. 1, pp. 1-39; and *Urdu Dā'irah-yi Mā'arif-i Islāmiyyah* (Lahore: Dānishgāh-i Punjab, 1968), vol. 3, s.v. "inshā'."

46. In the Mughal administration, *wazīr* was the head of civil government, and, in particular, was responsible for fiscal matters. The terms *dīwān, dīwān-i a'lā,'* and *dīwān-i kul* are used as synonyms for *wazīr* in the historical chronicles. For further details of the jurisdictions and actions of important *wazīrs* in the Mughal administration, see Qureshi, *Administration of the Mughul Empire,* pp. 72-75. For a brief discussion on the role of *dīwān/wazīr* in provincial appointments, see the important work of John F. Richards, *Document Forms for Official Orders of Appointment in the Mughal Empire. Translation, Notes and Text* (Norfolk, England: Gibb Memorial Series, 1986), pp. 13-14.

47. The term used in the administrative manuals and historical chronicles for such official is *muḥtasib.* Some scholars argue that Akbar discontinued this office and combined it with *kōtwāl* (head of the police). For details, see Qureshi, *Administration of the Mughul Empire,* pp. 203-204. We have definite information that Awrangzēb, after his accession to the throne in 1658, appointed Mulla 'Iważ Wajīh, a learned person and an emigre from Turan, to this office (Bakhtawar Khan, *Mir'āt al-'Ālam: The History of Awrangzēb,* edited by Sajida S. Alvi [Lahore: Research Society of Pakistan, University of the Punjab, 1979], vol. 1, p. 156). Also, see Ibid., p. 301, for details of Wajīh's replacement by Khawājah Qādir in the sixth year of Awrangzēb's reign. For a broader Islamic context, see *Encyclopaedia of Islam*[2], edited by B. Lewis, *et al* (Leiden: E. J. Brill, 1971), vol. 3, s.v. *"ḥisba."*

48. Bāqir employed the term *ṣāḥib-i khabrān* (as used by Niẓām al-Mulk), but he likewise gave no details. Niẓām al-Mulk covered the subject in two sections, and made a distinction between spies (*jāsūsān*) and reporters (*Siyāsat Nāmah,* edited by Muḥammad ibn 'Abd al-Wahhāb Qazwīnī [Tehran: Tahuri Bookseller, 1334H.S.], pp. 66-76 and 79-94). From historical and other sources, we know that the Mughals had a two-group reporting

system. One group was known as *waqā'i nawīs/swāniḥ nawīs* (recorders of events and incidents) and the other as *khufiah nawīs* (secret reporters). Bāqir and his contemporary writers did not discuss in detail the significance of an efficient intelligence system, leading to the speculation that the system was so well-established that they did not need to devote a separate chapter to it.

49. As discussed in the Introduction, Niẓām al-Mulk expressed similar views. The usual practice in the Mughal administration was to give one portfolio to one noble. There were, however, some exceptions. Jahāngīr, for example, after his accession to the throne, gave two portfolios of *wakīl* and *wazīr* to Sharīf Khān (*Tūzuk*, Urdu translation, vol. 1, p. 66; Qureshi, *Administration of the Mughul Empire*, p. 72, note 6). *Wakīl* or *wakīl-i mamlikat* was the highest minister at the imperial court and chief advisor to the emperor. This office should not be confused with *wakīl-i nafs-i nafīs-i humāyūn*, created by the Ṣafavid ruler Shāh Ismā'īl I (d. 1524). This official was the emperor's vicegerent and his representative in spiritual and temporal matters. For details, see *Cambridge History of Iran*, vol. 6, pp. 357-58.

50. *Amīn* and *'āmil* were the officials concerned with revenue matters. For the duties of *'āmil* and *amīn*, see Qureshi, *Administration of the Mughul Empire*, pp. 232-33. For confusion in the use of the term *amīn*, see ibid., p. 236. In the Mughal provincial administration, sometimes the duties of *amīn* and *faujdār* were also combined. For details, see Richards, *Document Forms*, pp. 35-38.

51. Lit.—would step in the valley of boldness . . .

52. The Mughal nobility was composed of many ethnically, culturally, and linguistically divergent groups—the Iranis, Turanis, Afghans, Rajputs, Marathas, and other Hindus. Competition and rivalry between these groups, particularly the high-ranking *manṣabdārs*, was intense. During Jahāngīr's reign, the number of Iranians holding high ranks in the empire more than doubled. For statistical charts, see Athar Ali, *The Apparatus*, Introduction, pp. xx-xxi. For the racial composition of nobility during Awrangzēb's reign, see (by the same author) *The Mughal Nobility under Aurangzeb* (London: Asia Publishing House, 1966), pp. 11-37; and for the later period, Satish Chandra, *The Parties and*

Politics at the Mughal Court (1707-1740) Aligarh: Aligarh Muslim University, 1959.

53. See the Introduction, note 122.
54. Lit.—should assay the coins of his affairs on the touchstone of trial and examination . . .
55. A legendary bird of good omen, foretelling of a crown upon the head that it overshadows.
56. Lit.—should not keep their subjects remote from their . . .
57. Lit.—the beauty of certainty does not emerge from behind the veil of suspicion . . .
58. Lit.—have covered up their temerity and rudeness with the skirt of oversight.
59. Lit.—found the reins of loosening and tying of the people under the control of his power . . .
60. Lit.—the bird of sedition lays eggs in the nest of his mind.
61. Lit.—would bite the finger of repentance in the teeth of bewilderment . . .
62. For a general discussion on *iqṭā'*, see *Encyclopaedia of Islam*[2], edited by B. Lewis, *et al* (Leiden: E. J. Brill, 1971), vol. 3, s.v. *ikṭā'*. For the replacement of the term *Iqṭā'* by *jāgīr* in India and various types of *jāgīrs* as revenue assignments, see Irfan Habib, *The Agrarian System of Mughal India* (Bombay: Asia Publishing House, 1963), pp. 257-73; and Qureshi, *Administration of the Mughul Empire*, pp. 107-8, 155-56.
63. Here Bāqir is referring to two groups of armed forces, one (called *aḥdīs*) maintained by the emperor and the other (called *tābīnān*) recruited and equipped by the *manṣabdārs*, and mobilized when the emperor needed it for his campaigns. The mode of payment to the *manṣabdār* was cash and *jāgīr* (see the preceding note). From Akbar's reign to Awrangzēb's, there was an evolution in the basic system. For details of the pay scale, recruitment, promotion, and inspection, see Abdul Aziz, *The Mansabdari System and the Mughul Army* (Delhi: Idarah-i Adabiyat-i Delli, 1972 reprint), pp. 1-12, 31-124; and Athar Ali, *The Mughal Nobility*, pp. 38-73. Another useful study in which the Mughal administration is discussed in a theoretical framework is Stephen P. Blake's "The Patrimonial-Bureaucratic Empire of the Mughals," *The Journal of Asian Studies* 39(1979): 77-94. Referring to Abū'l Fażl's *Ā'īn- Akbarī*, Book Two in this paper, Blake rightly

argues that "... the Mughal army is the adjunct of a household-dominated patrimonial-bureaucratic empire rather than the fighting arm of a highly structured, bureaucratically administered state" (p. 86).

64. This statement could be interpreted as a reference to deterioration in the inspection of armor and in the general readiness of armed forces for combat. Reorganization of the entire system by Shāhjahān raises some doubts about the efficiency of the system under Jahāngīr. The European travellers to Jahāngīr's India, such as Pelsaert, also commented on decline in law and order and nobility's somewhat casual attitude towards maintaining efficient troops. See Francisco Pelsaert, *Jahangir's India*, English translation by W. H. Moreland and P. Geyl (Delhi: Idarah-i Adabiyat-i Delli, 1972 reprint), pp. 58-9.
65. Lit.—they may bite the finger of remorse with the teeth of penitence . . .
66. Lit.—does not bring out the head of haughtiness from the collar of rebellion
67. Lit.—wisdom is in complete agreement with it that . . .
68. This passage in the *Mau'iẓah* is rather puzzling. Characteristics such as a keen sense of justice, the sophistication of Mughal emperors, and the loyalty of individuals (especially the high-ranking nobles) to the person of the emperor prevented the emperors from becoming whimsical, arbitrary, and unpredictable. Their actions, administrative and otherwise, were usually rational and well considered. If we compare, for example, emperor Jahāngīr with Sulṭān Muḥammad bin Tughluq of the Sultanate period, there is a marked difference in their political philosophy and code of conduct, especially in their dealings with the nobles, rebels, and enemies.
69. Bāqir, himself an influential *manṣabdār* and a patron of the arts, stresses the virtues of patronage. Mughal India—"a culture state," as correctly described by Qureshi (*Administration of the Mughul Empire*, p. 216)—attracted poets, writers, artists, physicians, and philosophers from other Islamic lands, particularly from Iran. Biographical dictionaries are full of the names of people patronized by Mughal emperors. Equally instrumental in enhancing the Mughal culture were the high-ranking *manṣabdārs*—through their literary, artistic, and architectural

patronage. 'Abd al-Raḥīm Khān-i Khānān, Abū'l Fatḥ Gilānī, Abū'l Fażl, and Faiżī are just a few of the high-ranking *manṣabdārs* of Akbar's period who themselves were accomplished writers and poets as well as generous patrons of poets, writers, and artists. Naẓīrī, 'Urfī, Shakaybī, Ẓahūrī, Malik Qumī, and Naw'ī Shīrāzī are some of the Persian poets affiliated with Khān-i Khānān's court. As discussed in the Introduction (note 78), Bāqir, along with other nobles of Jahāngīr's era, maintained this tradition. The example of Bakhtāwar Khān, a relatively low-ranking official in Awrangzēb's administration, may also be cited. He took an active interest in supporting the construction of numerous public works, patronized poets and litterateurs, and introduced many individuals of great promise to the imperial court. For details, see *Mir'āt al-'Ālam*, Introduction, pp. 18-19, notes 36-45.

70. The writer is probably referring to the Qur'ānic discussion that thinking people are the cream of creation. For details, see Fazlur Rahman, *Major Themes of the Qur'ān* (Minneapolis, MN: Bibliotheca Islamica, 1980), pp. 18-19.
71. Lit.—without seeing the glimpse of their grace, the candle of company does not give any light.
72. Lit.—in two three days when the writing of existence is inscribed on the folio of his body . . .
73. Lit.—run miles away from the company of . . .
74. In the text, there is a sentence that reads: "Just as association with moralistic individuals has all-encompassing benefits, [the] company of immoral persons results in unworthy consequences." It is the repetition of the previous idea; therefore it is not made part of the translated text.
75. Lit.—for ten times.
76. Lit.—herbs of the virtues of civilities.
77. Lit.—the scars of insolence . . . not discernible except in . . .
78. Lit.—inscriptions of degradation are not inscribed except on . . .
79. Lit.—the bird of no one's heart turns away from the love of . . .
80. Lit.—they spread the carpet of happiness . . .
81. Lit.—throw both of them from the shore of existence into the whirlpool of annihilation.
82. This phrase is repeated in the Qur'ān three times: first, one is asked to travel in order to observe the end of the evildoers

(27:69); second, one is encouraged to travel in order to see the wonders of the world and the rise and fall of civilizations (29:20); and third, one is encouraged to travel in order to see the end of the corrupted and irreligious societies (30:42). For complete text and commentary, see 'Alī, *The Holy Qur'ān*, pp. 995, 1033, and 1063, respectively.

83. Lit.—They bubble around you . . .
84. Lit.—if he embraced the beloved of his goal, that was his desire.
85. See above, note 24.
86. The Persian text of the next three pages is missing in the *Mau'iẓah* and is taken from the *Kulliyāt*.
87. Lit.—the bureau of sustenance . . .
88. This is certainly not one of the more imaginative verses in this work. Because of its odd construction and meaning, it is difficult to translate.
89. Lit.—they should make the lips of happiness laugh . . .
90. Lit.—opens the door of happiness to his heart . . .
91. Lit.—putting the head of leisure on the knee of seclusion . . .
92. Lit.—tears of blood are to be swallowed . . .
93. Qur'ān, 28:88. For commentary, see 'Alī, *The Holy Qur'ān*, p. 1027.
94. Father of Rustam, a mythical character in the epic poem, *Shāh Nāmah*, of the famous Persian poet Firdawsī (d. 1020).
95. One of Rustam's titles. For the etymological description of Tuhmatan, see *Lughat Nāmah-i Dihkhudā* s.v. "Tuhmatan."
96. Nephew of Rustam. For a brief narration of his activities, see ibid., s.v. "Bīzhan." It may be noted here that poet Firdawsī, his life, and especially his monumental epic poem, the *Shāh Nāmah*, attracted enormous scholarly attention over the years. Detailed works have been written on the characters of the *Shāh Nāmah*, including those noted above. To cite some: M. Awrang, *Zāl-o-Rūdābah* (Tehran: Chāp-i Rangin, 1966); Ibrāhīm Pūr-i Dā'ūd, *Bīzhan-o-Manīzhah, Dāstānī az Rūzgārān-i Pahlavan-i Iran* (Tehran: Shirkat-hā-yi 'Āmil-i Naft-i Irān, 1965); and Eḥsān Yār-e-Shāṭer, *Dāstān-hā-yi Shāh Nāmah* (Tehran: Bungah-i Tarjumah wa Nashr-i Kitāb, 1959). For more references, see *Encyclopaedia of Islam*[2], edited by B. Lewis, *et al* (Leiden: E. J. Brill, 1965), vol. 2, s.v. "Firdawsī."
97. Lit.—with the feet/steps of austerity . . .

98. Lit.—the ready money of life . . .
99. Qur'ān, 17:70.
100. Ibid., 7:179; 25:44.

تالیف

محمد باقر نجم ثانی

با تصحیح متن، ترجمه وحواشی و مقدمه

بکوشش

ساجده س. علوی

انتشارات دانشگاهِ ایالتِ نیویورک

فهرست مندرجات و موضوعات

موعظهٔ جهانگیری

موعظهٔ جهانگیری

[دیباچه]

[fol. 2a] سپاس و ستایش مر حکیمی را که بحکمتِ بالغه و صنعتِ کامله از عینِ حکمت بی دستیاری شریک و سهیم ، و بی آنکه بآلات[1] و ادوات محتاج شود ، و بمظاهرت و معاونت مفتقر[2] گردد ، بمجرد ابداعِ دو حرف کاف و نون این عالمِ گوناگون را از نهانخانهٔ عدم بعالمِ ظهور در آورد - و بقلمِ قدرت رقمِ خلقت را بر صفایح[3] بروز نگاشته ، کارخانهٔ آفرینش را بقالبِ وجودِ انسان تکمیل داد - و مرکزِ دایرهٔ هستی را بتمکن و استقرارِ بشر که مصدرِ خیر و شراست زیب و زینت بخشید -

[fol. 2b] و گم گشتگانِ بادیهٔ ضلالت و هاویهٔ غوایت[4] را برهنمونی هادی شریعت و راهنمای طریقت ، اعنی سیدِ انبیاء و سندِ رسل ، نوباوهٔ چمنِ کاینات ، فهرستِ مجموعهٔ مکونات ، محرمِ خلوتخانهٔ قرب و کرامت ، خورشیدِ آسمانِ نبوت و امامت ،

بیت

احمد مرسل که خرد خاکِ اوست
هر دو جهان بستهٔ فتراک[5] اوست

صلی الله علیه و آله وصیه و عترته[6] بسرِ منزلِ دانش و بینش رسانید[7]

اما بعد بر ضمایرِ اربابِ بصایر که مقتبس[8] از انوارِ فراست و منجلی از اشعهٔ حکمت و درایت[9] است ، مخفی و محجوب نخواهد بود که درین عالمِ ناسوت که مرآتِ عالمِ لاهوتست ، هیچ گوهری زیبا تر از سخنِ نیکو نیست - و بکیمیای سخن مسِ قلب را زرِ تمام عیار توان ساخت - بتخصیص سخنی که مبنی باشد بر مسایلِ حکمت و مشتمل بر میامنِ [fol. 3a] نصیحت -

---

O : The original/basic copy (I.O. Pers Ms. 1666).

K : *Kulliyat* (I.O. Pers. Ms. 1330).

1, *K* : ادواد 2. *O* and *K* : مفتعر 3. *K* : صفحات 4. *Ibid.*, عوانت 5. *O* : مراک 6. *K* : عرته 7. *Ibid* , رساند ; رساند - صلی الله is cited in verse form. 8. *Ibid.*, معتبس 9. *Ibid.*, درآیت

شعر[1]

جنبش ِ اول که قلم بر گرفت — حرف ِ نخستین ز سخن در گرفت
چون[2] قلم آمد شدن آغاز کرد — چشم ِ جهانرا بسخن باز کرد
پردهٔ[3] اول که بر انداختند — جلوهٔ اول بسخن ساختند
گرچه سخن خود ننماید جمال — پیش ِ پرستنده مشتی خیال[4]
ما که نظر بر سخن افگنده ایم — مردهٔ اوئیم و بدو زنده ایم
تا سخنست از سخن آوازه باد — جان و دل ِ من بسخن تازه باد

پس خرد مند ِ فرزانه آنست که زبدهٔ اعمار و خلاصهٔ اوقات را صرف ِ[5] مطالعهٔ سخنان ِ بی نظیر و کلمات ِ دلپذیر نموده این معنی را سرمایهٔ هر موعظت[6] و وسیلهٔ هر منفعت میدانسته باشد - اگرچه همچو آفتاب روشنست که این دلهای تیره بمشعلهٔ موعظت روشن نخواهند شد و ظلام ِ جهل و ضلالتی که در ذات ِ آدمی [fol.3b] سرشته شده[7] به پرتو ِ نصایح منتفی[8] نخواهد گشت - ونصیحت باطباع ِ خود پسند همان مثلست که آواز ِ نرم در گوش ِ کرّ ِ مادر زاد ، و یا ضرب ِ پای مورچه بر روی صخرهٔ صما - اما شاید که باره[9] از ورطهٔ خونخوار ضلالت که منشاء آن اخلاق ِ ناپسندیده است خلاصی روی نماید - چه توسن ِ سرکش را جز بتازیانهٔ حکمت رام نتوان کرد و طباع ِ مغرور را جز بموعظهٔ حسنه باصلاح نتوان آورد -

لا جرم این نامستعد ، هیچ مدان ، محمد باقر نجم ِ ثانی ببدرقهٔ عنایت ِ بیغایت ِ ربّانی همواره مایل ِ استماع ِ داستان ِ نصیحت فرجام و راغب ِ مطالعه کلام ِ حکمت انجام بوده ، هرگاه دست بدامن ِ فرصت میرسانید[10] ، و از مضیق ِ مجالست ِ یاران ِ رسمی که مصاحبت ِ اغلب ِ ایشان از زهر ِ افعی کار گر تر است و از مخاطرهٔ جان دادن دشوار تر، کالبرق الخاطف نجات می [fol. 4a] یافت ، این معنی را فوزی عظیم دانسته بتزکیهٔ[11] خویش مشغول می شد و اوقات ِ عزیز را صرف ِ سخنان ِ بدایع نگار و کلمات ِ

---

1. *Ibid.*, omits شعر 2. *Ibid.*, جون 3. *Ibid.*, برده

4. *Ibid.*,The order of lines in the verse is reversed. 5. *Ibid.*, واقف

6. *Ibid.*, مواعظت 7. *Ibid.*, شد 8. *Ibid.*, مشفی 9. O پاره

10. *K*: میرساند 11. *Ibid.*, بنزکیه

غرایب[1] آثار نموده ، خزانهٔ دل را از جواهرِ سخنانِ موعظت آمیز پُر می ساخت. و از هر جا فقره و عبارتی که غذای[2] دل و راحتِ جان می شد ، بقلمِ خیال بر لوحِ خاطر ثبت نموده میخواست بزبانِ قلم در آورد. لیکن تا غایت بنا بر[3] اشغالی که آدمی را ازان چاره نیست[4] ، عروسِ این مراد از پسِ پردهٔ مقصود جلوه نمیکرد ، و این آرزو از قوّت بفعل نمی آمد[5] ، چه حصولِ این مطلوب[6] بی جمعیتِ خاطر محال بود و طرحِ خلوت انداختن که موجبِ جمعیتِ ظاهر و باطن است میسر نه.

درینولا که از اتفاقاتِ حسنه دو سه روزی عنانِ اختیارِ خود را بقبضهٔ[7] اقتدارِ خویش دید ، بخاطرِ فاتر رسید که آنچه از دررِ [fol. 4b] غرر در صدفِ خاطر جای گرفته ، در سلکِ تحریر انتظام دهد و آن جواهرِ زواهر را بیش ازین در درجِ ضمیر مستور نگذارد. بنا برین [با] قلمِ شکسته رقمِ سخن پردازی[8] آغاز کرده[9] بنانِ بیان[10] روی بصوبِ تحریر در آورد. و آن دررِ[11] غرر را با چندی از خزف ریز های خود بمضمونِ مصراع :

بر دستهٔ گل نیز ببندند[12] گیا را

در یک سلک پیوسته ، جهتِ سر رشته نیک و بد بدست آوردن ، جریدهٔ این صحیفه را بجواهرِ عباراتِ نصیحت آمیز و زواهرِ کلماتِ حکمت انگیز که انواعِ فوایدِ حکمت و میامنِ نصیحت دران[13] مندرجست و چون ترکیبِ زر و گوهر صفتِ ترصیع دارد ، زیور بست[14] و مسمی بموعظهٔ جهانگیری نموده ، بدو باب[15] و ده فصل مرتب ساخت. و این فقیر اگرچه در ارتکابِ این امرِ خطیر خود را هدفِ سهامِ ملامت می بیند ، اما امیدوار است [fol. 5a] که اگر یارانِ ستم ظریف در معذور داشتن توجه مبذول نفرمایند ، جمعی که موصوف بصفتِ انصاف باشند ، بذیلِ عفو و اغماض بپوشند.

---

1. *Ibid.*, عراتب 2. *Ibid.*, غدای 3. *Ibid.*, برابر 4. *Ibid.*, نباشد 5. *Ibid.*, نمی آید 6. *Ibid.*, مطلب 7. *Ibid.*, در قبضه 8. *Ibid.*, سخن پرداز 9. *Ibid.*, نموده 10. *Ibid.*, سان سان 11. *Ibid.*, repeats : و آن درر 12. *Ibid.*, به بندد 13. *Ibid.*, درین 14. *Ibid.*, زیوریست 15. *Ibid.*, نمود و بمقدمه و دو باب مرتب

بیت[1]

چشمِ هنر بین بود از عیب پاک
بی هنر ار عیب کند زو چه باک

بابِ اول[2] : در نصیحتِ پادشاهان ـ و این باب مشتملست بر مقدمه[3] و شش فصل ـ

فصلِ اول : در عدالت و سیاست که آن نیز بر قانونِ عدالت بامد[4] ـ

فصلِ دویم : در سخاوت و شجاعت و حلم که محتاج الیه یکدیگرند ـ

فصلِ سیم : در مشورت و تدبیر ـ

فصلِ چهارم : در احتراز نمودن از دشمنان ـ

فصلِ پنجم : بسخنِ صاحبِ غرض عمل نکردن[5] و ساعی و نمام را در مجلس راه ندادن ـ

فصلِ ششم : در تربیتِ[6] ملازمان ـ و این فصل مبنی است بر دو قسم :
قسمِ اول : در تربیتِ[7] پادشاهان ملازمانرا
قسمِ دوم : در آدابِ خدمتِ پادشاهان ـ

[fol. 5b] **بابِ دویم** : در نصیحتِ زیردستان و اخوانِ زمان ـ و این باب مبنی است بر چهار فصل :

فصلِ اول : در مصاحبت و مخالطتِ یاران ـ

فصلِ دویم : در مذمتِ بیچیزی[8] و سعی نمودن در طلبِ دولت ـ

فصلِ سیم : در رضا بقضای الٰهی دادن و قناعت و عزلت ـ

فصلِ چهارم : در تحصیلِ کمالات و استرضای الٰهی ـ

---

1. Omitted in *O* 2. *K* adds مقدمه در توطه اسم سامی و نام نامی جهانگیری خلد الله ملکه' ابداً 3. *Ibid.*, omits مقدمه و 4. *O* omits بامد
5. *K* reads در عمل نکردن بسخن صاحب غرض 6. *Ibid.*, ترتیب
7. *Ibid.*, ترتیب 8. *Ibid.*, تنگدستی

بابِ اول

در نصیحتِ پاشاهان که مبنی است بر مقدمه و شش فصل[1] ـ

مقدمه[2] : بدانکه چون طبقهٔ انسان بر حسبِ تباینِ قابلیاتِ اصلی و تفاوتِ استعداداتِ جبلی باصنافِ متعدده[3] منقسم است و هر کس را ازین طایفه استحقاقِ آن نه که بتوسطِ اجتهادِ نفسِ خویش مبادی عالیه تشبث نماید و معرفتِ حضرتِ الوهیت[4] حاصل کرده بمقصود واصل شود و بمجرد راهنمایی عقلِ شبه اندوز سلوکِ مسالکِ [fol. 6 a] هدایت نموده گردِ سرادقاتِ عزت گردد و نیز بجهتِ انتظامِ[5] مصالحِ عالم و انتساقِ[6] امورِ بنی آدم قانونی باید که بدان قانون با یکدیگر معاش کرده بر هیچکس حیفی و ستمی نرود ـ لا جرم حضرتِ مهیمن متعال جلت[7] آلاوه و عمت نعماءه از همان جنسِ انسان ، انبیاء و رسل که هر یک درِ دریای صفا و دری برجِ اهتداء اند ، متسم بسمتِ تعلق و تجرد و متصف بصفتِ[8] تقید و تفرد ، برانگیخت تا بمناسبتِ[9] تجرد و تفرد فیض از عالمِ قدس گرفته ، در عالمِ تعلق و تقید سرگشتگانِ فیافی[10] ضلالت و لب تشنگان بوادی غوایت را بسرِ منزلِ هدایت و سر چشمهٔ عنایت دلالت نمایند ـ و قانونی که آنرا شریعت گویند گذارند که هرکس بر جادهٔ احکام آن مستقیم باشد ، از سطوتِ قهر الهی ایمن بوده[11] به نعم و تلذذاتِ جاودانی فایز گردد ـ و هرکس که [fol. 6b] ازان طریقِ قویم انحراف ورزد ، بسخطِ[12] جبارِ منتقم مبتلا گشته بعقوباتِ مولم[13] گرفتار شود ـ پس مدتی دعوتِ[14] ایشان متعاقب و متواصل بود تا[15] نسیمِ مرحمت از مهبِ مکرمت وزیدن گرفت ، و صبحِ سعادت از مطلع سیادت دمیدن آغاز نهاده ـ بدرِ منیر از افقِ عزت طلوع نمود و آفتابِ رسالتِ محمدی از مطلع بطحا طالع شده ، نورِ نبوتِ احمدی از مشرقِ امّ القری شارق[16] گشت ـ

و چون بعد از آنحضرت که ختمِ رسل و خاتمِ پیغمبرانست جهت انتظام و استحکامِ قواعدِ دینِ مبین[17] وتنسیقِ اعمال و ترفیه عباد و حصولِ نعمتِ امن و

---

1. *Ibid.*, omits باب اول—شش فصل
2. *O* omits مقدمه 3. *Ibid.*, متعدد 4. *K* : الوهیت عز اسمه
5. *Ibid.*, انتساق 6. *Ibid.*, انتظام 7. *Ibid.*, حلب 8. *Ibid.*, بصفیت
9. *Ibid.*, omits به 10. *O*: معامی 11. *K* : بود 12. *Ibid.*, بسخط
13. *Ibid.*, مولمه 14. *Ibid.*, مدت دعوتی 15. *O* : ما 16. *K*: سارق
17. *Ibid.*, omits مبین

امان از وجودِ مدبری ذوی الاقتدار و فرماندهی رفیع المقدار که ذاتِ پسندیده[1] سماتش[2] بحلیهٔ نصفت و معدلت آراسته بود و از افراط و تفریطِ قوتِ غضبی بل سایر قوای نفسانی [fol. 7a] و حیوانی مجتنب و محترز باشد، چاره نخواهد بود تا خلق از مصالحِ خود غافل نشوند، و متابعتِ طبع و نفس بر ایشان غالب نگردد - و بملاهی[3] و مناهی و تباهی اشتغال ننمایند، و طبقاتِ برایا در مهادِ امن و استراحت مرفه و آسوده زندگانی کنند -

پس بضرورت برآن، برگزیده درگاهِ احدیّت که او را پادشاه گویند، لازم و متحتم است که متخلق با خلاقِ صاحبِ شریعت بوده، بنای[4] مهمات و اساسِ امورِ ملک و دولت را بر احکامِ شریعت گذاشته، خود را بصفتِ[5] چند که طرازِ[6] لباسِ سلطنت تواند بود موصوف گرداند[7] - و تمامی همتِ خود را بر فهمِ اشاراتِ حکماء و کشفِ رموزِ علماء مصروف داشته، مواعظ و نصایح و حکمِ ایشانرا دستور العمل سازد، تاهم فرقِ ملّت با فسرِ دولت سرافراز باشد و هم لباسِ [fol. 7b] ملک بطرازِ اعزازِ دین مطـرّز - و هر پادشاهِ آگاه که مشـرّف به تشریفِ این صفاتِ حسنه بوده بزیورِ این اخلاقِ رضیه آراسته باشد، هم مملکتش آبادان و هم رعیتش خوشدل و شادان بوده، دلها بسلسلهٔ اطاعت و متابعتِ او در آیند و گلشنِ سلطنتش با برگ و نوا بوده، سالهای سال و قرنهای بیشمار نامِ او به نیکوئی بر صفحهٔ روزگار باقی ماند -

چنانچه[8] پادشاهِ فریدون فـرّ، همایون[9] فال، صدر نشینِ بارگاهِ ایلخانی، فروزندهٔ چراغِ گورگانی، مشـیّدِ ارکانِ خلافت[10] و بختیاری، موسّسِ اساسِ سلطنت و کامگاری، مرتقی معارجِ جاه و جلال، رافعِ مدارجِ عظمت و اقبال، آنکه تا نـیّرِ اعظم عطیه بخشِ عالمست، چشمِ زمانه اینچنین شهنشاهی ندیده و دستِ روزگار مثلِ این پادشاهی [fol. 8 a] بر تختِ سلطنت و فرماندهی ننشانده، اعنی خاقانِ جمجاه گیتی پناه[11]، ستاره سپاه -

---

1. *Ibid.*, بسنبدیده 2. *Ibid.*, صفاتش 3. *Ibid.*, ملاهی 4. بناهی
5. *O* : بصفی 6. *K* omits طراز 7. *Ibid.*, گردانیده تمامی 8. *Ibid.*, چنانکه
9. *Ibid.*, همیون 10. *Ibid.*, ارکان دولت خلافت 11. *Ibid.*, بناه

مصراع[1] : زلالِ چشمهٔ امیدِ نقدِ اکبر شاه

ابو المظفر نورالدین محمد جهانگیر پادشاه -

در تمهیدِ قواعدِ جهانداری و تشییدِ مراسمِ فرمان فرمایی و ترویجِ احکامِ شریعتِ غرّا[2] و تاسیسِ مبانی ملّتِ بیضا کوشیده با نامل عنایتِ بیغایت ابوابِ مرحمت و احسان بر روی خلایق کشوده است و بساطِ معدلت و امتنان[3] در بسیطِ ربع مسکون بنوعی گسترانیده و سایهٔ عاطفت بر مفارقِ عالمیان بنهجی مبسوط گردانیده که صیتِ معدلت و کامگاری او در اطراف و آکنافِ عالم سایر ، و صفتِ عظمت و شهر یاری او چون نیّرِ اعظم در نصف النّهار ظاهر است - از یمنِ معدلتش مقناطیس[4] از جذبِ[5] آهن در گذشته و کاه ربا [fol. 8b] دستِ تعرض از دامنِ کاه کوتاه ساخته ، میش با گرگ عهدِ خواهر خواندگی آغاز نهاده ، و شیر با آهو عقدِ مواخات بسته -

بیت[6]

بره وگرگند بهم در خرام　　　آهو و شیرند بهم گشته رام

در زمانِ دولتِ ابد مقرونش نه آهو را از چنگِ پلنگ نهیب است و نه تیهو را از مخلبِ عقاب آسیبی - بادِ صرصر را یارای آن نیست که غباری بکس رساند - و بازِ بلند پرواز را زهرهٔ آن نی که هوای صیدِ کبوتر بخاطر گذراند - در روزگارِ سلطنتِ روز افزونش ، جمهورِ خلایق از ظلماتِ ظلم و اعتساف بسر چشمهٔ عدل و انصاف رسیده اند - و طبقاتِ امم در ریاضِ امن و سلامت و حدایقِ فراغ و رفاهیت آسوده اند[7] - و لهٰذا سلاطینِ نامدار ، حلقهٔ اطاعتِ او در گوشِ جان کشیده و پادشاهانِ رفیع مقدار غاشیهٔ عبودیتِ او بر دوشِ دل گرفته اند و یقین که بیمنِ این اطوارِ حمیده و صفاتِ پسندیده[8] سالهای سال عامه برایا در ظلِ ظلیل ابدی التظلیلش هم آغوشِ امن و راحت بوده ، هم اساسِ سلطنتش استحکام خواهد داشت [fol. 9a] و هم ذکرِ جمیلش تا انقراضِ عالم[9] بر اوراقِ روزگار و الواحِ لیل و نهار باق و پایدار خواهد بود -

---

1. *Ibid.*, م　2. *Ibid.*, اعزا　3. *O* : احسان　4. *K* : مقیاطیس　5. *Ibid.*, حدت　6. *O* omits بیت　7. *K* omits اند

8. *O* omits سالهای سال - اساسِ سلطنتش　9. *Ibid.*, omits تا انقراضِ عالم

امید که ایزد تعالی و تقدس این[1] پادشاهِ جمجاه را در سلطنت و جهانبانی و دولت و کامرانی بر وفقِ امال و امانی باقی و پایدار داراد و کافهٔ عباد را از میامنِ نصفت و معدلتِ این پادشاهِ جهانگیرِ کامگار[2]

ع تا چرخ را مدار بود ارض را قرار

ممتع و برخوردار دارد[3] ـ

تا بود در جهان جنوب و شمال　　تا بود ماه را مدار و مسیر
تخت بادش همیشه چرخِ بلند　　تاج بادش همیشه بدرِ منیر
جگرِ دشمنش ز خنجر چاک　　روی بدخواهِ او چو برگِ زریر

این دعا را قدسیان از عرش آمین گفته اند[4] ـ

---

1. *Ibid.*, omits این پادشاه جمجاه—کافه　2. *K* omits کامگار

3. *Ibid.*, گرداناد ; and *O* adds : و در شمولِ سلطنت و جهانبانی و حصولِ دولت و کامرانی بر وفقِ آمال و آمانی باقی باد

4. *K* omits این دعا ـ گفته اند

فصل اول

در عدالت و سیاست

بدانکه سلطنت و جهانداری منزلتی[1] رفیع و مرتبتی منیع است و بکوشش خود پای آرزو بران پایه نتوان نهاد - و جز بتایید آسمانی و سعادت سرمدی و دستیاری دولت و پایمردی بخت بدان درجه نتوان رسید - و چون باتفاق[2] [fol. 9 b] حسنات این صورت میسر شد ، و حق سبحانه و تعالی دربارهٔ یکی از بندگان خود این چنین کرامتی فرموده ، افسر اختیار با فرق اقتدار اوگذاشت، این دولت را عزیز و مکرم باید داشت - و در ضوابط قواعد و حفظ مراسم آن بعدل و انصاف مبالغه باید نمود که اگر شحنهٔ عدل بضوابط احوال مردم اهتمام ننماید ، دزد فتنه[3] بدستیاری ستم دمار از روزگار خاص و عام بر آورد - و اگر پرتو شمع انصاف کلبهٔ تاریک دردمندان را روشنایی نبخشد ، ظلمات ظلم اطراف و اکناف مملکت را چون دل ستمکاران تیره سازد - چه ملوک سایهٔ آفریدگار باشند ، بی آفتاب عدالت ایشان عرصهٔ عالم منور نگردد - و جز در ظلال مرحمت و احسان ایشان آسایش عالمیان در مهاد امن و امان وجود نگیرد - و پادشاه عادل پناه مظلومان و دستگیر افتادگان باشد - و در خبر آمده که یکساعته عدل پادشاه در پلهٔ میزان راجح[4] تر است از عبادت شصت ساله - زیرا که نتیجهٔ عبادت جز بعابد نمیرسد ، [fol. 10a] و فایدهٔ عدل بخاص و عام واصل میگردد - و حکماء گفته اند که عدالت نه جزویست از فضیلت بلکه همه فضیلتهاست و جور که مقابل اوست نه جزویست از رزیلت بلکه همه رزیلتهاست - و از فضیلت عدالت یکی آنست که خاک در اجزای سلطان عادل تصرف نمیکند - و اگر این سلطان عادل مسلمان نیز بوده باشد - در قیامت آتش دوزخ هم باوکار[5] نخواهد کرد -

و بی شبه ملوک را تسخیر ملک آخرت بدستگیری[6] مظلومان و فریاد رسیدن محرومان میسر تواند شد - و هر بادشاه آگاه که مدار کار خود بر قانون عدالت گذاشته از جادهٔ عدالت انحراف نورزد ، قواعد[7] دین و دولت و بنای ملک

---

1. *Ibid.*, adds منزلتی امت 2. *Ibid.*, باتفاقات حسنه 3. *Ibid.*, درد فسنه
4. *Ibid.*, راجحه 5. *Ibid.*, یادکار 6. *Ibid.*, omits به 7. *Ibid.*, و قواعد

و ملتش ببرکت[1] آن قایم و منتظم خواهد شد[2] - و[3] اگر از جادهٔ عدالت قدم بیرون گذارد، بزودی[4] اساسِ دولتش منهدم و بنای سلطنتش متزلزل خواهد شد -

که حکماء گفته اند پنج کس را طمع از پنج چیز بباید برید ، و از حصولِ آن امید منقطع باید ساخت - اول : پادشاهِ ظالم را از ثباتِ[5] ملک [fol. 10 b] و دوامِ دولت ، دویم : متکبرِ مغرور را از ستایشِ[6] مردم ، سیوم : مردمِ بد خُلق را از بسیاری دوستان ، چهارم : خیره روی بی ادب را از برخورداری و مرتبهٔ بزرگی ، پنجم : بخیل را از نیک نامی -

پس ملوک و سلاطینِ نافذ الامر را که رشتهٔ امنیتِ اهلِ زمین بوجودِ ایشان باز بسته و حکمِ[7] ایشان بر جان و مالِ آدمیان جاری و فرمانِ ایشان چون قضای نازل در مجاری [و] حل و عقد امور سایر است - باید که بر تخت نشستن را از بهرِ داد دادن نه از بهر شاد زیستن دانسته ، عدل و انصاف را موجبِ بقای سلطنت و دوامِ نامِ نیکو و احرازِ ثوابِ آخرت تصور نمایند - و هیچ چیز واجب تر از[8] اشغال[9] بمصالح بندگانِ خدای ندانسته ، از سخن گفتن با رعایا و ضعفاء و عجزه و مساکین عار ندارند - و گوش بسخنِ داد خواهان کرده ، بنفسِ خود بر حقیقتِ احوالِ مظلومان برسند[10] و روی عاطفت بساختنِ مهمِ[11] ایشان آورده از بسیار گفتن به تنگ نیایند که پادشاه حکمِ طبیب دارد و داد خواه بمثابهٔ بیمار - اگر مریض تمامِ احوالِ [fol. 11a] خود را پیشِ طبیب نگوید و بمرضِ او مطلع نشود ، تشخیصِ مرضِ نا کرده چگونه حکم تواند کرد -

اما این را بباید دانست که بیخِ درختِ عدل برشحاتِ سحابِ سیاست تازه و سیرابست که آن سیاست بر قانونِ عدالت باشد[12] - و گفته اند سلطنت بمثابهٔ نهالست و سیاست بمنزلهٔ آب - پس لازمست بیخِ سلطنت را بآبِ سیاست تازه داشتن تا ثمرهٔ امن امان حاصل آید که اگر ضبط و سیاست نباشد ، مهمات بر نسق نماند - و اگر تعذیب و تادیب نبود ، کارها تباه شود - زینتِ ملک و ملّت و مصلحتِ دین و دولت در سیاست است ، و بی ضابطهٔ سیاستِ ملوک نه احکامِ شرع رواج یابد و نه اساسِ سلطنت استحکام پذیرد[13] - و اگر تیغِ سیاست از

---

1. *Ibid.*, omits به 2. *Ibid.*, خواهد بود 3. *O* omits و 4. *K* : و بزودی
5. *Ibid.*, اثبات 6. *Ibid.*, سایش 7. *Ibid*, omits بازبسته و حکم
8. *O* omits از 9. *K* : اشتغال 10. *Ibid*, omits به
11. *Ibid.*, مبهم 12. *O* : باید 13. *Ibid.*, omits پذیرد

نیامِ انتقام کشیده نشود ، بنیادِ فتنه منهدم و اساسِ ستم متزلزل نگردد ـ و اگر بآتشِ قهر[1] خس و خاشاکِ بیداد سوخته نشود ، نهالِ امانی در گلشنِ آمال پرورش نیابد ـ مردمِ فتنه انگیزِ فتان[2] چون بینند که آتشِ سیاست تیز[3] است گوشه گیرند ـ و اگر اندک دهشتی[4] درکارِ سیاست مشاهده [fol. 11b] شود از[5] هر طرف شورشی پدید آید و انواعِ فتنه بظهور رسد ـ پس ملوک باید که رحمتی باشند از خدای تعالی بر نیکان و مصلحان و خشم خدای بر بدان و مفسدان[6] ـ نیشِ قهرِ[7] شان با نوشِ لطف آمیخته و زهرِ هیبتِ شان با شکرِ مرحمت انگیخته ، سیاست را با عدالت قران باید[8] داد ، تا ریاضِ آمالِ نیکان را از رشحاتِ لطف سرسبز دارند و بنیادِ حیاتِ بدان را بصرصرِ سیاست از بیخ بر کنند ـ

---

1. *K* : مهر 2. *Ibid.*, omits فتان 3. *Ibid.*, بتر
4. *Ibid.*, دهنی 5. *Ibid.*, and *O* و از 6. *K* : مفسدان و بدان
7. *Ibid.*, مهر 8. *Ibid.*, مامد

فصل دویم

در سخاوت و شجاعت و حلم

بدانکه هیچ صفتی آدمیانرا[1] خصوصاً اشراف و سلاطین را بهتر از جود و سخاوت نیست ـ چه عیبی که جمیع هنرها بدو پوشیده ماند بخل است و هنری که همه[2] عیب ها را بپوشاند سخاوت ـ سعادت دین و دنیا به جود و کرم حاصل شود ـ سعادت دین[3] اینکه خدای تعالی میفرماید که من جاء بالحسنة فله عشر امثالها[4] ـ و سعادت دنیا آنکه مرغ دل خلق را بکرم صید توان کرد چنانکه گفته اند مرغ وحشی را بدام توان رام کرد و آدمی را بانعام و احسان صید توان ساخت ـ

و[5] سخاوت [fol. 12a] و احسان سبب نیکنامی و دوستکامی و خجسته فرجامیست ـ و حق سبحانهٔ و تعالی مردم بلند همت را دوست میدارد و تخم احسان جز سعادت دنیا و کرامت آخرت بر ندهد ـ و رفعت ارجمند باهمت بلند پیوندی دارد که جدایی ایشان از یکدیگر محال است ـ از معلم[6] اول نقل کرده اند که فاضل ترین صفتی از صفت باری تعالی آنست که او را جوّاد گویند ، چه جود او در جمله موجودات سیران[7] کرده و کرم او کل مخلوقات را فرا رسیده ـ و صاحب نبوت کبری صلوات الله علیه فرموده که جود نهالیست در چمن جنت رسته و برکنار جویبار کوثر نشو و نما یافته که السخاوة شجرة فی الجنة ـ

سلاطین را همت عالی پیشکاریست کافی و مددگاریست وافی و هر کرا از ایشان همت بیشتر بقدم شوکت بیش تر ـ و لیکن شجاعت را بر سخاوت مقدم باید دانست ، زیرا که شجاعت مستلزم سخاوتست و هر گاه نفس را تحمل اخطار امری که مظنهٔ هلاکت باشد ملکه[8] گردد ، بذل مال[9] که اعتباری ندارد ، یقین که ترد او ننماید ـ و استلزام سخاوت شجاعت را [fol. 12 b] اکثری نیست ، اگرچه مستلزم[10] دیگر ملکاتست ـ هر پادشاهی را که شجاعت نباشد چون ابریست که باران ندارد ـ و حکماء گفته اند که بقای ملک و استقامت دولت ملوک جز بچهار چیز ممکن نباشد :

اول : حزمی کامل که چهرهٔ فردا را[11] در آئینهٔ امروز مشاهده نماید ـ

---

1. *Ibid.*, آدم یاران 2. *O* omits همه 3. *K* omits دین
4. *al-Qur'an* 6 : 160 5. *O* omits و 6. *K* متعلم 7. *Ibid.*, اسیران
8. *Ibid.*, بلکه 9. *Ibid.*, امال 10. *O* استلزام 11. *Ibid.*, omits را

دویم : عزمی راسخ که فتور و قصور در عزیمتِ او راه نیابد -

سیوم : رای صایب که از صوبِ اعتدال بجانبِ خطا و خلل منحرف نباشد -

چهارم : شمشیرِ تیز که چون برقِ جهانسوز آتش در خرمنِ جانِ مخالف زند -

و مقرر است که روضهٔ دولت و اقبال بی آبِ شمشیرِ نصرت مآب نضارت و سرسبزی نیابد - و نهالِ امانیو آمال بی آبیاری تیغِ ضیمران مثال میوهٔ فیروزی بار نیاورد - هم از روی صورتِ بهشت ، امن و امان در ضمانِ شمشیرِ خسروان برقرار ماند - و هم از راهِ معنی فردوسِ برین رهینِ تیغِ سلاطینِ معدلت آیین تواند بود که **الجنة تحت ظلال السیوف** - چشمِ امیدِ گیتی ستانی بمشاهدهٔ جمالِ مرادِ روشنایی یابد که سرمهٔ دیده از غبارِ معرکه سازد - و دستِ آرزوی جهانبانی بگردنِ عروسِ مقصود حایل گردد که با طلعتِ [fol. 13a] سرو قامتِ نیزه عشق بازد - طالبانِ ملک را خوبترین لباسها زره است و بهترین تاجها خود و خوشترین منزلها معرکهٔ حرب و زیباترین شرابها خونِ خصم و خوبترین محبوبان شمشیر -

بیت[1]

عروسِ ملک کسی درکنار گیرد چست
که بوسه بر لبِ[2] شمشیرِ آبدار زند

پادشاهانِ کامگار وقتی با مخدره مملکت دستِ عشرت در آغوشِ مراد توانند کرد که آبِ شمشیرِ آتش بارشان نامِ خصمِ بد اندیش را از لوحِ حیات بشوید و خسروانِ نامدارِ آنزمان ساغرِ مراد بلبِ راحت توانند رسانید که پیمانهٔ تمنای دشمن را به سنگِ ظفر درهم شکنند - والحق لذتِ سلطنت در سه چیز باشد : **اول** : دشمنانرا منکوب و مخذول[3] کردن ، **دویم**: دوستان و هوا خواهانرا سر بر افراختن[4] ، **سیم**[5] : : حاجتِ مظلومان بر آوردن و بیچارگانرا نواختن -

---

1. *Ibid.*, omits بیت 2. *Ibid.*, بر دم
3. *K* : مخذول و منکوب کردن 4. *Ibid.*, برا فراختند 5. *Ibid.*, سیوم

و هر پادشاه که در وقتِ نام و ننگ و در روزِ جنگ بعواقبِ کارها التفات ننموده[1] ، هنگامِ نبرد جان و مال را بیقدر و بی قیمت و کلفت شمرد ، جنگ را[2] بهتر از محو شدنِ نام و ننگ داند ، البته با شاهدِ ظفر [fol. 13b] هم آغوش خواهد شد ـ اگرچه شمشیر دو روی دارد و باد را از هر دو جانب امکانِ و زیدن باشد ـ اما حق سبحانهٗ و تعالی مردمِ شجاع را دوست میدارد و حافظ و ناصرِ ایشانست ـ نه بینی که اکثر در کارزار بددلان و ترسندگان علفِ شمشیر میشوند و دلیران و مبارزان بسلامت بیرون می آیند ـ هرکس را بویِ از گلشنِ شجاعت بمشامِ[3] او رسیده است ـ هزار زخم خوردن را دوستر دارد[4] از آنکه در بسترِ بیماری همچو پیرِ زالان بمیرد ـ

اما باید دانست که حکماء سخاوت و شجاعت و حلم را[5] محتاج الیه یکدیگر گرفته اند و اکثری ازیشان حلم را که با ثبات و وقار آمیخته باشد بر سخاوت و شجاعت هر دو[6] ترجیح داده گفته اند که شجاعت همیشه بکار نیاید و در عمر ها روزی بدان احتیاج افتد و سخاوت و حلم که[7] همیشه باین هر دو احتیاج می افتد[8] ـ باز فوایدِ سخاوت مخصوصِ طایفه باشد و گروهی خاص از مواهبِ انعام بهره مند توانند شد ـ و لیکن خرد و بزرگ [fol. 14a] و وضیع و شریف را بحلمِ حاجتست و منافع خوشخویی خواص و عوام و سپاهی و رعیت را شامل و[9] چون احکامِ ایشان بر خون و مال و مِلک و ناموسِ جهانیان نافذ است ، و اوامر و نواهی ایشان بر اسافل و اعالی و اصاغر و اکابر جاری ، اگر حلم و بردباری را پیرایهٔ روزگار و سرمایهٔ کارِ خود نساخته اخلاقِ خود را[10] بحلم و ملایمت آراسته ندارند[11] ، یمکن که بیک درشتخویی اهلِ اقلیمی را آزرده و رنجور گردانند و بسی مالها و جانها در معرضِ تلف افتد ـ و اگر چنانچه پادشاهی در سخاوت و شجاعت نامِ حاتم واسفند یار را[12] از صفحهٔ روزگار

———

1. *Ibid.*, بنموده 2. *Ibid.*, omits را

3. *Ibid.*, بمشام رسیده هزار 4. *Ibid.*, دارند

5. *Ibid.*, که محتاج 6. *K* omits هر دو 7. *O* adds که

8. *K* : حلم همیشه محتاج الیه اند باز 9. *Ibid.*, omits و

10. *Ibid.*, خویش را 11. *Ibid.*, بدارند 12. *Ibid.*, omits را

محو نماید و از حلم و[1] بردباری بهره نداشته باشد ، بیک جفا سرچشمهٔ سخاء را تیره سازد و بیک عربده هزار دشمن جانی برانگیزد - و اگر از گلشن سخاوت و شجاعت هیچ کدام بویی بمشام او[2] نرسیده باشد ، برفق و دلجویی و خوشخویی رعیت و لشکری را راضی و شاکر تواند ساخت [fol. 14b] و عالمیانرا در سلسلهٔ اطاعت و هواداری تواند در آورد[3] -

و گفته اند که[4] حلم از جملهٔ اخلاق پیغمبرانست و غضب وسوسهٔ شیطان - و سلطان انبیاء علیه الصلواة والسلام فرموده که سعادت دنیوی و مرادات اخروی بر حلم و نیکو خویی[5] متفرع است و نزد اهل تحقیق مقرر است که تا کسی[6] بر غضب مستولی نگردد بدرجهٔ صدیقان نتواند رسید - و بزرگی گفته است که ترک غضب جامع جمیع مکارم اخلاق و محاسن خصالست و ترک نکردن آن مستجمع تمام قبایح اعمال و فضایح افعال - و حکماء گفته اند که قوت آدمی را به فرو نشاندن[7] شعلهٔ خشم توان دانست و در هنگام اشتعال نایرهٔ غضب خود را در قید ضبط در آوردن - والحق هیچ چاشنی در کام عقل خوشتر از شربت زهر آمیز حلم و بردباری نیست - چه ستوده تر خصلتی که خدای تعالی آدمیانرا بدان آراسته گردانیده است ، زینت حلم و فضیلت وقار است، و حلیم محبوب قلوب باشد -

اگرچه غضب بموقع پادشاهانرا بمراتب بهتر از حلم بی موقعیت[8] و جا باشد [fol. 15a] که البته غضب را کار باید فرمود که اگر حلم بجای آورند ، موجب خفت و باعث انهدام مبانی سلطنت ایشان شود - اما محل هر یک را بباید دانست - و چون آدمی از سهو و خطا خالی نیست ، اگر در ازای[9] هر جرمی عقوبتی بظهور رسد ، خلل کلی در ارکان مملکت راه خواهد یافت - هر که بنور عقل آراسته و بزیور خرد متحلی[10] است و بعنایت ازلی اختصاص یافته در اطفاء نایرهٔ غضب میکوشد و چندانکه میتواند آب حلم بر آتش خشم میریزد و

———

1 *Ibid.*, omits و 2. *K* : بوی او بمشام 3. *Ibid.*, تواند آورد
4. *O* omits که 5. *K* : نیک خویی 6. *Ibid.*, تاکسی
7. *Ibid.*, نشانیدن 8. *O* : بی موقعست
9. *K* : درازی 10. *Ibid.*, متجلی

میداند که در نوشیدنِ شربتِ عفو اگرچه بغایت تلخ نماست ، اما[1] حلاوتِ مسرت درو[2] مندرجست و تحمل نمودن بر مشقتِ حلم و بردباری هر چند مزاجِ زهر دارد تریاقِ بهجت را متضمن -

هر آئینه ملوک را بشکرانه[3] قدرت بر انتقام ، گنه گارِ خجلت زده را به بشارتِ عفو باید نواخت ،که اگر گناه نبودی عفو که بهترین فضایلست از ایشان صادر نشدی - و در جمیع کارها خصوصاً در خون ریختن تامل واجب باید دانست که اگر کشتن لازم آید فرصت باقیست ، [fol. 15b] و اگر عیاذا بالله تعجیل نموده بیگناهی را بقتل آورده باشند و بعد ازان معلوم شود که استحقاقِ کشتن نداشته ، تدارکِ آن از دایرهٔ امکان بیرون بوده ، خون و وبالِ آن تا ابد در گردنِ ایشان خواهد ماند - چه خون ریختن کاری صعب و اساسِ[4] حیاتِ جانوری را منهدم ساختن مهمی دشوار است و گذشته را باز آوردن و مرده را زنده کردن خارج از دایرهٔ قدرتِ بشری - پس ملوک و سلاطین را باید که خود را بصفتِ[5] حلم و بردباری[6] موصوف کرده ، شربتِ ناخوشگوارِ غضب را بکشاده پیشانی تجرع نمایند - و همیشه چاشنی عفو را بر تلخی عقوبت ترجیح داده ، هر چند گناه بزرگ باشد عفو را بزرگتر دانند -

و چون طبیعتِ عالم صفتِ مکافات را متضمن است و ممکن نیست که اگر کسی از ساغرِ ستمکاری جرعه نوشد ، بخمارِ بلا مبتلا نگردد - و یا در چمنِ اعمال نهالِ بیدادی نشاند ، ثمرهٔ عقوبت و عذاب بر ندارد - تا می توانند بناحق گردِ آزارِ هیچکس نگردیده ، هر چه خود را و فرزندان و متعلقانِ خود را نپسندند در بارهٔ [fol. 16 a] دیگران روا ندارند تا فواتحِ امور و خواتیمِ مهماتِ ایشان بنامِ نیکو و ذکرِ جمیل متحلی[7] باشد و یقین دانند که هرگز[8] نیکو کاری ضایع نمیشود و جزای بدکرداران در توقف نمی ماند و هر[9] کرداریرا جزایی مقرر است و اگر تاخیر درمیان آفتد مغرور نباید شد که دو سه روزه مهلت مجال

---

1. *O* omits اما 2. *Ibid.*, omits درو

3. *K* : ملوک بشکر از قدرت بر انتقام 4. *Ibid.*, omits اساس

5. *Ibid.*, نصفت 6. O : برده باری 7. *K* : متجلی

8. *Ibid.*, هرکه 9. *Ibid.*, س

است ِ[1] و اندیشهٔ نایافتن ِ سزا و جزا خیال ِ محال - هر تخمی که در مزرعهٔ عمل بکارند بسی بر نیاید که بر ِ او بردارند -

و حکماء جهانرا که دار ِ مکافاتست بکوه تشبیه کرده اند که هر چه از بد و نیک بدو گویی جواب ِ خود همان شنوی - هرکه بد کند طمع نیکی نباید[2] داشت و هر که نیشکر طلبد حنظل نباید کاشت - بلکه سلاطین را باید که بشکرانهٔ اینکه فراش ِ قضا بارگاه ِ دولت ایشانرا بر افراشته، و کار فرمای قدر نوبت ِ کامگاری و جهانداری با ایشان گذاشته است، سعی نمایند که تا کاری که موجب ِ نیکنامی دین و سبب ِ نجات ِ درجات ِ عقبی[3] باشد از ایشان بوجود آید - و کار ِ خود را باصلاح آوردن و نیت بر افعال و اعمال ِ حسنه مصروف داشتن را از فرایض و لوازم دانسته، [fol. 16b] باران ِ احسان بر مفارق ِ عالمیان می باریده باشند - تا در روضهٔ ان احسنتم احسنتم لانفسکم[4] گلهای مراد ببار آمده در دنیا و عقبی[5] مشکور و مستحسن باشند -

شعر[6]

اگر بد کنی چشم ِ نیکی مدار　　که حنظل نمی آرد انگور بار
مپندار ای در خزان کشته جو　　که گندم ستانی بوقت درو
مثل اینچنین گفت آموزگار　　مکن بد که بد بینی از روزگار
کسی نیک بیند بهر دوسرای　　که نیکی رساند بخلق خدای

———

1. *Ibid.*, محالست 2. *Ibid.*, نبایدش 3. *Ibid.*, در عقبی
4. *Qur'ān* 17:7 5. O : دینی و عقبی 6. *K* omits شعر

فصل سیم

در مشورت و تدبیر

بدانکه اکثری از حکماء رای و تدبیر را بر شجاعت تفضیل داده گفته اند که آنچه بتدبیر[1] توان ساخت به شمشیر و تیر از پیش نتوان برد ـ چنانکه گفته اند ، شجاعت بمثابه تیغ است[2] و رای و تدبیر بمنزلهٔ دست قوی که آنرا کار فرماید ـ هرکرا دست بی تیغ بود همه کار تواند کرد ، اما از تیغ بی دست هیچ کار نیاید و ضایع و بیکار باشد ـ و هر چند مرد مبارز و دلیر و شجاع بود در مصاف با ده تن [fol. 17a] یا بیست ' نهایتش با صد تن برابری تواند کرد ـ اما مرد دانا بیک فکر صائب ملکی را پریشان سازد و باندک تدبیری لشکریرا بشکنند ، بتخصیص بادشاهانرا برای صائب و تدبیر درست مطالب حاصل شود که بخزاین و[3] دفاین بسیار و خدم و حشم بیشمار میسر نشود ـ

هر پادشاه آگاه که از میامن عقل بهره مند شده ، اساس احکام خلافت و بنای مهمات سلطنت[4] خود را بمشورت و تدبیر گذاشته باشد و بحکم **شاورهم فی الامر** [5] ، بی تدبیر و مشورت بزرگان خورده دان در مصالح ملک مدخل ننماید و تمام نظام اعمال و احکام خود را بتدابیر[6] وزیران کامل و مشیران[7] عاقل باز بسته[8] ، به رای ناصحان امانت گذار مقبول القول استظهار جوید ـ لا شک بحکم **ما یشاور قوم الا هداهم الله ولا رشد [فی] امور[9] لا مشورة فیها** ، هر چه از ایشان صادر شود بصلاح مقترن[10] و امنیت عالم و جمعیت حال بنی آدم را متضمن خواهد بود و ملک او پایدار و دولت او برقرار خواهد شد و هر که بسخن ناصحان اگرچه درشت و بی محابا گویند التفات [fol. 17 b] ننموده از جادهٔ مشورت و تدبیر انحراف ورزد ، از پیرایهٔ حزم و دور اندیشی عاطل و در میدان خرد و عاقبت بینی راجل باشد و عواقب امورش از ندامت خالی نخواهد بود ـ و در قبضهٔ اختیار و اقتدارش جز حسرت و پشیمانی باقی نخواهد ماند ـ

---

1. *Ibid.*, بتدبر 2. *Ibid.*, لغت
3. *Ibid.*, omits و 4. *O* omits سلطنت
5. *Qurān* 3 : 159 6. *K* : تبدبیر 7. *Ibid.*, مبشران
8. *Ibid.*, بار بسته 9. *O* : لا مور 10. *K* : مقرن

چون بیماری که بفرمودهٔ طبیب عمل نکرده ، غذا و شربت بحسب ِ آرزوی خود[1] خورد و هر لحظه[2] ضعف و ناتوانی در وی بیشتر استیلا یابد - و یقین باید دانست که تدبیر ِ چندین عقل از تدبیر ِ یک عقل صایب تر و پر[3] فایده تر خواهد بود - و تدبیر ِ باصواب[4] را صیدی گفته اند که بدست ِ یک کس در نیاید و اگر جمعی باشند از دست ِ ایشان بیرون نتواند رفت -

پس بر[5] سلاطین واجبست که تدبیر و مشورت را پیشکار ِ خود دانسته هر عقده که پیش آید بسر انگشت ِ تدبیر بکشایند[6] - و کارهای خود را بمقتضای رای صایب پرداخته ، در مراعات جانب ِ حزم[7] و احتیاط جهد ِ موفور [fol. 18 a] بجای آورند - و در هر کار از آغاز ِ مهم نظر بر انجام انداخته ، نفع و ضرر ِ آنرا بمیزان ِ عقل بسنجند - و چون ایشانرا قضیه روی دهد با اهل ِ حکمت و اصحاب ِ تجربت و مردم ِ دور اندیش و پیران ِ عاقبت بین و جمعی که جوهر ِ تدبیر ِ ایشانرا بمعیار ِ عقل سنجیده باشند ، درمیان نهاده مداخل و مخارج ِ آنرا ملاحظه نمایند - و آنچه موافق ِ مصلحت[8] و تدبیر بوده باشد بعمل آورند - اگر تدبیر موافق ِ تقدیر آمد ، خود بر سریر ِ اقبال و مسند ِ کامرانی متمکن شوند - و اگر قضیه منعکس شد ، هم دوستان عذر می پذیرند و هم طاعنان مجال ِ وقیعت نمی یابند - و حکماء گفته اند که عاقل آنست که در فاتحه هر کاری نظر بر خاتمهٔ آن انداخته ، پیش از نشانیدن ِ نهال ثمرهٔ او را ملاحظه کند - و در هر چیز وخامت ِ کار و شامت ِ خاتمت ِ مهم ِ خود بشناسد تا از کرده پشیمان نشود - و عاقبت ِ آن کار بفوز و نجاح مقترن[9] گشته بر مقصود ظفر یابد[10] - [fol. 18 b] -

و در کارها شتاب زدگی ننموده بجانب ِ تامل و تأنی گراید که مضرت ِ تعجیل بسیار و منفعت ِ صبر و سکون بیشمار است - و تأنی همه کاریرا بیاراید و به سبب ِ تعجیل بسی مهمات بزیان آید - و شتاب کاری بارباب ِ خرد[11] نسبتی ندارد ، چه حکماء آنرا از وساوس ِ شیطانی شمرده اند - و[12] هر آینه هر که در کارها زمام ِ

———

1. *Ibid.*, omits خود 2. *Ibid.*, هر ساعت 3. *Ibid.*, omits پر
4. *Ibid.*, omits با 5. *Ibid.*, omits بر 6. *Ibid.*, بکشاید
7. *Ibid.*, جزم 8. *O* : موافق و مصلحت 9. *K* : انجاح مقترن
10. *Ibid.*, تابد 11. *O* : خود 12. *K* omits

اختیار بدستِ تعجیل دهد ، آخرِ کارش به پشیمانی و خاتمهٔ احوالش بحسرت و ندامت و تاسف خواهد کشید و هر که بنای کارِ خویش بر صبر و ثبات و اساسِ مهامِ خود بسکون و وقار استحکام دهد ، بی شبه عواقبِ اعمال و خواتیمِ احوالش به فتح و فیروزی مقرون خواهد شد - چه عاقبتِ شتاب پشیمانی و شرمساریست[1] و مردِ تعجیل کننده[2] همیشه از حصولِ مراد محروم باشد - و صبر صفتی بغایت مقبول و مرضی است و صبر مفتاحِ فرجست و درِ خانهٔ راحت جز بکلیدِ صبر نتوان کشاد - و در هر چه بآدمی حادث شود ، چون بعروهٔ وثقای[3] صبر تمسک جسته ، طریقِ مشورت و تدبیر مسلوک دارد ، [fol. 19 a] عاقبت الامر چهرهٔ مراد در نظر آید - هر مهمی که به تأنی و آهستگی دران شروع نمایند ، اکثر آنست که بر حسبِ دلخواه صورت می یابد - و هر کاری که به شتاب و سبکباری دران خوض نمایند ، غالب آنست که بمراد از[4] پیش نرود - و[5] سبکباری همچو تیریست که از کمان رفت باز نتوان آورد و آهستگی چون[6] شمشیریست در دست ، اگر خواهند کار فرمایند و الا هیچ ضرر نکند -

اما ملوک را با هر کس طریقِ مشورت مسلوک نباید[7] داشت و اسرارِ مملکت را چون مهماتِ عرفی و معاملاتِ رسمی نباید دانست - و[8] تا بدین و دیانت و عقل و فطانت کسی را بارها نیازموده باشند ، سرِ خود درمیان نباید نهاد که نه هر مستشاری مؤتمن باشد و گفته اند که فاش شدنِ اسرارِ پادشاه از جانبِ اربابِ مشورتیست که بحلیهٔ امانت آراسته نباشند و آنچه از مشاورت[9] و تدبیر حاصل آید و رای بدان قرار گیرد نهان باید داشت که درکتمانِ سر و اخفای ما فی الضمیر دو فایده[10] متضمن است : [fol. 19 b]

یکی آنکه هر مهمی که نهان سازند زود تر بانجاح مقرون گردد -

دویم آنکه اگر آن تدبیر موافقِ تقدیر نباشد و آنچه در ضمیر است ، از قوت بفعل نیاید ، شماتتِ اعداء و عیب جویان بران مترتب[11] نگردد - و

---

1. *Ibid.*, بود 2. *Ibid.*, تعجیل کنند 3. *O* : بعروة الوثقی ; *K* : غروه
4. *K* : بمرادار 5. *O* omits و 6. *K* : همچو
7. *Ibid.*, نیامد 8. *O* omits و 9. *K* : مشورت
10. *Ibid.*, دو قاید 11. *Ibid.*, مرست

اظهارِ اسرار نتیجهٔ نیکو ندارد[1] - و در امثال آمده که هر که سر از دست بدهد سر بنهد -

مصرع[2] : خواهی که سر بجای بود سِرّ نگاهدار -

ملوک را در نگاهداشتنِ اسرار احتیاطی تمام لازمست ، خاصه از دوستانِ نومید و از دشمنِ[3] هراسان - و حکماء گفته اند که پادشاه را در افشای اسرارِ خود به هفت طایفه اعتماد نباید کرد :

اول : هر که بدرگاهِ ایشان جرمی و جنایتی کرده ملالتی دیده باشد و رنج[4] و مشقتِ او مدتی کشیده باشد -

دویم : کسی که مال و حرمتِ او در خدمتِ ایشان بباد رفته و معیشت برو تنگ شده باشد -

سیم[5] : آنکه از عملِ خود معزول شده دیگر باره امیدواری بر یافتِ عمل نداشته باشد -

چهارم : شریری که فتنه جوید و بجانبِ ایمنی و آرامش مایل نبود -

پنجم : گناهکاری که [fol. 20 a]ابنای جنس او راگوشمالی داده ، در حقِ او زیاده مبالغه رفته باشد -

ششم : آنکه خدمتِ پسندیده کند و محروم باشد و دیگران بی خدمتی نموده[6] بیشتر از وی تربیت یافته باشند :

هفتم : آنکه بدرگاهِ ایشان قبول نیافته باشد و نزدیکِ دشمن مقبول باشد -

و بادشاهانرا بعضی اسرار باشد که از خود نیز نهان باید داشت[7] ، یعنی در اخفای سر مبالغه بدان حد باید نمود که گویا خود هم[8] محرم آن نمی توانند[9] بود ، فکیف که[10] با دیگری ازان رمزی توان گفت - باید که خود

---

1. *Ibid.*, نیکو یندارد

2. *O* : نظم 3. *K* : دشمنان 4. *O* adds مدتِ رنج

5. *K* : سیوم 6. *O* omits نموده 7. *K* : باید بنهان داشت

8. *O* omits هم 9. *K* : تواند 10. *Ibid.*, omits که

محرمِ اسرارِ خود بوده کسی را بر سرِ خود مطلع نگردانند - و بعد از آنکه مکنونِ ضمیرِ خود با دیگری آشکارا کنند ، اگر او نیز بدیگری گوید جای رنجش نبود - چه هر گاه خود باوجودِ فرزانگی و تائیدِ آسمانی و همتِ بلند و خاطرِ ارجمند رازِ خود اخفا نتوانند کرد و بارِ خود نتوانند کشید ، دیگران که بپایه از ایشان[1] فروتر و بعقل و خرد کمتر باشند ، چگونه محافظتِ آن توانند کرد ، و تحملِ حملِ آن توانند داشت -

راز مکشای بهر کس که درین عالمِ خاک
سیر کردیم بسی محرمِ اسرار نبود

1. *Ibid.*, ازو

فصل چهارم [fol. 20 b]
در احتراز نمودن از دشمنان

بدانکه دو چیز است که اندک آنرا بسیار باید دانست۔

اول : آتش که اندکِ آنرا در سوختن همان ضرر است که بسیارِ آنرا۔

دویم : دشمن که هر چند خوار و ضعیف بود ، کارِ خود بکند۔

و حکماء گفته اند که هر چه ازان مضرتی توان تصور کرد[1] ، بچیزِ دیگر مندفع توان کرد ، مگر کینه که دفعِ آن بهیچ چیز در حیز امکان نیاید۔ مثلاً آتش اگرچه سوزنده است آن[2] را بآب تسکین توان داد و شعلهٔ حقد و خصومت بآبِ هفت دریا فرو ننشیند[3]۔ و زهر اگرچه کشنده است ، ضررِ آنرا به تریاق از بدن بیرون توان برد ، زهرِ کینه بهیچ تریاق از بدن بیرون نرود ، بتخصیص عداوتی که ذاتی باشد ، چه هیچ دشمنی آنقدر اثر ندارد که عداوتِ ذاتی۔ زیرا که اگر میانِ دو کس عداوتِ عارضی پدید آید ، باندک چیزی رفعِ آن ممکنست ، اما اگر دراصل دشمنی آفتاده باشد و با عداوتِ قدیمی خصومتِ مجدد نیز منضم شده باشد ، مدافعه آن [fol. 21 a] بهیچوجه در دایرهٔ امکان داخل نیست و عدمِ آن بانعدامِ ذاتِ هر دو باز بسته خواهد بود۔

نظم[4]

امید دوستی نو ز دشمنانِ کهن چنان بود که طلب کردن گل از گلخن

چون هیچ حصاری محکمتر از حزم و احتیاط نیست و از جمله حزم یکی آنست که بهیچ وجه بر دشمن اعتماد نکنند ، چه حکماء درین باب مبالغه کرده گفته اند که اعتماد بر دوستِ نا[5] آزموده کردن از عقل دور است ، تا[6] بدشمنِ کینه جوی چه رسد۔

پس سلاطین را باید که در هیچ باب طریقِ حزم را[7] فرو نگذاشته خصم را خورد[8] و خوار ندانند که حکماء گفته اند دوستی هزار تن در مقابله دشمنی

---

1. *Ibid.*, تصور توان کرد
2. *O* : اورا
3. *K* : بنشیند
4. ***Ibid.***, omits نظم
5. ***Ibid.***, ما
6. ***Ibid.***, باد بدشمن
7. O ; omits را
8. ***K*** : خود

یک شخص در نیاید ، و دفع ایشانرا اهم ِ مهمات دانسته بتلطف و چاپلوسی ایشان مغرور نشوند - و هر چند تملق پیش آورده تضرع پیشتر کنند ، اعتماد ننموده ، متاع روی اندود ِ تزویر و شعبدهٔ نفاق آلود ِ ایشانرا نخرند و افسون ِ جانگذاری ایشانرا در گوش راه ندهند - و هر چند تلطف و ملایمت بیش بینند در بدگمانی و خویشتن داری[1] بیفزایند - و چندانکه خصم قدم ِ ملایمت پیش نهد ، [fol. 21 b] دامن ِ موافقت پیشتر در چینند - که گفته اند بقول ِ دشمن فریفته نباید شد اگرچه مودت کند ، و بسخن ِ خصم اعتماد نباید کرد هر چند در مصادقت مبالغه نماید ، چه از ایشان بهیچ رو[2] دوستی نیاید - و دشمن اگر به هزار نقش[3] بر آید ، هنوز رنگ ِ عداوت بر دلش باقی خواهد بود - وگفته اند کینه در سینهٔ دشمن چون انگشت ِ[4] فسرده باشد - اگرچه حالی اثر ظاهر نکند ، اما چون شراره بوی رسد ، افروخته گشته فروغ ِ خصومت بالا گیرد و جهانی را سوخته دود ِ آن بسی دماغها را خشک و بسیار دیدها را تیره سازد و ممکن نیست که تا[5] ذرهٔ از انگشت ِ کینه در کانون ِ سینه باشد ، از مضرت ِ شعلهٔ خصومت ایمن توان بود -

باید که خصم هر چند خورد و ضعیف و ایشان بزرگ و قوی باشند ، احتراز واجب دانسته ، چون بر ایشان[6] دست یابند و این گوهر ِ مراد بچنگ[7] در آورند ، در اطفاء نایرهٔ حیاتشان تهاون نورزندکه دیگر تدارک صورت [fol. 22a] نبندد - و چند انکه پشیمانی خورند فایده ندهد - و اگر درکار ِ ایشان غفلتی ورزیده ، رخنه کشاده گذارند ، دشمن که مترصد ِ این حالست ، ناگاه کمین کشاده تیر ِ تدبیر بهدف ِ مراد برساند و در آنوقت قوت ِ تدارک فوت شده ، حسرت و ندامت بهیچ وجه سود ندهد - و لا شک هرکه بچرب زبانی و تلطف ِ ایشان فریفته شده جانب ِ هشیاری و حزم و عاقبت اندیشی را فرو گذارد ، تیر ِ آفت را از جان ِ خود هدفی ساخته ، آتش ِ بلا را برافروخته باشد ، چه دشمن ِ دانا برای مصلحت ِ کار ِ خود کمال ملاطفت بظهور میرساند - و ظاهر[8] را بخلاف ِ باطن آراسته دقایق ِ مکر[9] و لطایف ِ حیله بکار می برد - و در ضمن ِ آن فکر های کلی و تدبیر های عجیب تعبیه میکنند و بعذر و مکر آتش ِ حیله بر می انگیزد

---

1. *Ibid.*, omits داری
2. *Ibid.*, بهیچوجه
3. *Ibid.*, نفس
4. *Ibid* , انکست
5. *O adds* اگرتا
6. *O* : بدیشان
7. *K* : بجنگ
8. *Ibid.*, ظاهراً
9. *Ibid.*, بکر

که[1] بهیچوجه زبانهٔ او را بآبِ تدبیر فرو نتوان نشانید ـ

اما اگر چنانچه[2] قوت و قدرت و شوکتِ خصم زیاده بود و خوف آن باشد که فسادِ استیلای او در ممالک [fol. 22 b] منتشر شده ، رعایا و عجزه و مساکین در معرضِ هلاک و ورطه تلف[3] آفتند و قوتِ مدافعه و مقابله نداشته باشند[4] درین حال جز باضطرار جنگ اختیار نتوان کرد ـ و مادامیکه بیرون شده[5] ، کارِ او را طریقِ دیگر ندانند ، طرحِ منازعت نباید افگند و بلکه نقشِ حیلتی بر آورده کعبتینِ خصم را بلطف باز باید مالید ـ و مال را سپرِ ملک و ناموسِ سلطنت باید ساخت که بر بساطِ تجبر[6] و تکبر با آنکه نقشِ خصم می نشیند ، داؤ طلبیدن و نردِ مخاصمت باوجودِ آنکه قوتِ حریف زیاده بود باختن از حکمِ خرد دور است ، و دشمن را برفق[7] و مدارا زود تر مستاصل توان کرد که بجنگ ـ چنانچه آتش با صولت اگر بد رختی آفتد بها نقدر تواند سوخت که بر روی زمینست و آب با لطافت و ملایمت هر درختی که ازان قوی تر و بزرگتر باشد از بیخ بر کند ـ

و هر آینه هر که بی تامل و اضطرار در مقامِ انتقامِ خصم درآمده داعیهٔ محار به کند ، بر گذرگاهِ سیل خوابیده ، بر رویِ آبِ روان خشت زده باشد چه [fol. 23 a] بر قوتِ خود اعتماد کردن و بزور و شجاعتِ خود مغرور شدن از عقل دورست - و لیکن مراعات جانبِ حزم را بدان مقدار واجب باید دانست که کارِ خود را از پیش ببرند[8] و دران باب بمرتبهٔ افراط نباید رسانید که نفسِ خود را خوار کرده دلیری دشمن بیفزاید و ابوابِ چاره اندیشی را بر روی خود بسته باشند ـ و اگر چنانچه ملاحظه نمایند که دشمن قصدِ جانِ ایشان دارد ، درین حال لابد بحکمِ غیرت و بمقتضای حمیت قرارِ مقابله و مقاتله بخود داده ، دل در عنایتِ بی غایتِ[9] مسبب‌الاسباب بندند ، و دل از جان برداشته در میدانِ مبارزت در آیند ـ و[10] تا ممکن و مقدور بوده باشد کوشش نمایند که اگر سعی و کوشش[11] فرو گذارند در خونِ خود سعی کرده باشند و چون بکوشند حال از دو

---

1. *Ibid.*, omits که
2. *Ibid.*, جناجه
3. *O* : تلطف
4. *Ibid.*, باشد
5. *O* : شد
6. *K* : تجر
7. *O* : بروفق
8. *K* : برند
9. *O* : بی علت
10. *Ibid.*, omits و
11. *K* : و سعی کوشش

بیرون نخواہد بود : اگر فیروز[1] آمدند ، خود نامِ مردی بر صفحهٔ روزگار خواہند گذاشت و اگر کاری از پیش نرود باری بعدم مردی[2] و حمیت موصوف نخواہند شد ـ

و چون [fol. 23b] حق سبحانهٗ و تعالی مردمِ شجاع را دوست میدارد ، و حافظ و ناصرِ ایشانست ، بیشتر آن بوده است که ہر کس از روی مردی و مردانگی قدم در میدانِ مبارزت گذاشته دل از جان برداشته است[3] ، با شاہدِ مراد ہم آغوش شده قرینِ فتح و فیروزی گردیده است ، چه جلادت[4] و شجاعت دندانِ طمعِ دشمن را برمیکند و ترس و بد دلی خصم را دلیر میگرداند ـ و بمصدوقه کم من فئة قلیلة غلبت فئة[5] کثیرة باذن الله[6] ، بسیار اقل بر اکثر ظفر یافته و بسیار ضعیف قوی را شکسته است چنانچه نی ہر چند بزرگ و قوی بود به چوبِ باریکی شکسته شود و کلنک ہر چند بزرگ جثه و قوی ہیکل باشد بچنگالِ بازِ ضعیف گرفتار آید ـ

---

1. *Ibid.*, فروز 2. *Ibid.*, omits مردی و
3. *Ibid.*, omits است 4. *K* : حلاوت
5. *O* : فیه 6. *Qur'ān* 2 : 249

فصل پنجم

در عمل نکردن بسخن صاحب غرض ، و ساعی و نمام[1] را در مجلس راه ندادن

شهریاری که فرق دولت او سزاوار تاج سرافرازی و خنصر[2] سعادت او شایسته خاتم جهانداری باشد ، [fol. 24 a] او را باید دانست که با کدام طایفه مجالست[3] باید ورزید و سخن ایشانرا[4] که از روی دولتخواهی و موافق صلاح دولت گویند بسمع رضا اصغاء باید کرد - و از کدام جماعت اجتناب نموده ایشانرا راه سخن نباید داد ، چه از ملازمان عتبهٔ سلطنت اندک جمعی باشند که کمر خدمت بر میان جان بسته در نیکنامی دنیی و نجات عقبی صاحب خود سعی نمایند ، بلکه اغلب ایشان برای جر منافع یا دفع[5] مکاره از خود طریق ملازمت مسلوک دارند - و چون مدار مهم ایشان بر طمع است جمعی بجهت کم و بیش عزت و منصب بر یکدیگر حسد برند و چون حقد و حسد درمیان ایشان پدید آید انواع حیلها انگیخته صورتهای غیر واقع بعرض رسانند -

و اگر این پادشاه از حلیهٔ[6] احتیاط عاری بوده ، سخن ایشانرا بسمع رضا اصغاء نماید[7] و بتفحص حالات و تحقیق آن التفات نکنند ، انواع خلل و ضرر تولد کرده ، اصناف فساد مترتب[8] [fol. 24 b] گردد[9] - اما چون این پادشاه بیدار دل هوشمند بوده بغور مهات برسد و تفتیش کلیات و جزویات[10] نموده ، فروغ راستی را از تیرگی دروغ امتیاز کند و صدق و کذب هر سخن را معلوم خود نماید ، هم در دنیا اساس دولت او از خلل ایمن باشد و هم در عقبی بدولت نجات و رفعت درجات رسد و اگر تحقیق صدق و کذب نا کرده ، سعایت این در حق آن و غمازی آن در بارهٔ این استماع نماید ، نه[11] بر پادشاه و نه بارکان دولت او اعتماد توان کرد ، جهت آنکه هر گاه خواهند مخلصی را در معرض تهمت توانند در آورد - بیگناهان در گرداب فنا گرفتار مانند و مجرمان بر ساحل نجات بسلامت[12] و ایمنی گذرانند و نتیجه این[13] کار این خواهد بود که حاضران از قبول

———

1. *K.*; تمام 2. *Ibid*, خضر
3. *Ibid.*, محالست 4. *Ibid.*, omits را
5. *Ibid.*, حلب 6. *Ibid.*, حیله 7. *Ibid.*, نمایند
8. *Ibid.*, مرتت 9. *Ibid.*, omits گردد 10. *Ibid.*, جزئیات
11. *Ibid.*, omits نه 12. *Ibid.*, omits بسلامت 13. *Ibid.*, omits این

عمل امتناع نموده غایبان از خدمت تقاعد نمایند و هزار خلل در ارکانِ دولت راه یافته بزودی اساسِ سلطنت انهدام [fol, 25 a] یابد و بزرگان گفته اند پنج طایفه را در مجلس راه نه باید داد -

اول : حسود که زهرِ حسد را بهیچ تریاق علاج نتوان کرد - و حقد و[1] حسد اذلِ صفات و خوار ترین خصایل است و حسد را از نتایجِ جهل گرفته اند ، چه حسود همیشه از راحتِ دیگران در مشقت است - و هر کس پای نشاط بر زمین می نهد ، او دستِ حسرت بر سر میزند -

دویم[2] : بخیل و ممسک که مردودِ[3] خلایق اند - و چنانچه سخا پوشنده عیبها ست بخل و امساک نیز پوشنده هنرها ست[4] -

سیوم : مردمِ بسیار گوی که بیهده‌گوی باشند و در سخنِ ایشان سهو و غلط بسیار بود -

چهارم : مردمِ غدار حق ناشناس که حقوقِ نعمت را نشناخته شکرِ منعم را بکفران مبدل سازند -

پنجم : ساعی و نمام[5] که ایشان فتنه انگیزند و عاقبتِ کارِ ایشان بغایت وخیم است - و چون ایشان در مجلس راه یافتند بحیلهٔ تمام جالِ یقین را بحجابِ کذب پوشانند و بسخنانِ[6] [fol. 25 b] فریب آمیز بادشاه را از طریقِ مروت منحرف ساخته به بیوفائی و بد عهدی موسوم گردانند و این معنی سوجبِ خرابی رکنِ دولت و شکست پایهٔ سلطنتِ او شود -

پس عقلِ دور اندیش و رای عالم آرای را که شرفِ جوهرِ آدمی بصفای خردِ ارجمند است ، در هر[7] صورت که پیش آمد و هر حادثه که روی[8] نماید ، حاکمی عادل و ممیزی کامل باید شناخت - و تفحص و استکشاف را[9] از لوازم دانسته احتیاط و استفسار بر وجهِ کلی بجای باید آورد و آنچه بدیشان رسد تفکری نموده ، توسنِ غضب را بلگامِ شکیبائی از سرکشی منع باید کرد و تاریکی آن شبهت را بروشنایی عقل مرتفع ساخته گوشِ[10] استماع بسعایتِ هیچ ساعی نباید

---

1. *Ibid..* omits و 2. *Ibid.,* دوم 3. *Ibid.,* هر دو
4. *Ibid..* omits هنر هاست 5. *Ibid.,* تمام 6. *Ibid.,* omits به
7. *O* omits هر 8. *K* : روح 9. *Ibid.,* omits را 10. *O* : کوس

کشاد و در معایبِ شخصی سخنی که گویند قبول نکرده در بدگویی کسان از اندک و بسیارِ هر سخن که بعرض رسد آنرا تاویل باید کرد و راهِ سخن دیگران را باید بست ـ و تا ببرهانی باهر و دلیلی ظاهر مشاهده [fol. 26 a] نرود ، ترهاتِ اربابِ غرض[1] را نباید شنید و بر قولِ ایشان عمل نباید[2] کرد و[3] چون معلوم کنند که خالی از غرض و ریاست ، بسرحدِ قبول باید رسانید ـ

و باید که چون کسی را بتقربِ خود سرافرازی دهند ، سخنِ دیگران در بابِ شکستِ او بعزِ قبول نرسانند که نزدِ[4] پادشاهی هر که مقرب شد هر آینه محسودِ اکفا و اقران خواهد گشت و جمعی بر[5] او حسد خواهند برد ـ و چون اساسِ عنایتِ سلطان در بارهٔ او محکم بینند ، بلطایف‌الحیل در نقصِ حرمتش کوشیده از روی دولتخواهی سخنانِ فریبنده مکر آمیز بعرض رسانند ، تاوقتیکه مزاجِ سلطانرا بروی متغیر کرده درین ضمن مقصودِ ایشان بحصول پیوندد و چون راهِ این معنی یافتند اکثر ارکانِ دولت او را منکوب و مخذول ساخته از اینجهت خللِ کلی بپادشاه سرایت کند و خاتمتِ کار بفساد انجامد و دفترِ نشاط و بهجتِ او بر طاقچه عدم آفتد ، بلکه چون این صفت [fol. 26 b] از کسی مشاهده کنند ، هر چند زود تر[6] آتشِ سعایتِ[7] او را بآبِ شمشیر فرونشانند تا دودِ آن عرصهٔ عالم را تیره و چشمِ روزگار را خیره نسازد ـ و اگرچه علمای دین و عارفانِ معارفِ حق الیقین در فضیلتِ عفو و منقبتِ[8] احسان مبالغها کرده اند ـ اما درین امورکه اثرِ آن در فسادِ عالم و ضررِ آن در نهادِ بنی آدم شایع باشد ، عقوبت بمراتب از عفو اولیست ـ و در اینجا عفو و اغماض را مجال نباید داد و تنبیه و تادیبِ مفسدانرا از لوازم باید شناخت ـ

بیت[9]

هر آنکس[10] است که بآزارِ خلق فرماید عدوی مملکتست آن به کشتنش فرمای

---

1. *K* : عرض 2. *Ibid.*, نشاید
3. *Ibid.*, adds : ورای سخن 4. *Ibid.*, نرود 5. *Ibid.*, برو
6. *Ibid.*, تردد تر 7. *Ibid.*, شعایب 8. *Ibid.*, منقب
9. *O* : نظم 10. *Ibid.*, هر انکست

فصل ششم

در تربیتِ ملازمان

و این فصل منقسم[1] بر دو قسم است - **قسمِ اول** : در تربیتِ پادشاهان ملازمانرا - **قسمِ دویم** : در آدابِ خدمت ملوک که چون تقربِ خدمتِ ایشان بهم رسد بچه عنوان سلوک باید کرد -

قسم اول : [fol. 27 a] در تربیتِ[2] پادشاهان ملازمانرا - بدانکه سلاطین و ملوک را از ارکانِ دولت و اعیانِ حضرت و سایر ملازمان گریز نیست و حاجتِ پادشاهان بکافیانِ ناصح و عاملانِ امین[3] که استحقاقِ محرمیتِ[4] اسرار و استعداد و استقلال[5] در مهمات داشته باشند ، خود مقرر است - و گفته اند که قصرِ سلطنت را چهار قایمه است که اگر یکی نباشد اساسِ مهمات استحکام نیابد -

اول : امرای عظام که اصحابِ سیف اند و اطرافِ مملکت را محافظت کرده شرِ دشمنانرا از شاه و رعیت باز دارند و ایشان رکنِ[6] دولت و اساسِ سلطنت باشند -

دویم : وزراء کافی کفایت و عمالِ صاحبِ دیانت که ایشان پیرایهٔ ملک و سببِ استحکامِ بنای سلطنت و انتظامِ امورِ مملکت اند - و مهمِ والی مملکت بی اربابِ قلم متمشی نشود[7] و بلکه بچند وجه اینجاعت را بر اصحابِ سیف تفوقست[8] : یکی[9] آنکه شمشیر دشمنانرا [fol. 27 b] بکار آید نه دوستانرا ، و قلم هم برای نفعِ دوستان بکار آید و هم برای دفعِ دشمنان - و کاری که بقلم توان پرداخت به شمشیر نتوان ساخت - **دویم** : آنکه اصحابِ سیف را هوسِ ملک داری در سر پدید آید و از اهلِ قلم هرگز این حرکت در وجود نیاید - **سیم**[10] : آنکه اصحابِ سیف خزانه را تهی سازند و اربابِ قلم خزانه را پر کنند و محلِ دخل عزیز تر از محلِ خرج باشد -

هر آینه هر پادشاه که زمامِ مصالح و مهماتِ خود را بوزیری دانای[11] هوشمندِ نیک سیرت ، بی طمع ، بلند همت ، متدین سپارد ، هرگز دستِ ناکامی بدامنِ اقبالِ او نرسد و پای حوادث گردِ ساحتِ سلطنتِ او نگردد - که[12] اگر بر خلافِ این

---

1. *K* : منقسم است   2. *Ibid.*, ترتب   3. *Ibid.*, آمین   4. *Ibid.*, محرمست
5. *Ibid.*, استقبال   6. *Ibid.*, برکن   7. *Ibid.*, نگردد and omits the following و   8. *Ibid.*, تعولست   9. *Ibid.*, اول   10. *Ibid.*, سیو دویم
11. *Ibid.*, داناء   12. *Ibid.*, چه

بود ، وزیرِ بد نیت ، ناپاک طنیت در مهمات مدخل نماید - هر چند پادشاه بذاتِ خویش عادل وکم آزار و نیکوکار بود ، منافع عدل و رافتِ او از رعایا و مردم منقطع [fol. 28 a] گشته ، از خوفِ او قصه پر غصه مظلومان بعرض نرسد - چنانچه آبِ شیرینِ صافی که در آن[1] صورتِ نهنگی معاینه بیند[2] ، هیچ تشنه هر چند بغایت متعطش باشد نه دست بران تواند کشاد و نه پای در آن[3] تواند نهاد -

سیم[4] : حاکمی از جانبِ سلطان که تفحصِ احوالِ خلایق نموده ، دادِ ضعیف از قوی بستاند و اہلِ فسق و فجور را مخذول و مقهور گرداند -

چهارم : صاحب خبرانِ امین که پیوسته احوالِ مملکت و اعمالِ عمال و حالاتِ رعیت را معلوم نموده ، خللی از شایبهٔ غرض و ریا بخدمتِ سلطان عرض کنند که چون خبرِ مملکت و ولایت از پادشاه پوشیده گردد ، از دوست و دشمن و نیک و بد غافل بوده هر که هر چه خواهد بکند ، و چون او بیخبر باشد از اطراف و جوانب انواع فتنها برخاسته[5] ، ازین سبب بنای سلطنت متزلزل گردد - بس جهاندار آن باشد که گروهی را که بکمال خرد و صلاح و هنر [fol. 28 b] و عفاف و امانت و دیانت و تقوی و حق گذاری و هوا خواهی آراسته بوده ، از اقران باین صفات ممتاز باشد[6] ، تربیت[7] نموده - حیثیت آنکه هر یک بچکار آیند ، و هر کدام چه عمل را شایند حاصل کنند ، و فرد فرد را فرا خورِ حال و اندازه رای و شجاعت و مقدارِ[8] عقل و کیاست و کفایت بکاری نامزد فرمایند -

و یک کس را دو عمل ندهند که دو[9] عمل بر مراد ساخته و پرداخته نگردد که از هر[10] فردی کاری آید و هر مردی عملی را شاید - و خود تفحصِ احوال و اشغالی که بعمال و امینان[11] تفویض میفرمایند ، بجای آورده معلوم کنند که از مباشرانِ عمال[12] کدام رعیت پرور و[13] متدین است وکدام جفا گستر و خاین - او را که بصفتِ رعیت پروری و امانت موصوف بوده[14] از عهدهٔ مهمی که بدو مفوض است بر وجهی که باید و شاید بیرون آید ، نوازش فرموده دران شغل

---

1. *O* : درو 2. *Ibid.*, بینند 3. *K* : بران 4, *Ibid.*, سیوم
5. *O* : برخواسته 6. *K* : باشند 7. *Ibid.*, ترتیب
8. *Ibid.*, omits مقدار 9. *O* omits دو 10. *K* : هرد
11. *Ibid*, بعمال ماهنا 12. *O* & *K* : اعمال
13. *K* omits و 14. *Ibid.*, بود

دستِ قوی دارد - و آنکه غمِ زیردستان نمیخورد و در لوازمِ [fol. 29 a] خدمتِ خود تهاون مینماید و خیانت[1] را از دست نداده بد نفسی را شعار و دثار خود می سازد ، نامش از جریدهٔ[2] عمل محو کرده در دفترِ عزل[3] ثبت نماید که اساسِ ستم را ویران[4] ساختن و اهلِ خیانت را گو شمال دادن موافق رضای خالق و ملایمِ طبع خلایق است - و نیکوئی با بد نفسان مشابه[5] بدی است با نیکوان[6] و زنده گذاشتنِ ستمکاران برابرِ کشتن پرهیزگاران -

وگفته اندکه اساسِ تربیتِ ملازمانرا بلطف و قهر هر دو باید نهاد - بقهر بگیرند تا مردم دلیر نشوند و بلطف بگذارند تا ملازمان نا آمید نشوند و لطف بر وجهی باید که سمتِ ضعف نداشته باشد و عنف چنان شاید که از وصمتِ ظلم خالی بود تا نه مخلصان از عنایتِ بیکرانه نا آمید باشند و نه مفسدان از بیمِ سیاست قدم در وادی جرأت نهند - و هر یک را در تربیت و تقویت بمرتبهٔ خاص نگهداشته دیگریرا [fol. 29 b] با او شریک و سهیم نسازند تا میانِ ملازمان حقد و حسد پیدا نشود ، بلکه همه را بر دوستی و موافقتِ یکدیگر ترغیب نموده از مخالفت منع نمایند که موافقت و مخالصتِ ایشان دخل[7] عظیم دارد و سخنِ هیچکدام را در بارهٔ یکدیگر که از روی رشک و حسد گویند بسمع رضا اصغا ننمایند[8] -

و نگذارندکه مردمِ نا اهلِ بدگوهر[9] با مردمِ اصیلِ پاک طینتِ[10] خردمند در مقامِ برابری در آیند[11] - و[12] نگاهداشتِ این مرتبه را در قوانینِ سلطنت و مراسمِ جهانداری اصلی معتبر دانند که اگر تفاوتِ مراتب از میان برخیزد و اراذل با اوساط و اوساط با اشراف لافِ همسری زنند ، هیبتِ جهانداری را زیان دارد و خللی کلی در ارکانِ مملکت پدید آید - و ازینجهته سلوکِ سابقه نگذاشتندی که مردمِ فرومایه بد اصل علمِ خط آموخته ، مسایلِ استیفاء و قانونِ سیاق بدانند - زیرا که چون این رسم استمرار یابد و اربابِ [fol. 30 a] حرفت در معرضِ اصحابِ دولت در آیند ، هر آینه مضرت این شایع گشته ، اسبابِ معیشتِ خاص و عام خلل پذیر شود -

---

1. *Ibid.*, جنایت 2. *Ibid.*, جرید 3. *Ibid.*, غضب 4. *Ibid.*, ویرا
5. *Ibid.*, مشابه 6. *Ibid.*, نیکان 7. *Ibid.*, دخلی 8. *Ibid.*, نمایند
9. *O* : adds بد گوهر خود را 10. *K* : طبیب 11. *O* : برابری آورد
12. *K* omits و

و چون خدمتگاران[1] کافی و ملازمان کاردان زیب و زینت بارگاه ملوک اند و زینت خدمتگاران سلوک عقل وکفایت است و زیب این طایفه دانش و درایت ، پادشاهانرا باید که نظر بر[2] محاسن اخلاق و متانت عقل و اصابت رای و کیاست و کاردانی و امانت و دیانت و اخلاص و هوا خواهی ملازمان و ارکان دولت کرده ، سزاوار تربیت[3] جمعی را دانند که عز اصالت با شرف فضیلت و امانت و دیانت جمع کرده باشند - و چون کسی را خواهند تربیت[4] کنند باید که اول نقود احوال او را بر محک آزمایش و امتحان زده ، عیار رای و دانش و عقل و درایت و اخلاص او را معلوم کنند و این سه صفت را[5] درو ملاحظه نمایند -

اول : امانت در فعل ، که چون مجاوران عتبه سلطنت بصفت [fol. 30b] امانت موصوف باشند ، هم مبانی سلطنت استحکام دارد و هم خلایق از ضرر ایشان ایمن اند که اگر چهرهٔ حال ایشان بخال خیانت سیاه بود و سخن ایشان نزد سلطان بدرجهٔ کمال رسیده باشد ، شاید[6] که بیگناهی[7] را در معرض بلیه افگنند -

دویم : راستی در قول ، که هیچ عیبی عظیم تر از دروغ نیست و هیچ چیز بدتر از دروغ[8] گفتن نه - و اگر کسی را همه فضایل جمع گردد[9] ، چون دروغ گویی بود اعتماد را نشاید - و هر کس شمشیر زبانش جوهر صدق نداشته باشد ، در نظر مردم او را شکوهی نباشد -

سیم : اصل پاک و همت عالی ، که فرو مایه و بی همت قدر انعام و اکرام نشناسد و پادشاه را از منهاج سخاوت منحرف ساخته نگذارد که هیچکس فیضی و کرامتی میرسانیده باشد و بزرگان گفته اند که هر که دراصل نسیب نیست ، امید را درو هیچ[10] نصیب نیست - و چون باین صفت موصوف بوده بحلیهٔ[11] فضایل متحلی و از شیمهٔ رذایل خالی [fol. 31a] آفتد و عفاف موروث و صلاح مکتسب را با یک دیگر جمع کرده از بوتهٔ امتحان بنوعی که تقریر آفتاد ملخص و بیغش بیرون[12] آید ، بنظر[13] تربیت در وی نظر کرده ، در تربیت او و تربیت مصالح نگاهدارند و بتدریج او را بمراتب تقرب و مدارج تمکن رسانند تا حرمت او در چشمها و

---

1. *O* adds خدمتگاران کاران　　2. *K* : بذ

3. *Ibid.*, ترتیب　4. *Ibid.*, ترتیب　5. *Ibid.*, omits را

6. *Ibid* , omits شاید که　7. *Ibid.*, نیکنامی　8- *Ibid.*, omits دروغ

9. *Ibid.*, جمع کرد و　10. *Ibid.*, omits هیچ　11. *Ibid.*, بحیله

12. *Ibid.*, آمد　13. *O* omits بنظر

هیبتِ او در دلها متمکن گردد -

و حکماء گفته اند که پادشاه در تربیتِ ملازمان چون طبیبِ حاذق می باید که تا اول از[1] حالِ بیمار و کیفیتِ علت و اسباب و علاماتِ[2] او استکشافی تمام و استفساری شافی ننماید ، در معالجت و مداورت[3] شروع نکند - همچنین پادشاهان نیز باید که بعد از تعرفِ حالِ خدمتگاران ، آغازِ تربیت کرده آسان بر کسی اعتماد نکنند[4] - و مردمِ عاقلِ فرزانه طلبیده ، کسانی را که در کارها غافل و از هنرها عاطل باشند بر مردمانِ فاضلِ هنرمند ترجیح ندهند و منصبِ خرد مندان را به بیخردان تفویض نکنند که حلیهٔ سر به پای بستن و پیرایهٔ پای بسر آویختن ست و هر جا که اهلِ هنر ضایع [fol. 31 b] مانند و اربابِ جهل و سفاهت زمامِ اختیار بدست گیرند ، خللِ کلی در ارکانِ سلطنت راه یافته شامتِ آن حال بر سپاه و رعیت برسد -

نظم[5]

[به] همای گو مفگن سایهٔ شرف هرگز
دران دیار که طوطی کم از زغن[6] باشد

و آن را که جوهرِ اصلی دارد لائقِ تربیت دانسته از تربیتِ بدگوهرِ بداصل اجتناب نمایند که هر سنگی جوهر نگردد و هر خونی مشکِ اذفر نشود - و آن را که خستِ ذات و دناءتِ طبیعت و خبثِ باطن بود ملاحظهٔ امانت و رعایتِ دیانت نکند - و چون صفتِ امانت و دیانت که اصل اللبابست از میانه مرتفع شد هر عیبی که در حیز امکان داخل است ازو توقع توان[7] کرد ، چه از کج مزاج بهیچگونه راستی نیاید و بد اصلِ زشت سیرت بتکلف ستوده خوی و پا کیزه خصلت نشود - کل اناء یتر شح بما فیه -

و گفته اند که نفسِ خسیس را پروردن آبروی[8] خود بردن و سر رشتهٔ کارِ خود کم کردن ست و در تهذیب [fol. 32 a] و تربیتِ چنین کسان سعی نمودن

———

1. *Ibid.*, omits از حال 2. *K* : علامة
3. *O & K* : مداوست 4. *O* : نکند 5. *K* omits نظم
6. *Ibid.*, adds بوده باشد 7. *Ibid.*, چنان 8. *K* adds ابروی آبروی

همچنان باشدکه شمشیر برسنگ آزمودن ، و از زهر ہلا ہل خاصیت ِ تریاق ِ فاروق طلب کردن ـ

قطعه[1]

هرکه دراصل بد گهر آفتاد هیچ نیکی ازان مدار آمید
زانکه هرگز بجهد نتوان ساخت از کلاغ ِ سیاه باز ِ سفید

اما ایشان را هم یکباره از عاطفت ِ خود چنان محروم نباید[2] گردانید که نا آمید شده ترک ِ ملازمت گیرند و بجانب ِ دشمن میل کنند ، بلکه باید همیشه میان ِ[3] خوف و رجا روزگار ِ ایشان گذشته ، سهم ِ ایشان بوعده و وعید و بیم و آمید باشد ـ چنانچه توانگری ایشان را مستقل[4] گرداند و آن سبب ِ طغیان و عصیان شود ، نا آمیدی نیز ایشان را دلیر سازد و این سبب ِ شکست ِ ملوک گردد ـ

بیت[5]

نوسید دلیر باشد و چیره[6] زبان کاری[7] مکن ای دوست که نوسید شوم

و نیز باید که زیردستان را از پیش ِ نظر ِ عاطفت دور ندارند که چنانچه بارکان ِ دولت و اعیان ِ حضرت [fol. 32 b] درکفایت ِ مهات احتیاج می آفتد ، یمکن که بدرگاه ِ ایشان مهمی حادث شودکه بمدد ِ زیردستان باتمام رسد ـ

مصرع : کاندرین راه چو طاؤوس بکار[8] است مگس ـ

کاری که از سوزن ِ ضعیف آید ، نیزهٔ سرافراز در ترتیب ِ[9] آن مقصر است و مهمیکه قلمتراش ِ نحیف سازد ، شمشیر ِ آبدار در اتمام ِ آن متحیر ـ و هیچ خدمتگار هر چند بیقدر و بیمقدار باشد ، از جذب ِ منفعتی و دفع مضرتی خالی نیست ـ چه چوب ِ خشک که بخروارها در رهگذارها آفتاده باشد ، امکان دارد که بروزی[10] بکار آید و اگر هیچ را نمی[11] شاید ازان خلال توان ساخت ـ

---

1. *Ibid.*, omits قطعه 2. *Ibid.*, نیامد 3. *Ibid.*, درمیان
4. I*bid.*, مغرور 5. *Ibid.*, نیت 6. *Ibid.*, جیره
7. *O* : ای دوست چنان مکن که 8. *K* : بشکار 9. *O* : تربیت
10, *O & K* : بروزنی 11. *K :* omits می

بیت

گر دستهٔ گل نیاید از ما	هم هیزمِ دیگ را بشائیم

گفته اند که مرتبهٔ سلطنت مشابه[1] رتبهٔ حسن و جمال ست ، چنانچه محبوبِ دلآویز را هر چند[2] عاشق بیشتر است ، حسنِ او را جلوتِ[3] ظهور زیادت بود[4] - سلاطین را نیز هر چند ملازم بیشتر باشد ، میلِ ایشان بر زیادتی خدم و حشم بیشتر بود [fol. 33 a] پس ایشان را باید که با امراء و ارکانِ دولت و سرانِ سپاه و ملازمانِ درگاه طریقِ عنایت و شفقت مسلوک داشته روز بروز در ازدیادِ ایشان میکو شیده باشند -

و چون کسی را تربیت[5] کنند بی سببِ کلی او را خوار نسازند و هر کرا بردارند بی آنکه امری عظیم ازو حادث شود[6] از نظر نیندازند که زود برداشتن و زود افگندن سطوتِ سلطنت را زیان دارد و بمجرد گمان ملازمان و نزدیکانِ خود را دور نگردانند - و تا جمالِ یقین از پسِ پردهٔ گمان روی ننماید در تضیع حقوقِ ایشان سعی ننمایند و بمجرد شنیدنِ سخنی از جا نرفته ، تا بدلیلِ روشن و برهانی ساطع[7] بر حقیقتِ مهمی اطلاع نیابند ، هیچ[8] حکمی[9] به امضا نرسانند که تیشه بر پای خود زدنست و از طریقِ مروت و منهاجِ حقیقت دور شدن - و بعد ازان که سخنِ اهلِ غرض در معرضِ قبول آفتاد و عملِ نا پسندیده در وجود آمد ، هر چند سخن چینِ صاحبِ غرض را بر وجهی [fol. 33 b] گو شمال دهند که عبرتِ دیگران شود ، اما خانهٔ عقلِ خود را خراب کرده باشند و پشیمانی[10] سود ندهد ، چه بهمه وقت چاکری که از عهدهٔ کفایتِ مهمات[11] بیرون آید نتوان یافت و ملازمی که محلِ اعتماد و لائقِ تربیت باشد بدست نتوان آورد - و چنانچه سخنِ دیگران را در بارهٔ او بسمعِ رضا اصغا نمی فرمایند ، باید که بسخنِ او نیز بدیگران استخفاف روا ندارند تا دیگر ملازمان و دولتخواهان از ملازمتش متنفر نشوند[12] و منافع خدمت و فوایدِ نصیحتِ ایشان منقطع نگردد ، چه ازین صورت آفتهای بزرگ بظهور رسد -

---

1. *Ibid.*, مشابه 2. *O* omits هر چند 3. *Ibid.*, omits جلوت
4. *K*: شود 5. *Ibid.*, ترتب 6. *O*: نشود 7. *K*: مبرهن
8. *Ibid.*, به هیچ 9. *Ibid.*, حکمی را 10 *O* adds پشیمانی را
11. *K* omits مهمات 12. *O*: نشده ; and omits the following و

که گفته اند آفتِ ملک و خطرِ سلطنت[1] یکی ازین سه[2] چهار چیز باشد ـ

اول : نیک خواهان را از خود محروم گردانیدن و اهلِ رای و تجربه را خوار داشتن ـ

دویم : هوا و هوس ، و آن مولع بودن است بزنان[3] و راغب بودن بشکار و مشغول شدن[4] بشراب و میل نمودن بلهو و لعب ـ [fol. 34 a]

سیم : تند خویی که افراط بودن درخشم[5] راندن و مبالغه در عقوبت و سیاست ـ

چهارم : جهل ، و آنچنان باشد که در موضع صلح بجنگ گرایند[6] و در محلِ جنگ بصلح میل نمایند و در وقتِ ملاطفت مجادلت نمایند ـ و آنجا که[7] سدِ قهر باید بست درِ لطف بکشایند ـ

پس باید که ملازمانرا باندک جریمه در معرضِ عتاب و خطاب در نیاورند که همواره سلاطین بآبِ[8] عفو و مرحمت ، نقشِ جرایم از جرایدِ احوالِ اصاغر فرو شسته اند و از روی شفقت دامنِ اغماض بر بی ادبی و جسارتِ ایشان پوشیده و چون از مقربان و ملازمان جنایتی بظهور رسد و بعفوِ ایشان مستظهر شوند ، دیگر باره از شربتِ عنایت سیراب گردانیده ، شرمندهٔ تفقدِ خود سازند که این شرمندگی ایشانرا بد تر [fol. 34 b] از انواعِ سیاست است ـ

بیت[9]

چوب را آب فرو [می] نبرد حکمت چیست
شرمش آید ز فرو بردنِ پروردهٔ خویش

و اگر احیاناً کسی را موردِ عتاب و خطاب فرمایند ، بزودی مشمولِ عواطف نسازند و هرگز حکمِ بیهوده نفرسوده[10] ، هر مهمی که بدان امر کنند و سخنی که بر زبانِ ایشان جاری شود ، بنقیضِ آن تا ممکن باشد تکلم نکنند که جمیعِ اینها محمول بر خفت است ـ و اگر میانِ خشم و لطفِ ایشان مدتی نگذرد اعتباری نداشته باشند[11] ـ

و باید که هر کس را تربیت کنند ، در تربیت[12] و تقرب او زیاده از حد

1. *Ibid.*, خطری ملک 2. *K* omits سه 3. *Ibid.*, بزبان
4. *Ibid.*, omits شدن 5. *Ibid.*, جشم 6. *O* omits گرایند
7. *K* omits که 8. *Ibid.*, باب 9. *Ibid.*, omits بیت
10. *Ibid.*, مفرموده 11. *Ibid.*, باشد 12. *Ibid.*, ترتیب ; and omits وتقرب

مبالغه جایز ندارند - که چون کسی دست ِ خود را در امر و نهی قوی و مطلق دید و زمام ِ حل و عقد ِ جمهور در قبضهٔ اقتدار ِ خود یافت ، مرغ ِ فتنه در آشیانهٔ دماغ ِ او بیضه نهاده ، هوای عصیان از سویدای دل ِ او سر بر خواهد زد و مخرب ِ بنای سلطنت خواهد شد - [fol. 35 a] پس چون یکی از خدمتگاران را بدرجه و حرمت و مال و حشمت مقابل ِ خود رسانند باید که پیش از فوات ِ[1] فرصت چارهٔ این کار بکنند و الا کار بجای رسد که انگشت ِ ندامت بدندان ِ تحیر گزند و سودی ندهد - چه از جمعی که بجان ایمن نتوان بود بخشودن خطاست و ایشان را بزندان ِ کور محبوس ساختن کار ِ عقلاء -

با آنکه دندان را با آدمی مصاحبت ِ دیرین ست ، چون درد گرفت جز بقلع از رنج ِ آن شفا نتوان یافت و طعام که مدد ِ حیوتست ، چون در معده فاسد شد جز بدفع از مضرت ِ آن خلاص نتوان یافت - و[2] انگشت که زینت ِ دست و آلت ِ قبض و بسط است ، اگر مار بران زخمی زند ، بجهته حفظ ِ[3] باقی جثه ببرند و مشقت ِ آنرا عین راحت شمرند - درین باب حکماء گفته اند که مردم سه گروه اند : عاقل ِ کامل ، نیم عاقل و جاهل ِ غافل -

عاقل ِ کامل آنست که دور اندیشی را [fol. 35 b] شعار ِ خود ساخته ، پیوسته اندیشهٔ عاقبت ِ امور میکرده باشد و پیش از ظهور ِ خطر چگونگی آنرا شناخته ، آنچه دیگران در خواتیم ِ کارها دانند ، او در مبادی آن بدیدهٔ عقل ِ دور اندیش دیده ، تدبیر ِ اواخر ِ امور در اوایل بکند[4] و چنین کس پیش از آنکه در گرداب ِ[5] فنا و بلا افتد ، خود را بساحل ِ خلاص تواند رسانید -

و نیم عاقل آنست که چون بلای برسد دل را بر جای داشته حیرت و دهشت بخود راه ندهد و برین کس راه ِ صواب و وجه تدبیر پوشیده نخواهد ماند -

و جاهل غافل آنست که در وقت ِ حدوث ِ واقعه و وقوع ِ حادثه سراسیمه و مضطرب و پریشان حال شده نتواند از ورطهٔ محنت و بلا خلاص شد -

و نیز پادشانرا باید که چون دنیا محل ِ حوادث است و کس نداند که در چه وقت حادثه روی خواهد داد و از کدام طرف فتنه پدید [fol. 36 a] خواهد آمد ،

---

1. *Ibid.*, فوت 2. *O* : ور 3. *Ibid.*, omits حفظ 4. *K* : کنند
5. *Ibid.*, بگرداب

ترتیبِ لشکر[1] را عمده کارها دانسته پیوسته لشکری را آراسته داشته برای حرب آماده و مهیا[2] باشند - و امراء و اعیانِ حضرت و ارکانِ دولت[3] را نیز درین باب تاکید و قدغن نموده هر امیری را فراخورِ منصب و جاگیرِ خود مقرر فرمایند که چه مقدار لشکر نگاهدارد - و سال بسال لشکرِ خود و امراء را[4] عرض دیده ، اهتمام نمایند که جمیع اسلحه و اسباب و ادواتِ حربِ ایشان آماده و مهیا باشد که اگر سلاطین و امراء بجمعِ[5] خزانه و[6] مال مشغول گشته لشکر جمع نکنند ، بوقتِ ضرورت در مانند و دران محل صندوقهای زر فایده نکند - و هر چند انگشتِ تاسف بدندانِ ندامت بگزند[7] سودی ندهد -

قسم دویم : در آدابِ خدمتِ ملوک

بدانکه خدمتِ سلاطین کاری پر خطر و مهمی سخت دشوار است و حکماء پادشاهانرا [fol. 36 b] بکوهِ بلند تشبیه کرده اند که اگرچه دران معدنِ جواهرِ قیمتی ست هم رفتن بران دشوار است و هم مقام گرفتن دران مشکل - و خدمتِ ملوک را نیز بدریا تشبیه کرده اند که بازرگانی[8] که سفرِ دریا اختیار کند[9] ، یا سودِ بسیار بدست آورد یا در غرقابِ هلاکت گرفتار شود - و گفته اند پنج چیز درین جهان بی پنج چیز نباشد : ملازمتِ سلطان بی آفت ، مالِ دنیا بی نخوت ، متابعت[10] بی محنت ، مجالستِ زنان بی بلیت ، مصاحبتِ لئیمان بی مذلت - هیچکس ملازمتِ ملوک اختیار نکند که بسلامت ازان ورطهٔ خونخوار بیرون آید - و هیچکس از خمخانهٔ دنیا جرعه نچشد که سرمست و بی باک نشده سر تجبر از گریبانِ عصیان بیرون نیاورد - و هیچکس در طریقِ هوا و هوس قدم ننهد که در معرضِ محنت[11] نیفتد - و هیچ مرد با زن صحبت نداردکه بانواعِ [fol. 37 a] فتنه مبتلا نشود و هیچکس با مردمِ لئیم شریرِ فتان اختلاط نکند که عاقبت خوار و ذلیل و[12] بیمقدار نشود -

و اربابِ حکمت پادشاهانرا بآتشِ سوزان تشبیه کرده اند که اگرچه بپرتوِ

---

1. *O* : لشکری را 2. *Ibid.*, adds داشته باشند

3. *K* : ارکانِ دولت و اعیانِ حضرت 4. *Ibid.*, omits را

5. *Ibid.*, بجمیع 6. *O* omits و 7. *K* omits بگزند

8. *O* : بازارگانی 9. *Ibid.*, omits کند

10. *Ibid.*, adds متابعت هوا 11. *K* omits محنت 12. *Ibid.*, omits و

عنایت کلبهٔ تاریک_ آمیدواران را روشن می سازند ، ولی بشعلهٔ سیاست نیز خرمن_ سوابق_ خدمتگاران را میسوزند - و خرد_[1] کامل برین متفق است که هر که بآتش نزدیکتر ، ضرر_ او بیشتر - اما جمعی که از دور تماشای نور_ آتش کرده از احراق بیخبر اند ، تصور_ لذتی و گمان_ منفعتی دارند و تقرب_ ملوک را خواهانند و فی الحقیقه نه چنانست - اگر چنانچه ایشان از سیاست_ سلطانی و هول و هیبت_ پادشاهی وقوف یابند بایشان روشن گردد که هزار ساله عنایت با یکساعه سیاست برابر نیست - و حکماء[2] گفته اند بیچاره[3] کسی که در خدمت_ پادشاهان آفتد ، زیرا که زمام_ عهد_ ایشان [fol. 37 b] سخت سست و بنای وفای ایشان بغایت ضعیف است - و همیشه رخسار_ مروت را بآسیب_ جفا خراشیده دارند و سر چشمهٔ فتوت را بخاک_ بد عهدی انباشته سازند - نه اخلاص و یکرنگی نزد_ ایشان حرمتی دارد و نه[4] سابقه خدمت و نه رابطهٔ ملازمت قدری و قیمتی -

گفته اند که صحبت با کسی که قدر_ آن نشناسد و خدمت_ شخصی[5] که قیمت_[6] آن نداند مشابه[7] آنست که کسی بر آمید_ محصول تخم در زمین_ شوره بیفشاند یا بر روی[8] آب_ روان غزلهای تر و تازه نویسد -

بیت[9]

ازین خوان کس نخاید لقمهٔ نان   که سنگی نایدش در زیر_ دندان

و گفته اند که خدمتگار_ ملوک در خوف[10] و خطر و بیم و دهشت همخوابه[11] پلنگ و همخانهٔ[12] شیر می ماند - اگرچه پلنگ خفته و شیر نهفته باشد ، عاقبت آن یکی سر برآرد و این دیگری[13] دهن بکشاید -

شعر[14]

مکن ملازمت_ پادشه ازان ترسم [fol. 38 a]
که همچو صحبت_ سنگ و سبو شود نا گاه

---

1. *Ibid.*, رای 2. *O* : حکماء و گفته 3. *K* : بیچاره که کسی
4. *Ibid.*, omits نه 5. *O* : کسی 6. *Ibid.*, قدر قیمت
7. *K* : مشابه 8. *Ibid.*, بروی 9. *Ibid.*, omits بیت
10. *O* : خدمت 11. *Ibid.*, بهمخوابه 12. *Ibid.*, بهمخانه
13. *K* : دیگر 14. *Ibid.*, بیت

هر که در خدمتِ ملوک بمرتبهٔ تقرب رسد جمله دوستان و دشمنانِ ملک خصم او شوند - دوستان از روی حسد بجهة جاه و منزلت[1] و دشمنان بجهت مناصحتِ وی در مصالح ملک و ملت - و هر گاه اجماع بر عداوت منعقد شد البته ایمن نتوان بود و خوشدل نتوان زیست که[2] اگرچه پای بر فرقِ کیوان نهد سربسلامت نبرد - **والمخلصون علی خطر عظیم** از آنست که اهلِ حقیقت پشت بدیوارِ امن و راحت نهاده اند و روی از دنیی نا پایدار بر تافته[3] عبادتِ خالق را بر خدمتِ مخلوق گزیده اند که در حضرتِ عزت سهو و غلط و غفلت[4] روا نیست و ظلم و ستم جایز نه ، جزای نیکی به بدی و پاداشِ طاعت بعقوبت نبندد[5] - و در احکامِ بادشاهِ پادشاهان از سمتِ عدالت گریز نباشد -

چه اکثر کارهای خلایق بر خلافِ صفتِ خالق [fol. 38b] بانواعِ اختلاف و تفاوت آلوده است ، و از اتفاق و ملاحظهٔ استحقاق بر طرف[6] افتاده ، گاه مجرمانِ لازم العقوبت را جزای کردارِ مخلصانِ صافی طویت ارزانی دارند و گاه ناصحانِ واجب التربیت را بعذابِ ذلتِ خاینان مؤخذ[7] نمایند - کسی باشد که خزاینِ روی زمین بخازنِ شاه سپارد بیک جو منت ندارند و دیگریرا بد شنامی سرِ رفعت با وجِ عزت بر آرند -

بیت[8]

بی نیازی بین و استغنا نگر   خواه مطرب باش و خواهی نوحه گر

پسِ هر کس را تقربِ ملوک حاصل شود ، چون بمیامنِ عواطفِ ایشان بمثابهٔ عزیز محترم[9] و نامی گردیده است که در ظلِ دولت و سایه[10] ملازمتِ ایشان پای افتخار بر فرقِ اکفا و اقران نهاده ، باید که حقوقِ اعطاف و اکرامِ ایشان را نابود ندانسته ، همتِ خود را بر متابعتِ ایشان مقصورگرداند و باخلاص و اعتقاد [fol. 39 a] و دولتخواهی تمام خدمت کرده در هیچ باب مصلحتِ ولی نعمت را فرو نگذارد و اگر او را هزار جان باشد فدای یکساعتِ فراغتِ صاحبِ خود ساخته ، برای آنکه جهتِ مخدومِ خود حق گذاری کند و نام هوا داری بر

---

1. *Ibid.*, omits بجهته جاه و منزلت   2. *O* omits که

3. *K* : پرداخته   4. *Ibid.*, غلت   5. *Ibid.*, ببندد   6. *Ibid.*, بطرف

7. *Ibid.*, مواخذ   8. *Ibid.*, omits بیت

9. *K* & *O* : و محترم   10. *O* : بسبب

جريدهٔ روزگار بگذارد ، خود را در ورطهٔ فنا بيندازد که باوجود اين از حقوق نعمتهای ايشان يکی[1] نگذارده[2] باشد -

و بنای کار خود بر امانت و ديانت و راستی نهاده بشعاع شعلهٔ رشوت ديدهٔ امانت خود را خيره نسازد - و حرص فتنه انگيز و طمع فريبنده را بر عقل راهنما مستولی نساخته کمر طمع نبندد - تا بمضمون **عز من قنع[3] و ذل من طمع** ، لباس عزتش به پلاس مذلت مبدل نشده ، از تيرگی طمع غبار خواری بر ديباچهٔ احوالش ننشيند - و حکماء گفته اند که امانت رکن اعظم ست از خصايل [fol. 39 b] حميده و ديانت اصل محکم است از اخلاق پسنديده - امانت و ديانت را علامت ايمان گرفته اند و امانت صفتی است که مردم خوار را[4] عزيز گرداند و خيانت مردم عزيز را خوار سازد - بس بايد که از جادهٔ راستی بهيچ وجه انحراف نورزيده ، سيرت خود را بر قانونی نگاهدارد که سبب نيکنامی صاحب و آبادانی مملکت و خشنودی خلايق باشد - و راحت و آسايش را بخود حرام کرده جهد کند که هميشه حاضر باشد - و از دروغ گفتن که قبيح ترين افعالست اجتناب نموده در برابر ملک را ستايش نکند که خوش آمد صريحست -

و آداب نصيحت بجای آورده سخن برفق و مدارا گويد[5] و از عنف و درشتی بجانب لطف و نرمی مايل بوده ، جانب تعظيم را رعايت تمام کند - و از جرأت و گستاخی احتراز لازم داند و اگر در قول و فعل بادشاه خللی مشاهده نمايد [fol. 40 a] و يا ملک خواهد که[6] در کاری خوض نمايد که عاقبتی وخيم و خاتمتی مکروه داشته باشد و مضرت او بصاحب عايد شود ، بعبارتی شيرين و رفقی تمام ضرر آنرا باز گفته در تنبيه[7] آن بمدارا[8] بکوشد ، و مثلهای شيرين دلفريب آورده[9] معايب ديگران در اثنای حکايت تقرير کند و آنچه بصواب نزديک باشد باز نموده از سوء[10] عاقبت آن او را بياگاهاند[11] و وجه[12] فساد آنرا روشن ساخته ، تا استقامت در رای و تدبير وی[13] پديد نيايد دست باز ندارد که اگر شرط امانت و نصيحت بجای نياورد[14] او دشمن ملک باشد - و اگر چنانچه کاری کند که

1. *K* omits يکی 2. *Ibid.*, بگذارده 3. *Ibid.*, قع
4. *O* omits را 5. *K* : گويند 6. *Ibid.*, omits خواهد که
7. *Ibid.*, دفع 8. *Ibid.*, بمدا 9. *Ibid.*, omits آورده
10. *O* : سوی عاقبت 11. *K* : نگاهدارد 12. *Ibid.*, omits وجه
13. *Ibid.*, omits وی 14. *Ibid.*, نيارد & omits the following او

بصواب نزدیک و صلاح دران باشد ، آنرا در چشمِ وی آراسته گردانیده فواید و منافع آنرا در نظرِ وی در آورد[1] ، تا شادی او بخوبی و راستی تدبیرِ او[2] بیفزاید -

و بطریقِ ملایمت [fol. 40 b] ظلم را در نظرِ پادشاه نکوهیده ساخته ، عدل را بتعریف و توصیف در دلِ او شیرین کند که اگر چنانچه پادشاه را بر ظلم ترغیب نماید او نیز دران مظلمه شریک باشد و از زنگارِ غرض دلِ خود را تیره نگردانیده جمالِ صواب را مشاهده نموده در نظرِ پادشاه جلوه نماید - و آنچه او را بخاطر رسد که موافقِ صلاحِ دولت بوده باشد بعرض رسانیده ، بهیچوجه طریقِ مناصحت فرو نگذارد - و بر کما هی احوالِ هر کس اطلاع یافته ، حقیقتِ هر یک از ملازمان را معروض دارد ، تا پادشاه اتباع و لواحقِ خود را نیکو شناخته بر اندازهٔ اخلاص و تمیز و رای و تدبیرِ هر یک واقف شده[3] ، هم از خدمتِ ایشان انتفاع گیرد و هم فراخورِ استحقاق هر یک را بنوازد - اما تا بار ها شخصی را نیازموده باشد و وثوق و اعتمادِ تمام بران شخص نداشته [fol. 41 a] باشد ، او را تعریف نکند که بوقتِ آزمایش شرمنده نشود -

و چون تقربِ پادشاهانرا اعتباری نیست و هر عملی را عزلی و هر دولتی را نکبتی در پی هست و در اندک فرصتی رقمِ نا امیدی بر صفحهٔ بختیاری و کامگاری کشیده میشود ، باید که باقتدار و اختیارِ خود[4] مغرور نشده تکیه بر عزت و احترام نکند و از رجوعِ خلق و ترددِ مردم به تنگ نیامده بوقتِ ملاقات با هر کس گره بر پیشانی نزند و[5] بدان مقدار که تواند با مردم نیکویی کرده با زیردستان چنان زندگی کند که خواهد[6] زیردستان با او معاش کنند که فایده تقرب و اختیار بدرگاه سلاطین آنست که فوایدِ احسان بخاص و عام رسانیده ، خورد و بزرگ را شرمندهٔ احسان و نیکویی خود کند[7] - هر که نیکی میکند بخود میکند و هر که[8] [fol. 41 b] خود را باین اخلاق و صفاتی که مذکور شد موصوف ساخت ، خدای

---

1. *Ibid.*, اندازند 2. *Ibid.*, omits تدبیر او 3. *Ibid.*, شد

4. *Ibid.*, خویش 5. *O* omits و

6. *K* omits زیردستان چنان زندگی کند که خواهد

7. *O* : کنند ; followed by a sentence: چه مردم ملازم تقرب و اختیار باشند

8. *Ibid.*, گاه

تعالی خواهد داد او را آنچه در دنیی و عقبی شاید و بکار آید ـ و پادشاه نیز روز بروز در ازدیادِ تقرب[1] و عزتِ او کوشیده پیوسته مایلِ صحبتِ او خواهد بود و بمیامنِ این اخلاق نامِ نیکو و ذکرِ جمیلِ او سالهای سال و قرنهای بیشمار در صفحهٔ روزگار مثبت بوده عند الخالق والخلایق مشکور و مستحسن خواهد بود ـ

نظم[2]

نیک ار کنی بجای تو نیکی کنند باز ور بدکنی بجای تو از بد بتر کنند
امروز هستی از بد و از نیک بی خبر روزی بود که از بد و نیکت خبر کنند[4]

1. *Ibid.*, ازدیاد و تقرب

2. *Ibid.*, بیت 3. *K* omits امروز نیستی ـــ خبر کنند

باب دویم

در نصیحتِ زیردستان و اخوانِ زمان که مشتمل بر چهار فصل است -

فصلِ اول : در مصاحبت و مخالطتِ یاران

بدانکه اکثری از حکماء صحبت را بر خلوت تفضیل داده گفته اندکه صحبتِ نیکو به از وحدتست - و وقتیکه[1] رفیقِ [fol. 42 a] شفیق و یارِ مشفق پیدا نشود ، وحدت به از صحبت - و چون تنهایی کاری صعب و امری دشوار است و آدمی را طرحِ خلوت انداختن و بمصاحبتِ ابنای جنس نپرداختن از قبیلِ محالات - هیچکس را درین عالم از مصاحبی[2] مناسب چاره نباشد[3] و از یارِ موافق گریز نه ، چه دوستی ثمراتِ پسندیده و نتایجِ برگزیده دارد -

و درین کاشانهٔ دنیا هیچ آرزو[4] با صحبتِ یارانِ موافق و دوستانِ مهربان برابر نیست - و هیچ درجه بلند پایه تر[5] ، از مصاحبانِ[6] مشفق نه - و اگر بهم رسد هر چند دوستان بیشتر باشند[7] بهتر ، اگر دوست هزار باشد یکی باید شمرد - و اگر دشمن یکی باشد بسیار باید دانست - لهذا نزدِ[8] هنرمندانِ کاملِ الذات و خردمندانِ ستوده صفات هیچ نقدی گرانمایه تر از وجودِ دوستانِ مخلص و ملاقاتِ یارانِ خالص نیست - و طایفهٔ عقلاء که خلاصهٔ عالمیان [fol. 42 b] و نقاوهٔ آدمیان اند با یکدیگر مصاحبتی افگنند و اساسِ محبتی بنیاد نهند - و آن را از سرِ خلوصِ نیت و صفای طویت به پایان رسانند - و آثارِ منافعش بر صفحاتِ احوالِ هر یک ظاهر گردد و در موافقت و معاضدت هم کمال ، و[9] صدقِ مودت در دولت و نکبت و ادای حقوقِ صحبت هنگامِ نعمت و شدت بجای آورند - و در نوایبِ ایام و حوادثِ زمانه باخلاصِ تمام ایستادگی نمایند تا ببرکتِ معاونتِ یکدیگر بر سریرِ معاشرت و مسندِ کامرانی خوشحال و فارغِ بال متمکن باشند[10] - هر آینه جمعی که سبیکهٔ محبتِ ایشان در دارالضربِ اخلاص بسکهٔ وفاداری آرایش یافته ، نهالِ مودتشان در روضهٔ اختصاص برشحهٔ یکجهتی پرورش

---

1. *Ibid.*, omits که 2. *O* : مصاحب 3. *K* : نیست
4. *Ibid.*, و 5. *Ibid.*, omits تر 6. *Ibid.*, صاحبان
7. *Ibid.*, باشد 8. *O* : تردد 9. *Ibid.*, omits و 10. *K* : ممکن باشد

یافته[1] باشد ، راحتِ روح و مددِ[2] فیض و[3] فتوحند - و در دنیی[4] هیچ شادی چون شرفِ مجالستِ ایشان نتواند[5] [fol. 43 a] بود و هیچ محنتی با فراقِ ایشان برابری نتواند[6] کرد - اما بباید دانست که هر کس دوستی را نشاید -

و حکماء در بابِ دوستی میزانی نهاده گفته اند که دوستی با یکی ازین سه طایفه واجبست - **اول** : اربابِ علم و فضیلت که ببرکتِ صحبتِ ایشان سعادتِ دنیوی و آخروی حاصل شود - **دویم** ، اهلِ مکارمِ اخلاق که خطای دوست را پوشانیده نصیحت از یار دریغ ندارند - **سیم**[7] : جمعی که بی غرض بوده بنای محبت و دوستی بر صدق و اخلاص نهند - و چنانچه دوستی این سه طایفه واجبست احتراز نیز از سه طایفه لازم است -

یکی[8] : فاسق و اهلِ فجور که همتِ ایشان بر مشتهیاتِ نفس مقصور بوده ، صحبتِ ایشان نه سببِ راحتِ دنیی و نه موجبِ رحمتِ آخرت باشد -

دویم[9] : دروغ گویان و اربابِ نفاق که صحبتِ ایشان عذابِ الیم و معاشرت با ایشان بلایی عظیم است [fol. 43 b] که پیوسته با دیگران از تو سخنانِ غیر واقع باز گویند[10] و از دیگران پیغامهای فتنه آمیزِ وحشت انگیز بخلافِ راستی باز نمایند -

سیم[11] : ابلهان و بیخردان که نه در جر منفعت بر ایشان اعتماد توان کرد ، و نه در دفعِ مضرت - و بسیار افتد که آنچه عین خیر و نفع تصور کرده باشند محض شر و ضر افتد و نکته درین که گفته اند :

مصرع : دشمنِ دانا به از نادان دوست

این تواند بود که دشمن چون بحلیهٔ عقل آراسته بود ، دور اندیشی را[12] شعارِ خود ساخته تا فرصت نه بیند زخم نزند ، و از حرکات و سکنات و افعال و اقوالِ او آثارِ انتقام مشاهده کرده خود را محافظت توان کرد - اما دوستی که از دولتِ دانش بی بهره باشد ، هر چند در تدبیرِ مصالح و مهمات مدد نماید[13] مفید نیاید -

---

1. *Ibid.*, بپرورش پذیرفته 2. *Ibid.*, omits مدد 3. *Ibid.*, omits و
4. *Ibid.*, وی 5. *Ibid.*, نتوانند 6. *Ibid.*, نتوانند
7. *Ibid.*, سیوم 8. *Ibid.*, اول 9 *Ibid*, omits دویم
10. *Ibid.*, omits باز گویند 11. *Ibid.*, سیوم
12. *K* omits را 13. *Ibid.*, نمایند

او بتو میرسد ، ہمگی ہمت بر دوستی و محبتِ او مقصور گردانیده شرطِ مخالطت[1] بجای آوری - و سر رشتهٔ اتحاد را انتظام داده دست از دامنِ صحبتِ او بهیچوجه باز نداری ، که حیف باشد بدشواری یاری بدست آوردن و بآسانی از دست دادن -

و ہر که بجهدِ بسیار دوستی آورد و بآسانی از دست بدہد ، از نتائجِ یاری محروم مانده ، دیگر دوستان از وی نا امید شوند و ترکِ مودت او گیرند - باید که چون دوستِ دانای مشفق بهمرسانیده با او قواعدِ محبت استحکام دہی [fol. 48 b] اول در تفحصِ عیوبِ خویش سعی بلیغ بجای آورده ، بعد از طولِ مجالست و موانست ازو استفسارِ عیوبِ خود نمایی و درین مبالغه و الحاحِ تمام بجای آورده ، ہر چند گوید "من از تو عیب نمی بینم" راضی نشوی ، و کراہیت اظهار کرده بر سوال اصرار نمایی - و چون بر عیبِ تو[2] ترا واقف کند ، نهایت محبت دانسته اظهارِ مسرت نمایی و بازالتِ آن عیب مشغول گشته شکرِ آن[3] بر خود واجب دانی - و این معنی را در حقِ خود احسانی شمری و دیگر چنانچه از جانبِ او توقع و چشمداشتِ این مراتب داری ، از جانبِ تو نیز آنچه لازمهٔ وفاداری و دوستداری و یکجهتی است باید که بجای آید -

که گفته اند پنج چیز علامتِ احمقی است : **اول** : توقع دوستی از مردمِ بیوفا[4] و از ایشان[5] رعایتِ حقوقِ یاری طلب[6] نمودن - **دویم** : براحت و تن آسانی دقایقِ علوم دانستن - **سیم** : بدرشتی و تند خویی با زنان عشقبازی کردن - **چهارم** : ثوابِ آخرت بی ریاضت چشم داشتن - **پنجم** : منفعتِ خود در مضرتِ دیگران دانستن [fol. 49 a] - و از جانبین عزیمتِ خلوص در صدقِ نیت و صفای طویت چنان باید که اگر از چشم و زبان که دیده بانِ[7] تن و ترجمانِ دلند خلافی دریابید[8] ، بیک اشارت ہر دو را از ساحلِ وجود بگردابِ عدم افگنید و با دوست ہم[9] دوست و با دشمنِ یکدیگر[10] دشمن باشید[11] - که گفته اند ہر که با دوستِ دشمن محبت ورزد و با دشمنِ دوست در آمیزد او را در اعدادِ اعداء داشتن **لا یتغیر** باشد -

---

1. *O* : مخالفت 2. *Ibid.*, omits تو ; *K* : تواتر 3. *Ibid.*, شپکران

4. *O* : بیوفاداری 5. *Ibid.*, omits از ایشان 6. *Ibid.*, omits طلب

7. *K* : دیدبان 8. *Ibid.*, دریانند 9. *Ibid.*, و بیم 10. *O* : ہم

11. *K* : باشند

و حکما گفته اند که دوستان سه گروهند : دوستِ خالص ، و دوستِ دوست ، و دشمنِ دشمن ـ و دشمنان نیز[1] سه فرقه اند : دشمنِ ظاهر ، و دشمنِ دوست ، و دوستِ دشمن ـ یارِ خود آنکس را باید دانست که یارِ دوستِ تو باشد ـ و دوستِ خود کسی را باید شناخت که در طلبِ رضای یارِ تو میکوشیده باشد ـ هر که بدوستِ تو پیوندد ، دوست داشتن تو نیز او را واجبست ـ اگر همه اغیار بود و هر که از و ببرد ، بریدن تو نیز از وی لازمست ـ اگر همه خویش و تبار باشد (lacuna) [fol. 49 b]

پندِ حکیم محض صوابست و عینِ خیر فرخنده بخت آنکه بسمعِ رضا شنید

---

1. *O* omits نیز

فصل دویم

در مذمتِ بیچیزی و سعی در طلبِ دولت نمودن[1]

بدانکه اهلِ دنیا جویای[2] یکی ازین سه مرتبه باشند ، **اول** : فراخی نعمت و سهولتِ اسبابِ آن و این مطلوبِ جمعی باشد[3] که همتِ ایشان در نوشیدن و پوشیدن و استیفاء لذاتِ نفسانی مصروف باشد - **دویم** : رفعتِ منزلت و ترقی رتبت ، و بزرگی جاه[4]، و این طایفه اهلِ جاه و منصب باشند و بدین دو مرتبه نتوان رسید الا بمال - **سیم** : یافتنِ ثوابِ آخرت و رسیدن بمنازلِ کرامت - و این گروه اهلِ نجات و در جاتند ، و حصولِ این مرتبه نیز بمالِ حلال میسر تواند شد **نعم المال الصالح للرجل الصالح** ، مجملاً مال سرمایهٔ دنیا و آخرت می تواند شد -

و هر چه از مراتبِ جهان کسی خواهد بسببِ مال بدست میتوان آورد - و شخصِ محتاج چنانچه از لذاتِ دنیا بی بهره است ، از درجاتِ [fol. 50 a] آخرت نیز محروم باشد[6]و سوید اینمعنی است ظاهرِ حدیث نبوی که **الفقر سواد الوجه فی الدارین**[5] ، زیرا که شاید در طلبِ روزی بر وجه نا مشروع نماید که موجبِ نکال و وبالِ آنجهانی گردد و[6] چنانچه درین عالم به محنتِ افلاس گرفتار است ، در عقبی نیز بزندانِ شقاوتِ ابدی محبوس باشد - گفته اند که[7] هر که مال ندارد چون مرغِ بی بال و پر است -

مال سرمایهٔ جرأت و پیرایهٔ قدرت و صیقلِ رای و پشتیبانِ قوت است - هر که مال ندارد یار ندارد ، و مردِ تهی دستِ مفلس هرکاری که کند با تمام نرسد و هر آرزو که از سویدای دلِ او سر بر زند بحصول نه پیوندد - چنانکه بزرگان گفته اند هر که برادر ندارد هر جا که افتد غریب باشد - و هر که فرزند ندارد ، نام و[8] ذکرِ او از صفحهٔ[9] روزگار محو شود - و هر که بی چیز بود نه از عمرِ خود تمتع یابد و نه از دوستانِ خود بهره - درویشی ظاهر و احتیاج اصلِ همه بلا هاست ، و واسطه دشمنی خلق و بر دارندهٔ حجابِ حیا و مخرب بنای مروت و مجمع شر و

---

1. *K* : در مذمت و تنگدستی و سعی نمودن در طلبِ دولت
2. *O* : جویان 3. *K* : باشند 4. *Ibid.*, بزرگی و جاه
5. *O* omits و سویداینمعنی — فی الدارین 6. *Ibid.*, omits و
7. *Ibid.*, omits که 8. *K* omits و 9. *Ibid.*, صحیفه

آفت [fol. 50 b] و قاطعِ زور و حمیت و سببِ خواری و مذلت ـ و هر که در دایرهٔ احتیاج پای بسته شد چاره[1] ای ندارد جز اینکه پردهٔ حیا از پیش بردارد ـ و چون رقم **الحیاء من الایمان**[2] از ورقِ حالِ او محو شد ، زندگانیش منغض گردد و به ایذا[3] و آزار مبتلا شود ـ شادی رخت از ساحتِ سینهٔ او برگیرد و لشکرِ غم بر نهادِ[4] خاطرِ او استیلا یابد و[5] شمعِ خردش بی نور بماند ـ و ذهن و کیاست و فهم و فراستش روی بقصور نهد ـ منافع تدبیرِ درست در حق وی نتیجهٔ مضرت دهد ـ باوجودِ امانت در معرضِ تهمت و خیانت آید[6] ـ گمانِ نیکو که در حقِ او مردم را بودی منعکس شود ـ اگر گناه دیگری کند ، جنایت بر او موجه[7] گردد ـ و هر صفتی که توانگر را مدح و ثنا گویند ، مردِ بی چیز را موجبِ[8] طعن و مذمت باشد ـ مثلاً اگر جرأت نماید حمل بر تهور کنند ، و اگر سخاوت ورزد ، اسراف نام کنند ـ و اگر در حلم کوشد عجز و بی غیرتی[9] شمرند ـ و اگر بوقار گراید[10] [fol. 51 a] گرانجانی و کاهلی گویند و اگر زبان آوری و فصاحت ظاهر کند ، بسیار گویی لقب نهند ـ و اگر به مامنِ خموشی گریزد ، نقشِ گرمابه اش[11] گویند ـ و اگر کنجِ خلوت گزیند بدیوانگی نسبت دهند و اگر بخنده رویی و آمیز کاری پیش آید ، از قبیلِ هزل و مسخرگی دانند ـ و اگر در خوردن و پوشیدن تکلفی کند تن پرورش گویند ـ و اگر با جبه و لقمه در سازد منکوب و مفلوکش تصور کنند ـ و اگر در یک مقام ساکن شود خادم[12] و سایه پرورش گویند ـ و اگر عزیمتِ[13] سفر نماید سرگشته ، و آواره گویند و بخت برگشته اش نامند[14] ـ و اگر در مجردی گذراند[15] ، گویند تارکِ سنت است ـ و اگر کد خدا شود گویند بد نفس و بندهٔ شهوتست ـ

حاصل الامر ، مردِ محتاج نزدِ ابناء زمان مردود و بیقدر باشد ـ و اگر باین حال **عیاذاً بالله** طمعی از وی[16] فهم کنند ، دشمنی او در دلها متمکن گشته

---

1. *Ibid.*, چاره جز این ندارد 2. *Ibid.*, الحیأمن الحیأ من الایمان
3. *O* : ایزا 4. *K* omits نهاد 5. *O* omits و 6. *Ibid.*, آمد
7. *K* : مورجه 8. *Ibid.*, omits موجب 9. *Ibid.*, بے عزتی
10. *Ibid.*, گر آید 11. *O* omits اش 12. *Ibid.*, خام
13. *K* omits عزیمت 14. *O* : آواره و بد برگشته اش گویند
15. *K* : گذارند 16. *Ibid.*, omits ازوی

هیچ حاجتش روا نکرده ازو بر بخند - چه[1] هر خواری که بآدمی [fol. 51 b] میرسد ، منشاءش طمعست - **عز من قنع و ذل من طمع** - مجملاً اگر کسی به بیماری در ماند که امید صحتی نباشد و یا بغربتی[2] افتد که نه روی باز گشتن باشد و نه اسباب اقامتش میسر شود ، آسانتر با شد از تنگدستی ، چه دست در دهان مار کردن و برای خود زهر هلاهل بیرون آوردن و از شیر گرسنه لقمه ربودن و با پلنگ خشم آلود همکا سه بودن آسانتر از احتیاج ، همچو[3] خودی بردنست - و مرگ بهمه حالت بهتر ازین حال تواند بود -

چون سنت الهی بران جاری شده که ظهور اکثر حالات این جهانی باسباب وابسته است - و حق سبحانه و تعالی مدار عالم بر اسباب و وسایط[4] گذاشته - و اگرچه قدرت او بی سبب مهم تواند ساخت - اما حکمت الهی آن اقتضا کرده که اکثر مهات بسببها ساخته و پرداخته گردد و بسبب آن قاعده افاده و[5] استفاده تمهید یابد - پس اگر کسی سبب فایدهٔ دیگری تواند شد بهتر از آنست [fol. 52 a] که به سبب دیگری فایده بگیرد **خیر الناس من ینفع[6] الناس** -

بیت[7]

چو باز باش که صیدی خوری و طعمه[8] دهی
طفیل خوار مشو چون کلاغ بی پر و بال

کسی که قادر باشد و ممکن بود[9] که نفع بدیگری رساند ، حیف باشد که کاهلی ورزیده از دیگری نفع گیرد - تا بر اوج مراد بکام دل ترقی توان کرد ، در حضیض خست و دناءت بنا کامی سیر[10] کردن حیفی عظیم باشد - و تا در چمن آسایش گل عشرت تماشا[11] توان کرد ، قدم در خارستان محنت[12] نهادن غبنی[13] فاحش - اما باید دانست که جد و جهد آدمی را بسر منزل[14] مقصود رساند - و بیابان مجاهده را بقدم سعی قطع کردن جمال مراد بنظر مشاهده در آورد - هر که در میدان همت علم جهد بر افراشت و در ارتکاب محنتها[15] صفت تن آسانی و فراغت

---

1. *Ibid.*, omits هر 2. *Ibid.*, بغریبی 3. *O* : بهمچو 4. *K* : واسایط
5. *Ibid.*, omits و 6. *Ibid.*, تنفع 7. *Ibid.*, omits بیت 8. *O* : لقمه
9. *K* omits و ممکن بود 10. *O* : سپردن 11. *Ibid.*, تماشان
12. *K* : محبت 13. *Ibid.*, عبنی 14. *O* omits منزل 15. *K* : محنت

را از[1] دست بداشت ، هر چند[2] زود تر بمقصود رسید ، هیچکس را بی تگاپوی[3] بلیغ آفتابِ [fol. 52 b] مراد از آفقِ آمید طالع نشده و بی جست و جوی کامل مقدمه رجا نتیجهٔ حصولِ مقصود نداده -

بیت

پادشاهی در چمن داند[4] گل را زانکه گل
باوجودِ نازکی از خار[5] بالین میکند

اگرچه آنچه مقرر شده است از مکمنِ[6] غیب بظهور میرسد و آنچه روزی نشده چندانکه در جست و جویش[7] سعی نمایند بهیچوجه فایده ندارد - و بی مظاهرتِ لطفِ ازلی و فیضِ لم یزلی سهمِ سعادت بهدفِ مراد نمیرسد - و لیکن جد و جهد را دخلی عظیم است - هر که آسایش الخمول راحة طلبد[8] ، دایم الوقت در زاویهٔ خواری و ناکامی خواهد ماند - و آنکه از خارستان[9] و الشهرة آفة نه اندیشد ، باندک فرصتی گلِ مراد چیده ، در چمنِ عزت بر مسندِ دولت خواهد نشست - گلِ طرب بیخارِ تعب نتوان چید و درِ گنجِ مراد جز بکلیدِ رنج نتوان کشاد - هوسِ استراحت مقدمهٔ خست و دناءت و[10] ارتکابِ مخاطرت نشانهٔ دولت و عزتست - [fol, 53 a] نوشِ ناز[11] و نعمت بی نیشِ آزار و محنت نیست - و هیچکس را[12] بی کشیدنِ رنجهای بیشمار و چشیدنِ شربتهای ناگوار[13] دست بدامنِ مقصود نتواند رسید[14] - و از جامِ آرزو بادهٔ[15] مراد[16] نتواند نوشید - مرد آنست که کمرِ سعی بر میان بسته بطلب بر خیزد - و همت بلند داشته بکارهای خسیس راضی نشود و منازل ادانی و اراذل نپسندیده چون عجایز بجزویات[17] سر فرود نیاورد - که هر که درجهٔ بلند یافت ، هر چند چون گل کوتاه زندگانی باشد ، خرد مندان بسببِ ذکرِ جمیل او را دراز عمر شمرند و آنکه بدناءت و دون همتی سر فرود آورد ، چون برگِ نار اگرچه دیر بپاید[18] ، نزدیکِ اهلِ[19] فضل قدری نداشته باشد - و از وی

1. *O* omits از 2. *K* omits هر چند 3. *O :* بی تگاپوی سعی
4. *Ibid.*, چمن دادند گل را زانکه او گل 5. *K :* جار 6. *Ibid.*, یکمن
7. *O* omits یش 8. *K :* راجه طلبید 9. *Ibid* , omits و
10 *Ibid.*, omits و 11. *Ibid.*, باز 12. *Ibid.*, omits را
13. *O :* بدگوار 14. *K :* رسانید 15. *O :* ساغر 16. *K :* نشاط
17. *O & K* بخرویات 18. *Ibid.*, نپاید 19. *Ibid.*, adds و

حسابی نگیرند[1] - و یقین باید دانست که ترقی بر[2] درجاتِ شرف بزحمت،[3] بسیار دست دهد - و تنزل از مرتبهٔ عزت باندک کلفتی میسر شود - چنانکه سنگِ گران را بمشقت از زمین توان برداشت ، [fol. 53 b] و بآسانی بزمین توان انداخت - و بواسطه اینست که جز مردِ بلند همت که تحملِ محنت داشته باشد کسی دیگر بکسبِ معالی رغبت نمیتواند کرد -

هر که ترسید از جفای خمار قدحی باده مراد نخورد

و اگر چنانچه در وطن امکانِ ترقی نبوده باشد ، ترقی کلی خواه از روی صورت و خواه از راهِ معنی در سفر دانسته بمصداقِ **قل سیرو فی الارض** [4] قدم بیرون گذارد -

بیت[5]

ای که داغی زوطن[6] مر همش از غربت[7] جوی
گو مشو[د] پاره[8] بمرگِ تو گریبانی چند

هر چند سفر درختیست که جز میوهٔ فراق بار نیاورد - و غربت ابریست که بموجب مضمون **الغربة کربة والفرقة حرقة** جز بارانِ مذلت نبارد[9] - و تفرجِ اطرافِ عالم و تماشای[10] ریاض ارم با یارانِ همدم و دوستان محرم خوش آید[11] - و چون کسی از سعادتِ دیدارِ والدین و اخوان و دوستان محروم شد ، پیداست که دردِ آن بتفرج آنها چه مقدار درمان [fol. 54 a] پذیرد و رنج او را[12] ازان مشاهده چه مایه شفا پدید آید - چه درد فراقِ یاران و رنجِ هجرانِ دوستداران صعب ترین همه دردها و سخت ترین سایر[13] رنجها ست - و در غربت هر چند رفاهیت و فراغتِ تمام حاصل بوده بعشرتی کامل روزگار گذرد[14] ، بی دیدارِ یارانِ جانی و مصاحبانِ روحانی چشمهٔ عیشِ او تیره و دیدهٔ بختِ او خیره خواهد بود - اما چون روزگار آراسته و سال و خواسته[15] باشد همه کس اظهارِ دوستی کنند[16] و

---

1. *Ibid.*, بگیرند 2. *Ibid.*, omits بر 3. *Ibid.*, برحمت
4. *Qur'ān* 27 : 69 ; 29 : 20 ; and 30 : 42 5. *K* omits بیت
6. *Ibid.*, واطن 7. *Ibid.*, غریب 8. *Ibid.*, یاره 9. *Ibid.*, نیارد
10. *Ibid.*, تماضای 11. *Ibid.*, آمد 12. *O* omits را
13. *Ibid.*, همه 14. *O* adds و 15. *K* : جواسته 16. *O* : کند

لافِ اتحاد و یگانگی زنند[1] ـ و هرگاه کسی حاجتمند شد و عیاذاً بالله غبارِ ادبار دیدهٔ اقبال او را تیره ساخت ، جمعی که چون ثریا صحبت او را انتظام دادندی مانند بنات النعش متفرق گردند ، برای آنکه دوستی مردمِ روزگار و محبتهای اهلِ زمانه بغرضهای نفسانی و نفعهای دنیوی مقصور باشد ـ

تا حطامی که هست مینوشند   همچو زنبور بر تو میجوشند

باز وقتی که ده خراب شود [fol. 54 b] کاسه چون کاسه رباب شود

ترکِ صحبت کنند و دلداری   دوستی خود نبوده پنداری

باز را بسببِ آن بر ساعدِ[2] سلاطین جای مقرر شده که سر بآشیانه فرود نمی آرد و جغد بواسطهٔ آن در پسِ دیوارِ خواری سانده که دل از ویرانه بر نمیدارد ـ

بیت

چو شاهباز بجولان در آی و سیری کن
چو جغد چند توان بود در پسِ دیوار

چون کسی در غربت بورطهٔ محنت آفتاد ، قطع نظر از دولت مودب و مهذب گردد[3] و او را تجربهای که مدت العمر بدان فایده توان[4] گرفت ، حاصل آید ، و محنتِ مسافرت او را پخته سازد ـ مجملاً هیچ سایه پرور[5] مرکبِ آمید در میدانِ مراد نتازد ـ و سفر آدمی را از حضیضِ[6] خمول و رزالت باوجِ عزت و جلالت رساند ـ و ترقیات تمام آدمی را در سفر دست دهد ـ چنانکه گفته اند السفر وسیلة الظفر ، شمشیر تاآز غلاف بیرون نیاید در معرکهٔ مردان سرخرو نگردد ، آسمان [fol. 55 a] که پیوسته در سفر است از همه بالا تر است و زمین که همواره در سکون ست پایمال هر اعالی و دونست ـ نه بینی که پیاده از سفرِ شش منزل از پیادگی مرتبهٔ فرزینی یابد و ماهِ سبک رو به سیر چهارده شب از مرتبهٔ هلالی بدرجهٔ بدری رسد ـ

---

1. *Ibid.*, زند   2. *Ibid.*, مساعد   3. *K* : کرده
4. *O* : تواند   5. *Ibid.*, پرورد   6. *Ibid.*, خضیض

قطعه

بجرم خاک و بگرددن نگاه باید کرد
که این کجاست ز آرام و آن کجا ز سفر

سفر مربی مرد است و آستانهٔ جاه
سفر خزانهٔ مالست و اوستادِ هنر

درخت اگر متحرک شدی ز جای بجای
نه جور اره کشیدی و نه[1] جفای تبر

غرض که چون ارتکابِ مشقت کارِ مردانِ[2] مرد و پیشه شیر مردانِ نبرد است ، مرد آنکس را توان شمرد که نخست دل از جان برداشته قدم در میدانِ طلب نهد و از تحمل مشقت نترسیده تا ممکن و مقدور باشد لازمهٔ سعی و جهد بجای آورد که حال از دو بیرون نخواهد بود : اگر چنانچه با شاهدِ مراد هم آغوش شد فهو المراد ، و الا عذرِ او نزدیک عقلاء [fol. 55 b] واضح خواهد بود . و علو همت او در طلبِ مفاخر و معالی[3] بر ضمایر هویدا .

همت چرا کنیم بهر کارِ مختصر
گردن چرا نهیم جفای زمانه را

سیمرغ وار زیر پر آریم بحر و بر
دریا و کوه را بگذاریم و بگذریم

یا مرد وار بر سرِ همت نهیم سر
یا بر مراد بر سرِ گرددن نهیم پای

---

1. *K* : نی 2. *Ibid.*, omits مردان 3. *Ibid.*, omits بر

فصل سیوم[1]

در رضا بقضای الٰهی دادن و قناعت و عزلت

اگر محولِ حالِ جهانیان نه قضا ست
چرا مجاری احوال بر خلافِ رضا ست

بلی قضاست بهر نیک و بد عنا نکشِ[2] خلق
بدان دلیل که تدبیرهای جمله خطاست

هزار نقش بر آرد زمانه و نبود
یکی چنانکه در آینهٔ تصور ماست

بر صفحاتِ تصوراتِ اهلِ تحقیق مصور است که هر چه هست بتقدیرِ ازلی و حکمِ لم یزلی متعلق ست ، و اصلِ همه قضای الٰهی و حکمِ لم یزلی[3] ست و انواعِ خیر و شر و اصنافِ نفع و ضر باحکامِ قضا و قدر باز بسته است و هر چه کاتبِ ارادت در دیوانخانه ازل بقلمِ مشیت بر صفحاتِ احوالِ مخلوقات[4] [fol. 56 a] کشیده ، لابد است که در عرصهٔ وجود بجلوه در آید ـ و احتراز و اجتناب ازان فایده ندارد ـ و بمقتضای قدر و قضا وسایط و وسایل ضایع[5] باشد ـ و از بندِ تقدیر بچاره و تدبیر رهائی نتوان یافت ـ و بسر انگشتِ تدبیر گرهٔ تقدیر نتوان کشود که از بیابانِ تدبیر تا به[6] سر منزلِ تقدیر راه بسیار است و از فضای[7] اندیشه تا سرحدِ قضا مسافت بیحد و نهایت ـ و چون آفریدگار سبحانه و تعالیٰ حکمی بنفاذ خواهد برساند[8] بمیلِ غفلت دیدهٔ بصیرت بینایان را خیره گردانیده ، نه دیدهٔ بصیرت را روشنایی ماند و نه تدبیرِ خرد نفع رساند ـ چون حاکمِ[9] نافذِ امرِ قضا سلسلهٔ ارادت در جنباند ، ماهی را از قعرِ دریا بفضای هوا رساند ـ و مرغ را از اوجِ هوا به حضیضِ زمین بکشاند[10] ـ بی مقتضای مشیت ربانی هر رقمی که اندیشهٔ رنگ آمیز بر لوحِ [fol. 56 b] خیال کشد ، بآخر نقشِ[11] خرابی پذیرد ـ و هر افسون که عزیمت خوانِ تدبیر[12] پیش آورد عاقبت رنگِ افسانه گیرد ـ

---

1. *O* omits فصل سیوم 2. *K* : کس
3. *Ibid.*, omits حکمِ لم یزلی 4. *Ibid.*, ممکنات 5. *Ibid.*, منافع
6. *O* omits به 7. *Ibid.*, قضای 8. *K* : رسانید
9. *Ibid.*, حکم 10. *Ibid.*, نشاند 11. *Ibid.*, نفس 12. *Ibid.*, تدبیرش

هیچکس را از بندِ قضا و قیدِ تقدیر رهایی ممکن نیست[1] - و هیچ یک از افرادِ انسانی با مقادیرِ[2] ازلی و قضای لم یزلی نمی تواند کوشید - و هیچ آفریده را در امرِ قضا و قدر بجز[3] تسلیم و رضا چاره نباشد - و جز آنکه سرِ تسلیم بر خطِ حکمِ الهی و تقدیرِ ربانی باید نهاد ، مسلکی قویم و منهجی مستقیم نه[4] -

و هر چند کسی بزیورِ انواعِ دانش و فضایل آراسته باشد ، چون قضای ایزدی با او یار نباشد هیچ ثمره نخواهد دید - و از مقدماتِ کمالِ خود نتیجه ای نخواهد یافت - چه بسیار دانایان که استحقاقِ دولت داشته اند ، از قوتِ یکروزه محروم بوده اند - و بسی جاهلانِ بی استعداد بر سریرِ عزت و شوکت نشسته اند و[5] هر آینه این حالت جز وابسته بحکم سبحانی و فرمانِ یزدانی نیست - هر گاه محقق شد که فاعلِ حقیقی جز ایزدِ متعال نیست و اگر او خواهد [fol. 57a] مقصودِ هر کس بی تعب و مشقت[6] بدست در آورد و اگر ارادهٔ ایزدی بحصولِ آن تعلق نگیرد[7] هیچوجه جد و جهد فایده نخواهد داد - بس ذرهٔ امکان[8] در درگاهِ وجوب جز رضامندی و خورسندی هر چه کند نشانِ بی دولتیست - و هر چه از جانبِ او در رسد بی شبه عینِ رحمت و محض کرامت باید دانست که اگرچه بنده بحقیقتِ آن و[9] لطیفه که در ضمنِ آن مندرجست بینا[10] نیست ، اما چون نیک[11] نگرد یقین که صلاحِ حال[12] وی[13] دران خواهد بود - چه طبیبِ ناشناسا که معالجه او متوهم است مر تلخ دارو که بخوردن دهد بکشاده پیشانی کشند و منت پذیرند - دادارِ جهان آفرین آنچه فرستد چگونه و چرا آزردگی راه دهد -

بدرد و صاف ترا کار نیست خوش در کش
که هر چه ساقی ما کرد عین الطافست

خرد مند آنست که از مقدراتِ الهی روی نه پیچد و با مقتضیاتِ قضا آلفت گیرد و هر چه از اقتضای قدر از بلا و عناء بدو رسد بخوشدلی و رغبتِ تمام در پذیرفته

---

1. *O* omits نیست 2. *K* : تقدیر

3. *K* omits بجز 4. *Ibid.*, omits نه 5. *Ibid.*, omits اندو

6. *Ibid.*, بی مشقت 7. *Ibid.*, omits نه 8. *O* adds را

9. *K* omits و and adds به 10. *Ibid*,, دانا 11. *O* omits نیک

12. *K* omits حال 13. *O* omits وی

خوشدل و شادمان گذراند و چون کودکِ کم خرد همواره [Kulliyāt, fol. 308b][1] میانِ خوشنودی [Ibid., fol. 309 a] و دماغ خشکی و میانِ گریه[2] و خنده نباشد که اگرش خوشی دهند و یادی ترنم نمایند بخندد و خشنود گردد و اگر یادی سختی نمایند و درشتی کنند بگرید و در خشم شود ـ و به نصیبی که از دیوان الرزق مقسوم نامزد کرده اند خرس بوده حرصِ نا پسندیده را همتِ عالی نام نکند و شره ناستوده را دیباچه بزرگی لقب ننهد و مزخرفات فانیه را وسیلهٔ کمال ندانسته پرتوِ التفات بر مال و جاهِ دنیاوی بی اعتبار نیفگند ـ و مالِ خود آنرا بداند که از پیش فرستد و متاعِ خود آنرا شمرد که در عالمِ آخرت ذخیره نهد ـ

چه گفتارِ نیک و کردارِ پسندیده و مکارمِ اخلاق و محاسنِ آداب محالیست که حوادثِ روزگار و گردشِ لیل و نهار را دران تصرفی نیست و از شا خسارِ رضا میوهٔ قناعت بدست آورده از شرهٔ نفس و حرصِ مال و تمنای جاه احتراز نماید که حکماء گفته اند هر که از دنیا بکفافی قانع نشده طلبِ فضولی نماید ، مشابه کسی است که بکوهِ الماس رود[3] ـ هر ساعت نظرش بر قطعه بزرگتر افتاده ، بخیال آن بیشتر زود تا بجای رسید که مطلوب بدست آید ، اما باز آمدن متعذر بود ـ ریزهای الماس پایهای او را خراشیده و تراشیده باشد و آن غافل در اندیشه حرص مستغرق شده ازان حال خبر نداشته باشد و آخر بحسرتِ تمام دران کوه هلاک شده بحوصلهٔ مرغان مقام گیرد ـ

از زیادت طلبی کارِ تو آید بزیان
سود اگر خواهی از اندازه زیادت مطلب

ساقی الطافِ یزدانی هر کس را در فراخورِ حال ساغری داده و هیچکس را از مشربِ عنایت و سر چشمه مرحمت محروم نساخته ـ بدانچه از دیوان خانهٔ ازل حواله شده خرسند باید بود و طلبِ فضولی نباید کرد [Ibid , fol. 309 b] که نه هر چه از آنها بخانهٔ آرزو سر بر زند بر وفقِ مراد محصل تواند شد ـ بسیار کس از غایتِ حرص و شره بامیدِ دولت در ورطهٔ محنت و نکبت افتاده و به وی منفعت در مهلکه مضرت گرفتار شده اند ـ گردنی که بسلسلهٔ حرص بسته شد ، عاقبت بتیغِ

———

1. The following text, fols., 308b to 310a, is taken from *K* and is missing from *O* 2. *K* : گره 3. *Ibid.*, کرد

ندامت بریده گردد و سری که سودای شره دران جای گرفت آخر بر خاکِ مذلت سوده شود -

زیاده از سرت ار یک کله بدست آری
بجا کپای غیریت که دردِ سر باشی

و از مردمِ خرد مند نزیبد که از پوشیدنِ خلعت لبِ نشاط خندان ساخته در نوشیدنِ جرعه محنت از دیده اشکِ حسرت بیارند - و به بسیاری مال شادی کرده باندکِ او غم خورند - و ندانند که راحتِ دنیا چون روشنایی برق بی دوام است و محنتش چون تاریکیِ ابر بی بقا - و حکما گفته اند که از پنج چیز توقع ثبات و بقا نتوان داشت : **اول** : سایهٔ ابرکه تا در نگری برگذرد - **دویم** : دوستی بغرض که باندک فرصتی چون شعلهٔ برق ناچیز شود - **سیوم** : عشقِ زنان که باندک سببی تسکین رباید - **چهارم** : جمالِ خوبرویان که بآخر ناچیز شود - **پنجم** : مالِ دنیا که با خداوندِ خود طریقِ وفا بپایان برساند و عاقبت در معرضِ فنا آید -

زہی بد بخت طایفه که در اوایلِ حال بزحمتِ بسیار مالِ دنیا بدست آورند و در اواخرِ کار بحسرتِ بیشمار بگذارند - عجب ازکسانیکه راحت در بسیاری مال طلبند و ندانند که از اندکِ آن آسایش توان یافت-و توانگری در جمع دنیا دانند و ندانند که از اندکِ آن بدرجهٔ بلند توان رسید - مرد آنکس را توان شمرد که رخشِ ہمت در میدانِ قناعت تاخته نه بوجودِ دنیا ابوابِ بہجت بر روی دل بکشاید و نه بعدمش اظهارِ تاسف نماید-و صفحه دل را [*Ibid*., fol. 310 a]

به نیرنگِ این پنج روزه خیال   که نادان نهد نام آن ملک و مال

مرقوم نساخته نقدِ حیات در تحصیلِ اسبابِ تجرد و ترکِ لوازمِ تعلق در بازد و دیدهٔ حرصِ شوخ چشم را بسوزنِ قناعت دوخته [*Mauʿiẓah*, fol. 57 b] دست از اسبابِ دنیوی بشوید-و چون اکثر مردمان[1] این روزگار به پیروی[2] نفسِ جفا جوی مظهرِ اخلاقِ ذمیمه چون حقد و حسد و ظلم و عجب و ریا و رعونت و نفاق و امثالِ اینها واقع شده اند و صحبتِ ایشان از زہرِ افعی کارگر تراست و مخالطت با ایشان از مخاطرهٔ جان دادن دشوار تر - حضور در وحدت و فراغت

———

1. *K* : مردم and omits این   2. *Ibid*., نیروی

درعزلت دانسته در صحبتِ دیگران بر روی خود ببندد و سرِ فراغت بر[1] زانوی عزلت نهاده خطِ بطالت بر صحیفهٔ[2] هوا و هوس بکشد که منافع عزلت از فوایدِ صحبت بیشتر است - و اینکه بعضی از حکماء مدتهای متمادی در کنج غاری یا تکِ چاهی[3] روزگار گذرانیده اند، نظرِ ایشان براینمعنی بوده :

رباعی[4]

از فتنهٔ این زمانهٔ شور انگیز   بر خیز بهر جا که توانی بگریز

ور پای گریختن نداری[5] [fol. 58 a] باری—دستی زن و در دامنِ خلوت آویز

اللهم خلصنا[6] عن الهواجس النفسانیة و الوساوس الشیطانیة و شرفنا بمقام الوصول و وصلنا بعالم العقول -

---

1. *O* : در 2. *K* : صفحه 3. *Ibid.*, یک جای 4. *O* omits رباعی
5. *Ibid.*, مداری 6. *K* : حضعلصنا

فصل چهارم

در تحصیل ِ کمالات و استرضای الٰهی

بدانکه این عالم ِ بیمدارا[1] سرائیست تشنه فریب و منزلیست پر[2] فراز و نشیب - بادهٔ عیش ِ این خمخانه را بخوناب ِ[3] غم آمیخته اند و بنای بقای این نگار خانه[4] را بآب و گل ِ فنا انگیخته اند - مستی این بزم را درپی خماریست و عاقبت ِ این سودا را در سر بخاری - کدام دل که جگر خون نیست و کدام دیده که خون فشان نه - این توده خاک گذشتنی[5] و گذاشتنیست[6] و این تیره مغاک پر کردنی و انباشتنی[7] ، پیوندها همه بریدنیست و خوناها همه کشیدنی - طغرا نویس ِ ازل نام ِ بقای جاودانی بر نامهٔ زندگانی هیچ آفریده رقم نفرموده و نقاش ِ صور ِ موجودات نقش ِ حیات بر صفحات ِ وجود ِ[8] ممکنات [fol. 58b] جز بقلم[9] **کل شیء هالک الا وجهه**[10] ثبت ننموده ، خیاط ِ کارخانهٔ قدم جامهٔ وجود ِ هیچ موجودی بی طراز ِ عدم ندوخته و فراش سراچه[11] قدرت شمع فراغتی بی تندباد ِ محنتی نیفروخته ، کرا برداشت که نیفگند و کجا نهالی نشانید که از بیخ[12] بر نکند[13] ، با که تکلفی کرد که خونش نخورد و بر روی که در ِ دولتی کشود که هزار محنت از پی در نیاورد -

این پیرزن ِ شوهر کش[14] که دنیاش خوانند زنیست نابکار که بسی مردان را در ِ قید ِ کمند ِ خود در[15] آورده ، و زالیست غدار که بسیار تهمتنانرا بیژن وار در چاه ِ بلا انداخته ، خود را در لباس ِ نو عروسان ِ جوان بر جهانیان جلوه میدهد ، و بزینت ِ ناپایدار و زیور ِ بی اعتبار دل ِ بیخردان ِ مغرور را در دام ِ محبت ِ خود می افگند - هرکه او را در عقد ِ ازدواج کشید ، دست ِ مرادش در آغوش ِ آرزو نرسید - و هرکه بحبالهٔ وصالش در آورد بکام ِ دل شبی ازو بر نخورد - بسی شیفتگان ِ [fol. 59 a] محبت خود را از[16] یافتن ِ مراد نا امید کرده و بسیار عاشقان خود را از پای در آورده ، کودک مزاجان سر کوی نادانی در دام ِ آفت ِ او افتاده بصورت ِ

---

1. *O* : بیمدار 2. *K* : بر 3. *Ibid.*, بخواب 4. *Ibid.*, کارخانه
5. *Ibid.*, گذشتی 6. گذاشتی است 7. انباشتی 8. *O* omits وجود
9. *K* : نقلم 10. *Qur'ān* 28 : 88 11. *K* : سراحة ; *O* : سراجه
12. *O* omits بر 13. *K* : نکنند 14. *Ibid.*, کس
15. *Ibid.*, omits در 16. *Ibid.*, omits از یافتن مراد نا امید کرده و بسیار عاشقان خود را

دلفریبش وابسته شده از خبث باطن و سستی عهد و دناءت طبع و ناپاکی سیرتش بیخبر مانده اند - و هر که دیدهٔ دلش بکحل الجواهر دانش و بینش روشن شده بمزخرفات فانیهٔ او التفات ننموده ، و دل در[1] محبت او نبسته[2] ، چه بدیدهٔ سیرت[3] و باصرهٔ بصیرت مشهود است که میل شاهین ترازوی زندگانی بکفهٔ فنا مایل تر است که به پلهٔ بقا -

و هرکه از کتم عدم بوجود آمد لابد باز بعدمش می باید رفت - و اگرچه مرگ خوابیست نا مرغوب و آسایشی است نا خواهان ، اما از دائرهٔ فنا و فوات هیچکس را خروج ممکن نیست - و هر که قدم در عالم وجود نهاد لابد شربت اجلش بباید نوشید ، و لباس هلاکتش بباید پوشید - دمبدم قدم در راه فنا می باید نهاد و عنقریب بهار عمر [fol. 59 b] که ایام جوانیست بخزان پیری مبدل شد - آخر سفر دور و دراز آخرت پیش باید گرفت و از ودیعت حیات مستعار هیچکس را چاره نیست - هر ابتدایی را انتهایی مقرر است و هر آغازیرا انجامی[4] مقدر - هیچ مشامی ازین گلشن بوی وفا نشنیده و هیچ کامی از دست ایام شربت راحتی نچشیده - عاقبت ازین[5] راه خطرناک آخرت رفتنی است و در[6] وحشت خانهٔ لحد[7] خفتنی - پیک اجل ناگاه در رسد و ودیعت حیات را وقتی معین و زمانی مقرر نباشد - و چون مدت عمر سپری شد و هنگام اجل فراز آمد ، یک چشم زدن مهلت صورت نه بندد - پس هرگاه حقیقت این حال منکشف شد ، مقتضی خرد آنست که مرغ محبت دنیا را در ساحت سینه جای نباید داد و بصورت او که چون مار منقش است فریفته نباید شد و نرمی و نازکی او را دوست نداشته - بر عمر که بمثابهٔ ابر تابستان و نزهت گلستان و حسن خوبرویان و وفای زنان زود زوالست[8] [fol. 60 a] اعتماد نباید کرد -

و عمر عزیز را که[9] چون برق درگذشتن است و اوقات زندگانی را که چون[10] موج ناپایدار است جوهر بی بدل باید دانست - و هر نفس که میگذرد غنیمت شمرده قیمت آن باید شناخت ، که از[11] زندگانی آنچه رفت[12] باز آوردن آن[13] از حیز امکان دور است - و آنچه مانده ، آن نیز در پردهٔ غیب مستور - میان ماضی

1. *Ibid.*, omits در 2. *Ibid.*, دربسته 3. *O* : سریرت
4. *Ibid.*, adds را 5. *Ibid.*, omits از 6. *K* omits در 7. *Ibid.*, خاک
8. *Ibid*, زوالیست 9. *Ibid.*, omits که 10. *Ibid.*, omits چون
11. *O* omits از 12. *K* : گذشت 13. *Ibid.*, omits آن

و مستقبل وقتی است که آنرا حال گویند ـ عمرِ خویش آن وقت را باید دانست ـ و در انتظامِ اسبابِ لا یعنی[1] صرف نساخته در تضیع آن نباید کوشید ـ و از خوابِ غفلت و مستی شرابِ جهالت بیدار و هشیار شده در بادیهٔ ضلالت و باویه غوایت[2] سرگردان و پریشان نباید شد ـ و هر نفس که بنا شایستگی از عمر بگذرد در شمارِ مدتِ موت دانسته امروز که قوتی و فرصتی هست چیزی ذخیره باید کرد که توشهٔ راه را شاید ، و تا گریبانِ حیات بچنگِ هادم اللذات نیفتاده سر بر خطِ فرمانِ نفس ننهاده [fol. 60 b] دست از دامنِ عقل باز نباید داشت ـ و فرصتِ تحصیلِ کمالات را که موجبِ استخلاصِ عقاب و نکالِ آخرتست از دست نداده همتِ خود را در طلبِ فضایل و تحصیلِ کمالات و تهذیبِ اخلاق و تزکیهٔ نفس و احرازِ ثوابِ آخرت که فوایدِ حیات و منافع زندگانی جز این مراتب نتواند بود مصروف باید داشت ـ و نوالهٔ زهر آلودهٔ دنیا را بکامِ آرزو نرسانیده بجای چاشنی راحتِ نفس و شربتِ هوا و هوس شورابهٔ ریاضت که در کامِ عقل بمنزلهٔ شهد است نوش باید کرد ـ

و از فوایدِ حیات استعدادِ سفرِ بادیهٔ فنا و فوات مهیا ساخته ، کسبِ فضایل و کمالات و استرضای الٰهی را سرمایهٔ سعادت و نجاتِ دنیوی و آخروی باید دانست ـ و صفحهٔ احوالِ خود را برقمِ عبادت که در دنیا واسطهٔ سلامت و در عقبی رابطه نجات و کرامتست آراسته باقدامِ ریاضت منهاجِ طاعت و عبادت [fol. 61 a] باید پیمود و روز[3] و شب بتدارکِ اوقاتی که گذشته مشغول شده توشهٔ راهِ عقبی بتوبه و انابت باید ساخت و نیتِ خود را در طلبِ خشنودی و رضای خدای تعالی بسته[4] خواهشِ خود را هیچ مدخل نباید داد که غرضهای نفسانی عملهای حقانی را تباه کند-و گفته اند که آدمی دو نصیب دارد : یکی ملکیه[5] که ازان مایل است بعلم و عمل و دیگر بهیمیه[6] که ازان حریص باشد بر محرمات ـ پس خوی عقل یگانه‌آنست که تا ممکن باشد بطرفِ بهیمی میل نباید کرد ـ و این دو سه روزه زندگانی را محصورِ لذات نفسانی ندانسته ، نقدِ عمر را سرمایه[7] سودِ عقبی و عرصهٔ زندگانی را مزرعهٔ دولتِ آخروی تصور باید کرد و سالکِ راهِ حقیقت بوده[8] دنیی و اسباب و متاعِ آنرا گاه برگی نباید دانست ، و از همه باید گذشت تا

---

1. *Ibid.*, مالا یعنی 2. *Ibid.*, غوایب

3. *Ibid.*, omits و 4. *Ibid.*, دانسته 5. *Ibid.*, ملکی

6. *Ibid.*, بهیمی 7. *Ibid.*, پرمایه 8. *Ibid.*, omits بوده

بمضمون **لا یصل الی الکل الا من یقطع علی الکل** بهمه رسی و بقدم شرف بر درجات **و لقد** [fol. 61 b] **کر منا بنی آدم**[1] ترقی نموده از غایتِ رذالت بدرکات **بل هم اضل**[2] محبوس نمانی و چون وقتِ استردادِ امانتِ روح فرا رسد ، سلوکِ آخرت بر سبیلِ سهولت میسر باشد -

ع این کار دولتست کنون تا کرا رسد

[خاتمه]

الهی مسود این اوراق را که درکشمکشِ کون و فساد گرفتار است بمحض عنایتِ ازلی و هدایتِ لم یزلی ، دردِ طلبِ[3] خود کرامت فرموده از بیدردی باز دار - و دستِ خواهشِ او را از تدبیرِ خودش باز داشته آنچه مرضی تست بدان هدایت نمای - چون این رساله که[4] دستورالعملِ بیدار دلان و هوشمندانست ، بسرحدِ اطناب رسید و این در های گرانمایه[5] در رشتهٔ انتظام فراهم آمد ، اخلاص و بندگی آن اقتضا میکند که بدعای دوامِ دولتِ روز افزون و بقای سلطنتِ ابد مقرون صاحب و ولی نعمت و قبله و کعبهٔ حقیقی خود اعنی

پادشاهِ ممالکِ عالم در تمامِ جهان بعدل و بعلم[6]
[fol. 62 a] تاج بخشِ شهانِ تخت[7] نشین مشرق و مغربش بزیرِ نگین
ترک و دیلم همه غلامانش قیصر از چاکرانِ دربانش
همه اجدادِ او خجسته شیم مالکِ تاج و تخت تا آدم

آنکه مکرر نامِ نامی و اسمِ گرامی آنحضرت را بزبانِ قلم در آوردن از ادب دور است٬سمتِ[8] اختتام یابد -

شعر

تا بود از شعشعه آفتاب سطح معلای فلک نوریاب
باد ز عدلِ شهِ روشن جبین روی زمین غیرتِ خلد برین

---

1. *Qur'ān* 17 : 70 2. *Ibid.*, 7 : 179 ; 25 : 44
3. *K* : در طلب 4. *Ibid.*, omits که 5. *O* : گرامی
6. *Ibid.*, بعدل علم 7. *K* omits تخت 8. *Ibid.*, بهمت

تاریخِ اتمام[1] موعظهٔ جهانگیری اینست[2] ـ

چون گشت تمام این صحیفه / از کوششِ طبعِ نکته پرداز
بودم ز برای سالِ ختمش / در عالمِ فکر در تک و تاز
ناگاه ز سوی هاتفِ غیب / در گوشِ دلم رسید آواز
کای طایرِ روحِ اهلِ دانش / در گلشنِ طبعِ تو پرواز[3]
در زنده نمودنِ معانی / الحق چو مسیح کردی اعجاز

چون موعظه [fol. 62 b] نامِ آن نهادی
ای در فنِ نظم و نثر ممتاز
از بهرِ رعایتِ تناسب
هم موعظه سال او رقم ساز
1021/1612

تحریراً فی تاریخِ دهم ربیع الثانی سن ۱۰۲۸
کتبه المذنب عبدالله شهابی غفر الله ذنوبه ـ

1. *O* omits اتمام 2. ***K*** : تاریخ اتمام کتاب 3. *Ibid*,. پرداز

INDEX